T0178531

Communications in Computer and Information Science 2112

Rationale

The CCIS series is devoted to the publication of proceedings of computer science conferences. Its aim is to efficiently disseminate original research results in informatics in printed and electronic form. While the focus is on publication of peer-reviewed full papers presenting mature work, inclusion of reviewed short papers reporting on work in progress is welcome, too. Besides globally relevant meetings with internationally representative program committees guaranteeing a strict peer-reviewing and paper selection process, conferences run by societies or of high regional or national relevance are also considered for publication.

Topics

The topical scope of CCIS spans the entire spectrum of informatics ranging from foundational topics in the theory of computing to information and communications science and technology and a broad variety of interdisciplinary application fields.

Information for Volume Editors and Authors

Publication in CCIS is free of charge. No royalties are paid, however, we offer registered conference participants temporary free access to the online version of the conference proceedings on SpringerLink (http://link.springer.com) by means of an http referrer from the conference website and/or a number of complimentary printed copies, as specified in the official acceptance email of the event.

CCIS proceedings can be published in time for distribution at conferences or as post-proceedings, and delivered in the form of printed books and/or electronically as USBs and/or e-content licenses for accessing proceedings at SpringerLink. Furthermore, CCIS proceedings are included in the CCIS electronic book series hosted in the SpringerLink digital library at http://link.springer.com/bookseries/7899. Conferences publishing in CCIS are allowed to use Online Conference Service (OCS) for managing the whole proceedings lifecycle (from submission and reviewing to preparing for publication) free of charge.

Publication process

The language of publication is exclusively English. Authors publishing in CCIS have to sign the Springer CCIS copyright transfer form, however, they are free to use their material published in CCIS for substantially changed, more elaborate subsequent publications elsewhere. For the preparation of the camera-ready papers/files, authors have to strictly adhere to the Springer CCIS Authors' Instructions and are strongly encouraged to use the CCIS LaTeX style files or templates.

Abstracting/Indexing

CCIS is abstracted/indexed in DBLP, Google Scholar, EI-Compendex, Mathematical Reviews, SCImago, Scopus. CCIS volumes are also submitted for the inclusion in ISI Proceedings.

How to start

To start the evaluation of your proposal for inclusion in the CCIS series, please send an e-mail to ccis@springer.com.

Arthur Gibadullin

Editor

Information Technologies and Intelligent Decision Making Systems

Third International Scientific and Practical Conference, ITIDMS 2023
Moscow, Russia, December, 12–14, 2023
Revised Selected Papers

 Springer

Editor
Arthur Gibadullin
National Research University "MPEI"
Moscow, Russia

ISSN 1865-0929 ISSN 1865-0937 (electronic)
Communications in Computer and Information Science
ISBN 978-3-031-60317-4 ISBN 978-3-031-60318-1 (eBook)
https://doi.org/10.1007/978-3-031-60318-1

This Springer imprint is published by the registered company Springer Nature Switzerland AG
The registered company address is: Gewerbestrasse 11, 6330 Cham, Switzerland

Paper in this product is recyclable.

Preface

The Third International Conference "Information Technologies and Intelligent Decision Making Systems" (ITIDMS 2023) was held as a virtual event, December 12–14, 2023, on the Microsoft Teams platform due to COVID-19.

The conference was held with the aim of developing and exchanging international experience in the field of information, digital and intellectual technologies, within the framework of which proposals were formulated for digital, intellectual and information transformation, the development of computer models and the improvement of automated and computing processes. A distinctive feature of the conference was that it presented reports of authors from China, Vietnam, Uzbekistan, Russia, Korea, Finland and Israel. Researchers from different countries presented the process of transition of the information and digital path of development, and presented the main directions and developments that can improve efficiency and development.

The conference sessions were moderated by Arthur Gibadullin of the National Research University "MPEI", Moscow, Russia.

Thus, the conference still facilitated scientific recommendations on the use of information, computer, digital and intellectual technologies in industry and fields of activity that can be useful to state and regional authorities, international and supranational organizations, and the scientific and professional community.

Each presented paper was reviewed by at least three members of the Program Committee in a double-blind manner. As a result of the work of the reviewers, 17 papers were accepted for publication out of the 54 received submissions. The reviews were based on the assessment of the topic of the submitted materials, the relevance of the study, the scientific significance and novelty, the quality of the materials, and the originality of the work. Authors could revise their paper and submit it again for review. Reviewers, Program Committee members, and Organizing Committee members did not enter into discussions with the authors of the articles.

The Organizing Committee of the conference expresses its gratitude to the staff at Springer who supported the publication of these proceedings. In addition, the Organizing Committee would like to thank the conference participants, the reviewers and everyone who helped organize this conference and shape the present volume for publication in the Springer CCIS series.

Arthur Gibadullin

Organization

Program Committee Chairs

Yuri Gulyaev	Institute of Radio-Engineering and Electronics, RAS, Russia
Alexander Bugaev	Institute of Radio-Engineering and Electronics RAS, Russia
Sergey Nikitov	Institute of Radio-Engineering and Electronics RAS, Russia
Vladimir Zernov	Russian New University, Russia
Andrey Kryukovskiy	Russian New University, Russia
Evgeny Palkin	Russian New University, Russia
Gulom Uzakov	Karshi Engineering-Economics Institute, Uzbekistan
Manuchehr Sadriddinov	International University of Tourism and Entrepreneurship of Tajikistan, Tajikistan
Arthur Gibadullin	National Research University "Moscow Power Engineering Institute", Russia

Program Committee

Oleg Zolotarev	Russian New University, Russia
Leonid Labunets	Russian New University, Russia
Maurizio Palesi	University of Catania, Italy
Yixuan Wang	Northwestern University, USA
Afroz Shah	Columbia University, USA
Ghali Naami	Sidi Mohamed Ben Abdellah University, Morocco
Jencia J.	Karunya Institute of Science and Technology, India
Pratap Sekhar Puhan	Sreenidhi Institute of Science and Technology, India
Priscilla Joy	Noorul Islam University, India
Meng Wei	Lanzhou Jiaotong University, China
S. G. Hymlin Rose	RMD College of Engineering, India
Ke Wang	University of North Carolina at Charlotte, USA
Rajanarayan Prusty	Alliance University, India
Kamal Saluja	Chitkara University Institute of Engineering and Technology, India

| Dmitry Morkovkin | Financial University under the Government of the Russian Federation, Russia |
| Dmitry Rastyagaev | Russian New University, Russia |

Organizing Committee

Arthur Gibadullin	National Research University "Moscow Power Engineering Institute", Russia
Elena Bovtrikova	Russian New University, Russia
Olga Matyunina	Russian New University, Russia
Dmitry Morkovkin	Financial University under the Government of the Russian Federation, Russia
Dmitry Rastyagaev	Russian New University, Russia

Organizer

Russian New University, Russia

Contents

The Structure and Principle of the Intelligent Micro-arc Oxidation System Operation

Ekaterina Pecherskaya$^{(\boxtimes)}$, Pavel Golubkov⑩, Vladimir Alexandrov⑩,
Kirill Nikishin⑩, and Ilya Kiryutkin⑩

Penza State University, 40, Krasnaya Street, Penza 440026, Russia
pea1@list.ru

Abstract. The purpose of the work is to create an intelligent technology for obtaining oxide coatings with specified properties through an automated system being developed. The developed intelligent system implements the method of micro-arc oxidation to obtain protective oxide coatings on products made of aluminum, titanium or their alloys. The intelligent system consists of hardware, software, and information content. The software is developed in the LabVIEW graphical programming environment. The intelligent application contains three subroutines: identification of the electrophysical model parameters and optimization of process parameters to obtain the required properties of oxide coatings; visualization of the coating parameters dependences in real time on influencing factors. The algorithm of the developed automated system functioning is presented. The presence of an intelligent application allows feedback for software, in which the process current source can change the oxidation mode depending on the coating state at a given time, taking into account the required target coating parameters (thickness, porosity, hardness, etc.). The advantage of the proposed intelligent system is the possibility of implementing a regime of controlled synthesis of oxide coatings with the required properties. In turn, it makes it possible to increase the reproducibility of the MAO coatings parameters, reduce the time for testing the technological process.

Keywords: Intelligent Automated System · Process Current Source · Information Content · Oxide Coating · Algorithm

1 Introduction

With the development of programmable logic controllers since the late 1960s, a new stage of the creation of methods and algorithms for controlling complex technical systems began. In the last decade, real-time object monitoring systems have become widespread in various fields, they are becoming intelligent tools capable of solving a wide range of management tasks. Such devices necessarily contain a microprocessor system for collecting and processing information. For example, [1] an intelligent integrated air pollution monitoring system with Internet of Things support, built on the basis of the Arduino hardware platform is presented.

© The Author(s), under exclusive license to Springer Nature Switzerland AG 2024
A. Gibadullin (Ed.): ITIDMS 2023, CCIS 2112, pp. 1–11, 2024.
https://doi.org/10.1007/978-3-031-60318-1_1

The article [2] contains the basic principles of building a multichannel system for collecting and preprocessing information about the control object state based on the precision analog microcontroller ADuC7060/61 Analog Devices in real time. The authors of the study [3] present the result of the development of a hardware sorting mechanism for peripheral computing devices with limited area and power consumption. It is important to use intelligent transport systems as part of a "smart city", which advisably can be presented in the form of a five-level hierarchical architecture, at the lower level of which there are sensors and actuators [4]. In control systems, feedback between sensors and actuators is organized thanks to programmable logic controllers. It opens up wide opportunities for the introduction of intelligent systems for automation of technological processes, control of technological parameters in real time. In [5–8], the possibility of automating the micro-arc oxidation (MAO) process for obtaining oxide coatings on products made of metals and alloys of the light group is described.

The recognized world leader in the field of micro-arc oxidation is Keronite, which offers its own range of automated process equipment. For example, an industrial installation with a capacity of 100 kW allows the application of MAO coatings in a pulsed bipolar mode with an adjustable voltage and current amplitude, pulse frequency and duty cycle [9, 10]. IBC Coatings Technologies (USA) has developed an MAO installation that allows performing various types of electrolyte-plasma treatment using a controlled source of rectangular high-voltage pulses of technological current [11, 12]. MILMAN THIN FILM SYSTEMS PVT. LTD. (India) has developed an automated Plasma electrolytic power supply installation, which is equipped with a remote touch control panel for the convenience of the operator [13]. The company "Mao Environmental Protection Technology Dg Co., Ltd" (China) produces MAO installations of three main types: fully inverter (4th generation); with the possibility of parallel connection (5th generation); based on a process current source with short pulses and low energy consumption (6th generation) [14].

The identified promising scientific and technical solutions were used in the development of an intelligent automated system structure for obtaining protective coatings of light alloys by the method of micro-arc oxidation, presented by the authors in this article.

2 The Structure of an Intelligent Micro-arc Oxidation System

The main functional parts of the proposed intelligent system for obtaining micro-arc coatings are hardware and software, as well as an information content subsystem (Fig. 1).

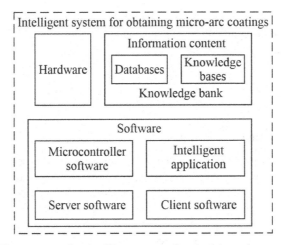

Fig. 1. The structure of an intelligent system for obtaining micro-arc coatings.

2.1 Hardware Part of an Intelligent System for Obtaining Micro-arc Coatings

The elements included in the hardware of the intelligent system (Fig. 2) are a galvanic cell, a process current source and a standby power source, measuring unit and control unit.

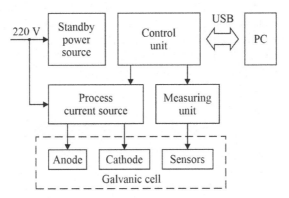

Fig. 2. Hardware part of the intelligent system.

The generation of a pulsed current for the formation of a micro-arc oxide layer on the sample is provided by a process current source. The process current source allows you to adjust a large number of electrical parameters of the output signal: amplitude, frequency, duration, polarity and pulse repetition mode, which makes it possible to effectively control the energy supply to the sample surface.

The standby power source is designed to power low-voltage circuits of measurement and control units, as well as other components of an automated system (for example, protection circuits). The standby power source is always on; it is used to control the switching on the process current source.

In the structure of the measuring unit, measuring channels, which are designed to measure both the control parameters of the technological process and the parameters of the oxide layers can be distinguished:

– Current strength, electrical voltage of the galvanic cell;
– The electrolyte parameters, which include its resistance, temperature and turbidity;
– Optical and acoustic parameters of micro-arc discharges;
– Coating impedance;
– Coating thickness (indirect determination by impedance).

The signals from the measuring channels are sent to the microprocessor control unit, which transmits them via the USB interface to the computer. Then, using the program, the measurement results are processed and used to construct the characteristic curves of the MAO process: the forming curve, dynamic current-voltage characteristics, etc. The output signals of the measuring channels also serve as an element of software feedback, through which the coating formation process is controlled.

The signals for controlling the nodes of the intelligent system are generated by the control unit, which provides a computer connection with the process current source and the measuring unit. The control unit includes a microcontroller, which, in turn, contains the following components: an analog-to-digital converter (ADC) for digitizing the analog output signals of the measurement module, a digital-to-analog converter (DAC) for controlling the process current source, a UART module (for communication with a computer), I/O ports for connecting external peripheral devices.

A galvanic cell is a bath with an electrolyte in which the anode (sample) and cathode are immersed. The bath is equipped with sensors of various physical quantities measured during the MAO treatment, as well as a protective fence. The galvanic cell is equipped with a cooling system on the Peltier element and a mixing system that circulates the electrolyte to maintain a constant temperature of the electrolyte and a continuous influx of ions to the sample surface.

2.2   Information Content Subsystem of the Intelligent System

The information content (Fig. 3) is a knowledge bank containing knowledge bases and databases. Conditionally, the knowledge bank contents can be divided into four subsystems. The MAO coatings subsystem contains information about the MAO coatings properties, as well as about the influencing factors of the MAO process. The subsystem of theoretical research concentrates knowledge about the physico-chemical laws applicable in the study and modeling of the MAO process, as well as about the currently existing mathematical expressions describing the relationship between the technological parameters of the MAO process, properties and quality parameters of coatings. The experimental studies subsystem includes information on methods and means of measuring the technological parameters of the MAO process and coating properties, their metrological characteristics, as well as on the technological modes used. The reference subsystem contains reference data on the MAO process mechanism and the MAO coatings application. All knowledge bases and databases available in the knowledge bank have the possibility of additions, which allows you to add new and refine existing mathematical models and technological modes of the MAO process, adjust measurement methods, thus improving the entire system operation.

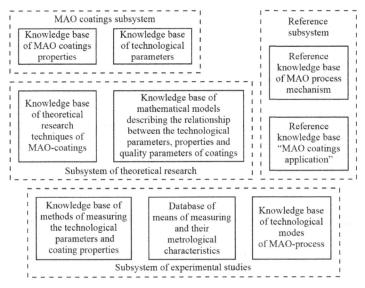

Fig. 3. Structure of the knowledge bank.

2.3 Software of the Intelligent Automated Micro-arc Oxidation System

The software includes microcontroller software and server software, an intelligent application that implements the methods of controlled synthesis of MAO coatings developed by the authors, and client software designed for user interaction. The microcontroller software is designed to control the process current source, process signals from measuring transducers and transfer the received information to a PC, as well as perform service functions (error messages, indication, etc.). The microcontroller software has been developed, which provides procedures for controlling the process current source; transmits signals for connecting measuring transducers and transmitting information from the output of measuring channels to a computer; performs service functions (for example, error reporting, indication, etc.). The server software is responsible for configuring the system and controlling the microcontroller. The intelligent application processes data from the output measuring transducers based on the proposed intelligent algorithms. In order to ensure the controlled synthesis of oxide coatings form control commands coming to the process current source, which varies the amplitude, duty cycle, frequency of current pulses intelligent algorithms and techniques are applied to the workpiece with a modifiable surface. The intelligent application structure is shown in Fig. 4.

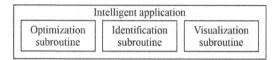

Fig. 4. The structure of an intelligent application.

The intelligent application contains three subroutines: optimization, identification and visualization. The optimization subroutine selects the technological regime parameters, which lead to obtaining coating properties as close as possible to the target ones, based on the information contained in the knowledge bases of technological parameters and properties of MAO coatings. The identification subroutine allows to identify the parameters of the electrical circuit of the galvanic cell corresponding to the resistance and capacitance of the coating, based on experimentally measured current-voltage characteristics of the galvanic cell for the selected optimal technological mode, taken from the knowledge base, by parametric identification. The visualization subroutine allows, using the parameters obtained by the identification subroutine, to simulate a change in the current-voltage characteristic of a galvanic cell to obtain the required target coating characteristics over the entire MAO processing interval, determine the deviation of experimental data from the calculated voltage curve and apply the appropriate control action to the process current source to minimize this deviation. It is how programmatic feedback is implemented.

3   The Algorithm of the Intelligent System Functioning

The algorithm of the intelligent system functioning is presented below. The exchange of information between different parts of the software is carried out using data packets, is shown in Fig. 5 (a). The presence of an intelligent application allows to implement software feedback, in which the process current source can change the oxidation mode depending on the coating state at a given time, taking into account the required target characteristics of the coating (Fig. 5 (b)).

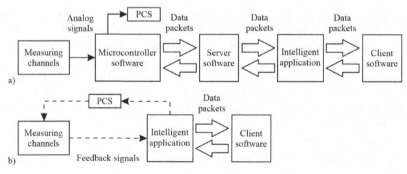

Fig. 5. Information exchange between different parts of the intelligent system software: a) as it is; b) with software feedback.

The software operates in two modes (Fig. 6):

- Experimental research mode;
- Controlled synthesis mode.

The experimental research mode is designed to establish experimental dependencies between the technological parameters of the MAO process and the properties of the coatings being formed in order to replenish the data bank. In this mode, the user sets the technological parameters of the process and starts the process current source. The intelligent application is not involved, the process proceeds in the usual way, the coatings properties are unknown in advance. The values of the applied technological parameters, the results of measurements of the electrical characteristics of the MAO process and the coating being formed are stored in the data bank.

The controlled synthesis mode is designed to produce MAO coatings with the required properties. In this mode of operation, the user sets the required coating charac-teristics. The required coating properties can be set either directly by entering a numeric value or by using limiting conditions. Next, the optimization subroutine as part of an intelligent application calculates the optimal variant of technological parameters and outputs a message to the operator. If the required parameters cannot be achieved (with the available set of modes in the database), two options are offered:

1. Pass to experimental research mode and get the missing data;
2. The set of coating properties closest to the target characteristics and the corresponding technological regime are calculated.

If the mode according to option 2 is acceptable for solving the problem, the operator starts the micro-arc oxidation process.

The micro-arc oxidation process includes two stages: preparatory and basic. At the preparatory stage, the protective enclosure condition of the galvanic cell and the electrolyte state are checked, provided that the part is already fixed in the galvanic cell. In addition, at this stage, the measurement channels of the galvanic cell impedance are automatically calibrated. If safety violations are detected (the protective fence is open), or improper electrolyte quality, warning messages should be sent to the operator's computer.

The program window in the oxidation mode is shown in Fig. 7. The user interface controls are located on the left side of the window on the "Oxidation" tab. The right side of the window is occupied by the digital oscilloscope screen.

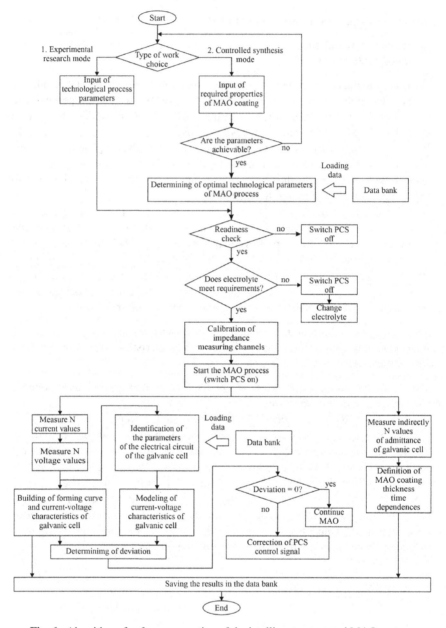

Fig. 6. Algorithm of software operation of the intelligent automated MAO system.

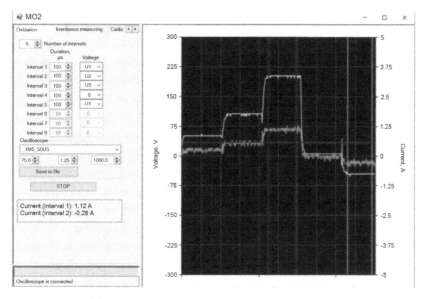

Fig. 7. The program interface in the oxidation mode.

When the preparatory stage is completed, the process current source is turned on, and the main stage - the MAO processing itself begins. At the same time, identification and visualization subroutines are included as part of an intelligent application, cyclic measurement of process parameters and formed coatings takes place, and software feedback is implemented according to the principle described above. The measurements results of the MAO process electrical characteristics (current-voltage characteristics of the galvanic cell, frequency characteristics of the impedance at specified times, forming curves), time dependences of the thickness of the formed coatings are stored in a data bank and displayed on the operators monitor. For example, Fig. 8 shows an experimentally obtained forming curve, the analysis of which allows us to judge the mechanism of growth of oxide layers under the influence of influencing factors and contains information about the formed coatings properties [7, 8].

The obtained dependences can be used both to study the MAO process and to improve the methods of controlled synthesis in order to improve the formed coatings quality.

The advantage of the controlled synthesis mode is that it allows to increase the reproducibility of the MAO coatings properties, the disadvantage is the need for a large set of experimental results in a data bank for different technological modes.

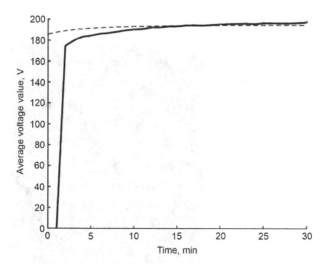

Fig. 8. Calculated and experimental time dependences of forming voltage.

4 Conclusion

The structure of an intelligent automated micro-arc oxidation system, which includes hardware, software, databases and knowledge bases as information content is proposed. The intelligent system provides the following functions:

- Setting process current parameters;
- Automated selection of technological parameters for obtaining MAO coatings with specified properties;
- Monitoring and correction of deviations of the MAO process from a given technological mode by means of software feedback;
- Real-time construction and graphical display of functional dependencies of the synthesized coatings parameters on technological modes for operator control of the process.

Acknowledgements. The work was carried out with the support of the Ministry of Science and Higher Education of the Russian Federation, the project "Fundamentals of the digital twin of the technological process of formation of oxide coatings with specified properties by the method of microarc oxidation", No. 123091800009-1.

References

1. Senthilkumar, R., Venkatakrishnan, P., Balaji, N.: Intelligent based novel embedded system based IoT enabled air pollution monitoring system. Microprocess. Microsyst. **77**, 103172 (2020)
2. Latenko, V., Ornatsky, I.A., Fil, S.O., Zaitsev, I.: Digital converters metrological specification for resistant thermal thermosensors compare. Tekhnichna Elektrodynamika **1**, 84–89 (2021)

3. Beitollahi, H., Pandi, M., Moghaddas, M.: Edge-sorter: a hardware sorting engine for area & power constrained edge computing devices. Microprocess. Microsyst. **105**, 105006 (2024)
4. Milik, A.: On hardware synthesis and implementation of PLC programs in FPGAs. Microprocess. Microsyst. **44**, 2–16 (2016)
5. Pecherskaya, E.A., Golubkov, P.E., Artamonov, D.V., Melnikov, O.A., Karpanin, O.V., Zinchenko, T.O.: Intelligent technology of oxide layer formation by micro-arc oxidation. IEEE Trans. Plasma Sci. **49**(9), 2613–2617 (2021)
6. Pecherskaya, E., Golubkov, P., Zinchenko, T., Kozlov, G., Alexandrov, V.: On the issue of modeling the process of microarc oxidation. AIP Conf. Proc. **2911**, 020018 (2023)
7. Melnikov, O.A., Pecherskaya, E.A., Golubkov, P.E., Kozlov, G.V., Alexandrov, V.S.: Modeling of the dynamic current-voltage characteristic of micro-arc oxidation. St. Petersburg State Polytech. Univ. J. Phys. Math. **16**(3.1), 335–340 (2023)
8. Golubkov, P.E., Pecherskaya, E.A., Gurin, S.A., Alexandrov, V.S., Artamonov, D.V., Maksov, A.A.: Influence of process parameters on the properties of microarc oxide coatings. St. Petersburg State Polytech. Univ. J. Phys. Math. **16**(3.1), 368–373 (2023)
9. Almashhadani, H.A., Khadom, A.A., Khadhim, M.M.: Effect of Polyeugenol coating on surface treatment of grade 23 titanium alloy by micro arc technique for dental application. Results Chem. **4**, 100555 (2022)
10. Troughton, S.C., Nomine, A., Nomine, A., Henrion, G., Clyne, B.: Synchronised electrical monitoring and high speed video of bubble growth associated with individual discharges during plasma electrolytic oxidation. Appl. Surf. Sci. **359**, 405–411 (2015)
11. Dehnavi, V., Luan, B.L., Shoesmith, D.W., Liu, X.Y., Rohani, S.: Effect of duty cycle and applied current frequency on plasma electrolytic oxidation (PEO) coating growth behavior. Surf. Coat. Technol. **226**, 100–107 (2013)
12. Wei, F., Zhang, W., Zhang, T., Wang, F.: Effect of variations of Al content on microstructure and corrosion resistance of PEO coatings on Mg-Al alloys. J. Alloy. Compd. **690**, 195–205 (2017)
13. Martin, J., et al.: The influence of metallurgical state of substrate on the efficiency of plasma electrolytic oxidation (PEO) process on magnesium alloy. Mater. Des. **178**, 107859 (2019)
14. Shi, M., Li, H.: The morphology, structure and composition of microarc oxidation (MAO) ceramic coating in Ca-P electrolyte with complexing agent EDTMPS and interpretation hypothesis of MAO process. Surf. Eng. Appl. Electrochem. **52**(1), 32–42 (2016)

Development of a Methodology for Implementing Object Storage of File Management System in a Microservice Architecture

Ahmed Magomedov[1] , Natalia Mamedova[1] (✉) , Huaming Zhang[2] ,
and Olga Staroverova[1]

[1] Plekhanov Russian University of Economics, 36, Stremyanny lane, Moscow 117997, Russia
nmamedova@bk.ru
[2] School of Economics, Shanxi University of Finance and Economics, No. 696, Wuchenglu,
Taiyuan 030006, Shanxi, China

Abstract. This paper describes the process and results of developing a methodology that contributes to the full implementation of an object storage file management system. The methodology is designed for use in the implementation of information systems with a microservice architecture. The sites of the digital platform became the pilot site of the study. A practical request for the development of the methodology is the need for digital platforms to organize the storage of website content and organize access to it. As a result of the conducted research, the effectiveness of the methodology for optimizing the process of filling in the content on digital platform sites when using a file management system is substantiated. The application of the file management system implementation methodology is designed to optimize the work with content. The solution can be scaling for other systems in the context of micro service architecture. This will require partial adaptation of the methodology to the current requirements and needs of the systems. The fact that the implementation of the methodology reduces the time for the implementation of the content filling process allows us to assume that the methodology can be tested in other systems after the analysis. The developed methodology has a great potential for development due to the expansion of functionality.

Keywords: Object Storage · File Management System · Microservice Architecture · Distributed System · Digital Platform

1 Introduction

The development of systems with microservice architecture is a complex and lengthy process. With such an architecture, the task of storing and processing files in file systems becomes non-trivial. Each microservice is independent of the other, and their file space functions independently. Choosing an implementation of a file management system that would ensure proper storage and effective interaction with files cannot have a single

A. Gibadullin (Ed.): ITIDMS 2023, CCIS 2112, pp. 12–25, 2024.
https://doi.org/10.1007/978-3-031-60318-1_2

solution. But want to demonstrate the best way to implement a file management system for digital platform sites. After all, the problem of organizing and managing content is key for them.

The intensive digitalization observed in the world due to the epidemiological situation, on the one hand, has marked new high requirements for the quality of content. On the other hand, there is a great potential for the growth of the digital component of the processes of customer interaction with digital platforms. And this trend is reinforced by external signals, such as an increase in the volume of data, an increase in demand for online services. It is quite natural that the tasks of storing information and organizing access to it remain relevant.

Object storage, as a computer data storage architecture, is a popular solution that has no critical drawbacks [1, 2]. Data management as objects provides storage of objects at several levels, including the device level (object storage device), the system level and the interface level. As a bonus of using object storage, you can designate, for example, interfaces that are directly programmed by the application, a namespace that can span multiple instances of physical hardware, as well as data management functions such as data replication and data distribution with object-level granularity.

Our area of interest is related to the organization of data protection [3, 4]. Definitely, data replication is needed for reliable storage in an object system. But at the same time, you do not need to arrange the amount of disk space, as in a block system. For example, if double or triple redundancy is required to implement the Redundant Array of Independent Disks (RAID) data protection method, then you use Erasure Coding technology in object storage. This technology saves hard disk space compared to replication and thereby maximizes available disk space and data protection.

Object storage is focused on working with unstructured data [5]. The efficiency of storing unstructured data in the form of files is directly related to their content and the context in which support should be provided. And, if structured data is created for the purpose of their further efficient extraction from databases, then for unstructured data, their contents and the spatiotemporal environment in which they are created are more important. This implies the dependence of the object storage on the quality of industry support. But, despite the evolutionary development of the concept of object storage, issues of such support still do not have widespread universal solutions [6, 7].

Two approaches are used to store data within the microservice architecture – centralized and decentralized approaches. The choice in favor of one of them depends on the current implemented information system, its requirements. The sources that contained the results of using the centralized storage approach in a single database for a file management system were studied [5, 8, 9], and they accepted the fact that this approach is optimal. Our own experience in the architecture of file management systems has shown that for a microservice architecture with a large number of services, where each service uses its own disk space, a centralized approach to management also has an advantage over a decentralized one.

Of course, there is a need to bear the costs of low-level design, since such a system has a high degree of complexity of implementation. After all, it should be able to work with several object repositories at once, be able to synchronize with them and provide an interface for file management to other services. However, in the long term, the maintenance of the system and its refinement will require much lower costs.

And although practice shows that the number of system failures with a centralized approach is lower than with a decentralized one [10], it would be unfair not to mention the lack of a centralized file management system in the microservice architecture. A system failure leads to the failure of files in all services. Working with files in the administrative system also becomes impossible. At the same time, the number of requests to the system increases. To work with files, the service will need to send a request to a centralized file management system each time, which increases the total number of requests to the system.

2 Materials and Methods

One understands the subject area of our research as the issues of developing an object storage file management system in a microservice architecture. The purpose of the study was to formulate a methodological solution for automating the process of filling in content on the site through the introduction of a file management system.

The objectives of the research included:

1. To study and describe file management systems in object repositories.
2. To study and describe the features of the current micro-service architecture using the example of a conditional dealer platform.
3. Analyze and compile business requirements and functional requirements for the file management system.
4. Analyze the content management processes that are the object of the study.
5. Develop a methodology for implementing a file management system in object storage.

The study was conducted within certain limits, which were formulated as follows:

– The ability to fill in content using only the file management system;
– The ability to use the file management system by company employees to create their own file data banks;
– The possibility of using the developed methodology only for the implementation of information systems with microservice architecture.

To fulfill the task of our research, one took as an example the conditional microservice architecture of the site and the digital platform (see Fig. 1).

Each server microservice has its own database, but the principle of storing files in file storage is different for the site and the digital platform. The site and digital platform use the Amazon Web Services (AWS) S3 compatible Minion object storage. The current storage conditions are as follows. There is no private part in the architecture of the digital platform. Reports or other files that need protection are not created for the digital platform. The file server has a closed part designed for creating reports for users of the administrative system. And also has a public part dedicated to images and files on the site.

Each microservice interacts with its disk using a set of development tools for the interaction of web Services Developed Kit (SDK) in Hypertext Preprocessor (PHP),

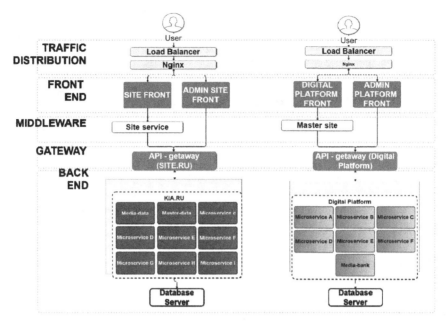

Fig. 1. Micro service architecture of the website and digital platform. Source: Compiled by the authors.

namely, the AWS SDK PHP. At the moment, it is a decentralized file management system in a distributed object storage. Since all files are stored on different disks, and file information is stored in each of the databases of each microservice, the services do not have access to other disks except their own.

The digital platform has only one "media bank" of disk space for all microservices of the system. Microservices of the digital platform interact only with it. But at the same time, each service interacts with the disk space independently. This is how a decentralized approach to managing a single object storage space manifests itself.

The process of the microservice working with the object storage is organized as follows. Each microservice implements the functionality of interacting with the object storage in the AWS SDK PHP. The main process of interaction is saving the file in the file storage. This process is implemented on each microservice. The process consists of three main stages, shown in Fig. 2.

The file is saved to the file storage only when any entity of the system is saved. At the same time, many files can be saved in some entities at once. All files are sent in one request by the HTTP1.1 protocol using the POST method. The file saving process goes through the following steps:

1. The administrative system sends a POST request with files and information about the entity to the microservice.
2. Microservice saves all files in the file storage and assigns unique identifiers to all files.
3. Microservice saves information about files in the files table.
4. The microservice saves the entity and specifies the file IDs for the entity.

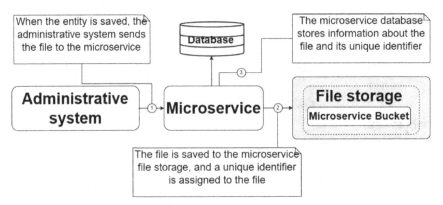

Fig. 2. The process of saving a file through the administrative system. Source: Compiled by the authors.

5. The microservice sends a response to the administrative system about the successful saving of the entity.

All information about files is stored in the files table in the database of each service. The table structure of each service is identical.

The features of this way of working with files and entities were determined. The fact is that the volume of the request size has limitations. They can be configured for each service, but this causes problems. For example, when a user adds a large number of images in a single request. As a result, the service cannot process it and issues server error 413. In addition, with large requests, the response speed increases proportionally. And the response time from the server may be longer than the waiting time for the browser response. In this case, the user will see a server error, although the item will be successfully updated.

Thus, it can be seen that the approach to organizing the work of the system with files on a digital platform and on a website is different. The digital platform has decentralized management and storage of file data in databases, and the files themselves are stored in a single object storage. While the site in the distributed object storage has decentralized management and storage of file data in databases. The principle of operation of the administrative system with microservices on the digital platform and the website is the same.

Hence, the methodological task for the solution being developed is formulated. As a result of the implementation of the methodology, the file management system should be able to work with both distributed object storage and a single object storage.

Approaching the solution of the problem, systems were studied that provide the ability to work with object storage [11–13]. Special attention was paid to systems implemented in php and the Laravel framework. This is due to the current IT architecture of the digital platform in question, which is a kind of functional limitation of study [14]. Frameworks that allow you to work with a Laravel-based file system have a similar set of functions. Some use a database to store information about files, some work directly with the file system. Summarizing the information received about the studied frameworks (alexusmai/laravel-file-manager; spatie/laravel-medialibrary), there was an indication of a common problem for them. It consists in the lack of integration with external services and the lack of data storage in a single database. One also concluded that at the moment there is no solution that would allow us to create a file management system in a microservice architecture with a single database and a management point. These solutions only partially cover the functional needs of the system.

To approach the problem of choosing a way to implement a file management system, one focused on modern approaches to organizing the work of object storage in a microservice architecture. And based our conclusions on the identified problem areas when implementing object storage in a microservice architecture. Functional recommendations for us were the results of an assessment of the current architecture of the digital platform and the site for which the file management system being developed will be implemented. The field of solutions includes all known approaches to the implementation of object storage file management systems. Based on the results of preliminary work, it was concluded that the optimal solution should correspond to the following parameters:

- Centralized data storage in the database;
- Centralized management and interaction with files;
- The system should allow working with distributed object file storage (physical file storage).

This solution was confirmed by the results of an expert assessment of reliability and scalability.

3   Results of the Study

The method of implementing the file manager of the file storage in the microservice architecture was developed based on the above functional requirements of the file management system.

The methodology is structured according to the following sections:

1. The general principle of the file management system microservice.
2. Data storage model of the file management system.
3. The mechanism of working with object storage.
4. The principle of interaction with public services.
5. Migration of object storage data to the file management system.
6. Administrative system, the interface of the file management system, which includes:

- working with object storage files;
- binding a file to an entity using the file management system interface.

The General Principle of Operation of the File Management System Microservice

The file management system microservice (hereinafter referred to as the media-bank microservice) will perform all basic operations and will become a link between the object storage and other systems. All requests related to files will be sent to media-bank. The microservice will work directly with object storage and bucket and have its own Application Programming Interface (API) for integrating external microservices that will work with files. Microservice of the file management system, has its own PostgreSQL database, the name of the media-bank database.

The media-bank microservice only serves as an interface for managing object storage, it provides a full range of storage management capabilities to other services that have access to management.

The interface of communication of the media-bank microservice with other services is implemented through the implemented API. The main manipulations with files are performed by the services of administrative systems, in our case, the administrative system of the digital platform and the website. Microservices designed to work with the public part of the site interact directly with the media-bank microservice via the API to obtain information about files and images. The process of interaction with the media-bank microservice is shown in Fig. 3.

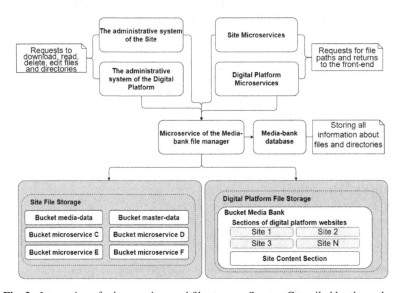

Fig. 3. Interaction of microservices and file storage. Source: Compiled by the authors.

The media-bank microservice is the central element of the system, which provides a connecting function of all other systems with object storage and database.

The methodology of developing a file manager when working with multiple object storages was described here, examples of a data storage model were also given, the data structure, the software used to implement the file manager, the database organization and the general principle of operation of the media-bank microservice with external services were described.

Data Storage Model of the File Management System

Data about file storages is stored in the media_library_storages table. All accesses to object stores are not stored in the database for security purposes. Special environment variables are provided for this function, which are passed to the microservice when it is initialized in the system.

Data about directories in file storages is stored in the media_library_sections table.

PostgreSQL allows you to use module JavaScript Object Notation (updated module JSOND) fields for filtering and other manipulations, so using JSOND format is optimal, both for queries and for future scaling of the system. A graphical representation of the data storage model with relationships between tables can be seen in Fig. 4.

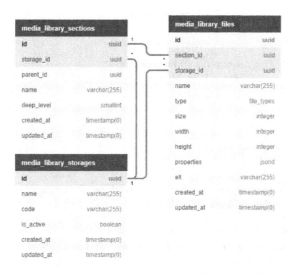

Fig. 4. Media-bank database data storage model. Source: Compiled by the authors.

The Mechanism of Working with Object Storage.

The microservice is written in php 7.2. The php league/fly system framework was used for development, which allows you to work with both local storage and object storage. It is compatible with AWS S3, which is the Minio object storage (see Fig. 2). To work with AWS S3, the package uses the standard AWS SDK PHP v3, which fully covers the needs of our implemented file management system.

To work with each of the repositories, accesses to it must be specified in the environment variables, accesses must be specified separately for each bucket, access settings are specified in a special config file/ filesystems.php. An example of access settings is shown in Fig. 5.

The 'media-bank' key is the 'code' field in the media_library_storages table, which is how the microservice identifies access to each of the bucket.

The construction of the format "env('MASTER_DATA_ACCESS_KEY')" is used to work with environment variables. This will allow you to hide and secure important information – to take it outside the code.

The Principle of Interaction with Public Services

One of the functions of the file management system is to provide information about the path to the file to display these files on the site.

Thus, each service that uses files on the public part of the site sends requests to the file management system to obtain the path of files and additional information. For example,

```
[
  'disks' => [
    'media-bank' => ['driver' => 's3',
      'endpoint' => env('MINIO_URL'),
      'key' => env('MINIO_ACCESS_KEY'),
      'secret' => env('MINIO_SECRET_KEY'), 'region' =>
      env('MINIO_DEFAULT_REGION'),
      'bucket' => env('MINIO_BUCKET'),
      'use_path_style_endpoint' => true,
    ],
    'master-data' => ['driver' => 's3',
      'endpoint' => env('SITE_MINIO_URL'),
      'key' => env('MASTER_DATA_ACCESS_KEY'), 'secret' =>
      env('MASTER_DATA_SECRET_KEY'),
      'region' => env('MASTER_DATA_DEFAULT_REGION'),
      'bucket' => env('MASTER_DATA_BUCKET'),
      'use_path_style_endpoint' => true,
    ],
  ],
]
```

Fig. 5. An example of access settings. Source: Compiled by the authors.

the algorithm of interaction between the service and the file management system for the entity "Banners" on the site looks like this:

1. The site service sends a request to the media-data service to receive banners.
2. Media-data processes the request, makes a request to the database for obtaining a list of elements of the "Banner" entity.
3. After receiving the list of entities, media-data processes the list and generates a list of identifiers of all files.
4. Media-data sends a request to media-bank transmitting an array of file IDs to get information about files.
5. Media-data receives a list of files with information, media-data forms a resulting array, where the path to the image is specified for each banner image (see Fig. 6).

Thus, for an external system, it is necessary to carry out 5 steps to process the entity. Since the request occurs inside the local network, the speed of the request and response is extremely low.

Migration of Object Storage Data to a File Management System

The process of implementing a file management system involves synchronizing the entire current file system with the file management system. The main purpose of synchronization is to fill the database of the file management system with up-to-date information about the system files. This is necessary, since when implementing a file management system for the digital platform and the site, all the current filled content, all the files added to the file storage should not disappear from the site. In the current implementation, all files are stored in a special files table for each microservice. It is necessary to transfer all file data from the files table to the file management system tables, keeping the unique identifier of each file. Additionally, when saving a file, you must specify in which disk space the file is stored.

All files from external services are obtained by HTTP requests to microservices. On the microservice side, an API is implemented that returns a list of all files for the file management system in JSOND format (see Fig. 7).

```
{ ▼
  "content": { ▼
    "22070daf-720b-4c47-b9f0-1fb6ca0aad25": { ▼
      "alt": null,
      "id": "22070daf-720b-4c47-b9f0-1fb6ca0aad25",
      "name": "22070daf-720b-4c47-b9f0-1fb6ca0aad25.jpeg",
      "path": "/media-bank/menu/22070daf-720b-4c47-b9f0-1fb6ca0aad25.jpeg",
      "size": 7341
    },
    "78b37cc1-0508-4bfb-bdb6-189cdd17678f": { ▼
      "alt": null,
      "id": "78b37cc1-0508-4bfb-bdb6-189cdd17678f",
      "name": "78b37cc1-0508-4bfb-bdb6-189cdd17678f.png",
      "path": "/media-bank/menu/78b37cc1-0508-4bfb-bdb6-189cdd17678f.png",
      "size": 66896
    },
    "ba478287-eeb7-457f-8a14-14b443d0c832": { ▼
      "alt": null,
      "id": "ba478287-eeb7-457f-8a14-14b443d0c832",
      "name": "ba478287-eeb7-457f-8a14-14b443d0c832.png",
      "path": "/media-bank/menu/ba478287-eeb7-457f-8a14-14b443d0c832.png",
      "size": 84940
    },
    "be7fe3df-14dd-4ab0-b8a4-a09434ad4f19": { ▼
      "alt": null,
      "id": "be7fe3df-14dd-4ab0-b8a4-a09434ad4f19",
      "name": "be7fe3df-14dd-4ab0-b8a4-a09434ad4f19.jpeg",
      "path": "/media-bank/menu/be7fe3df-14dd-4ab0-b8a4-a09434ad4f19.jpeg",
      "size": 21203
    },
    "ce45b93a-dde7-4f15-80a5-d10a21f1d044": { ▼
      "alt": null,
      "id": "ce45b93a-dde7-4f15-80a5-d10a21f1d044",
      "name": "ce45b93a-dde7-4f15-80a5-d10a21f1d044.png",
      "path": "/media-bank/menu/ce45b93a-dde7-4f15-80a5-d10a21f1d044.png",
      "size": 48154
    },
    "dd6ee9c2-136f-4cc6-ae09-4cce67eac279": { ▼
      "alt": null,
      "id": "dd6ee9c2-136f-4cc6-ae09-4cce67eac279",
      "name": "dd6ee9c2-136f-4cc6-ae09-4cce67eac279.jpeg",
      "path": "/media-bank/menu/dd6ee9c2-136f-4cc6-ae09-4cce67eac279.jpeg",
      "size": 11392
    }
  },
  "error": 0
}
```

Fig. 6. Example of a file management system response, a list of files for external services. Source: Compiled by the authors.

```
{ ▼
  "directories": [],
  "files": [ ▼
    { ... "alt": null, "basename": "Lease Payments", "extension": "svg", "filename": "Lease Payments.svg", "height": null, "id": ... },
    { ... "alt": null, "basename": "Car In Garage", "extension": "svg", "filename": "Car In Garage.svg", "height": null, "id": ... },
    { ... "alt": null, "basename": "Contract", "extension": "svg", "filename": "Contract.svg", "height": null, "id": "3173bf97-4..." },
    { ... "alt": null, "basename": "person", "extension": "svg", "filename": "person.svg", "height": null, "id": "03dbe0eb-d127-..." },
    { ... "alt": null, "basename": "Special Prices", "extension": "svg", "filename": "Special Prices.svg", "height": null, "id": ... },
    { ... "alt": null, "basename": "Call", "extension": "svg", "filename": "Call.svg", "height": null, "id": "fb62235d-b709-46da..." },
    { ... "alt": null, "basename": "Autopark", "extension": "svg", "filename": "Autopark.svg", "height": null, "id": "14cbc2b9-0..." },
    { ... "alt": null, "basename": "Choice", "extension": "svg", "filename": "Choice.svg", "height": null, "id": "6e6b2028-b8f2-..." },
    { ... "alt": null, "basename": "Balance", "extension": "svg", "filename": "Balance.svg", "height": null, "id": "4fc19ae9-c3f..." },
    { ... "alt": null, "basename": "Currency In Circulation (1)", "extension": "svg", "filename": "Currency In Circulation (1).s..." },
    { ... "alt": null, "basename": "Effective Tool", "extension": "svg", "filename": "Effective Tool.svg", "height": null, "id": ... },
    { ... "alt": null, "basename": "price doc", "extension": "svg", "filename": "price doc.svg", "height": null, "id": "1f609f42..." },
    { ... "alt": null, "basename": "car revert", "extension": "svg", "filename": "car revert.svg", "height": null, "id": "9d20c3..." },
    { ... "alt": null, "basename": "timer", "extension": "svg", "filename": "timer.svg", "height": null, "id": "35ac02a7-ab72-49..." },
    { ▼
      "alt": null,
      "basename": "person_percent_(1)",
      "extension": "svg",
      "filename": "person_percent_(1).svg",
      "height": null,
      "id": "b9fd0e42-e24c-406b-0a5f-8693e600be7d",
      "path": "master-site/icons/person_percent_(1).svg",
      "properties": null,
      "section_id": "fbec3d70-05f7-42e9-9ea2-fdc16b428406",
      "size": 735,
      "timestamp": 1618915182,
      "type": "file",
      "width": null
    }
  ],
  "result": { ▼
    "message": null,
    "status": "success"
  }
}
```

Fig. 7. Example of a response from the file management system to receive a list of directory files. Source: Compiled by the authors.

It is necessary to implement a script that will synchronize the file data of external microservices with the file management system.

The algorithm of the script:

1. Getting a list of disk spaces for synchronization. For each microservice with which integration is required, an entry for each integrated microservice must be added to the media_library_storages table.
2. Start the synchronization process of each item from the list:

- Request to microservice to get a list of files with all information about the file (path to the file, file name);
- Creating a list of directories based on the file path to write to the media_library_sections table, additional checking for the presence of an existing directory in the table;
- Formation of a list of files linked to a directory for writing to the media_library_files table;
- Writing the directory entity to the media_library_sections table;
- Writing file entities to the media_library_files table;
- Requests to write data to tables occur within a single transaction.

3. Completion of synchronization.

The synchronization script is needed only at the stage of implementing a file management system and filling it with up-to-date data. It will allow you to switch to an object storage file management system without problems associated with displaying images.

Administrative System, File Management System Interface

In addition to the microservice, which implements an API for manipulating files, the file management system includes an interface for interacting with the file system using a file manager. The file manager must provide an interface for sending requests to the implemented API. For dynamic and convenient work, the Vue framework in JavaScript will be used. As an example, the alexusmai/laravel-file-manager file manager interface is taken, the set of functions mostly meets current needs. As part of the implementation of its own interface, it is necessary to rewrite direct interaction with the file storage of the alexusmai/laravel-file-manager file manager to interaction with the API of the object storage file management system (see Fig. 8).

```
public function createDirectory(string $storageId, string $disk, ?string $dealerId, ?array $parentDir, string $name): array
{
    $parentId = $parentDir['id'] ?? null;
    $deepLevel = $parentDir['deep_level'] ?? 0;

    $directory = Repository::sections()->getUniqueSection($storageId, $dealerId, $parentId, $name);

    if ($directory) return $this->directoryExists();

    $params = [
        'id' => (string)Str::uuid(),
        'dealer_id' => $dealerId,
        'parent_id' => $parentId,
        'storage_id' => $storageId,
        'name' => $name,
        'deep_level' => $deepLevel + 1,
        'created_at' => Carbon::now(),
        'updated_at' => Carbon::now()
    ];

    Repository::sections()->create($params);

    return $this->createDirectorySuccess();
}
```

Fig. 8. Sample code for creating directories. Source: Compiled by the authors.

The interaction must be implemented using asynchronous requests using the HTTP 1.1 protocol, the JSOND data transfer format. After implementing the file manager, it is necessary to integrate it into the administrative system. Working with the file manager will take place in two modes:

- Working with object storage files;
- Binding a file to an entity using a file manager.

Working with Object Storage Files

It is necessary to create a separate page in the administrative system, when the page is opened, the file manager will be connected and displayed. The file manager is displayed within the entire free space of the page. A separate page is needed to upload files to disk space, without the process of linking files to the system entity.

Binding a File to an Entity Using the File Management System Interface

In the administrative system, the user can create or edit system entities. Some entities in attributes have bindings to files. To bind a file to such entities, you need to use a file manager. In the administrative system, in the file selection field, when you click on the "Select file" button, a file manager opens. A double-click user can select a file in the file manager. After that, the file ID will be written to the entity attributes. After saving the entity, the file will be linked to the system entity.

Developed in accordance with the methodology, the file management system has centralized management and storage of data on files, and also has the ability to work with distributed object storage. Based on this, it can be concluded that the methodology fully satisfies all the requirements put forward.

4 Discussion

According to the results of the study, the following results were obtained:

1. The necessity of developing a new methodology to optimize the process of filling in content on the dealer site when using the file management system is justified.

The developed methodology for implementing an object storage file management system in a microservice architecture describes the process of working with files in graphical and textual form. Based on the traditional approach to the development of information services [1], the business and functional requirements for the operation of the system are described. The developed system allows you to upload files from local storage to remote storage and use remote storage as a file management system for filling content. An option that has already become generally applicable [3] has also been added to these solutions – the system allows you to use previously added content from the shared and personal file space.

Adaptation to a service-oriented architecture is nothing more than a way to achieve mandatory requirements for reliability, archiving and recovery time [8, 13]. The use of microservice architecture makes it possible to unify processes at the technical level, which simplifies the processes of monitoring both the system itself and the processes of its implementation. The content management system for dealer organizations allows you to significantly reduce the time for filling in the content of dealers' websites.

2. A methodology has been developed for implementing a file management system to optimize work with content on the site.

A methodology for implementing and organizing the process of a file management system and implementing it into an information system is proposed. Within the framework of the developed methodology, the joint use of a service-oriented architecture, a microservice approach is proposed, which corresponds to the popular concept of storing files in distributed object storage [6, 7, 10].

Within the framework of the methodology, a scenario of interaction of all services and a file management system with both the public part of the system and the administrative part is proposed.

The methodology describes the process of implementing the methodology and the mechanism of operation of the main functions of the file management system. The structure of the mechanism is given below:

1. The general principle of operation of the file management system microservice.
2. File management system data storage model.
3. The mechanism of working with object storage.
4. The principle of interaction with public services.
5. Migration of object storage data to the file management system.
6. Administrative system, file management system interface:

– Working with object storage files;
– Binding a file to an entity using the file management system interface.

Due to the microservice approach to the system, the implementation takes a small amount of time. Also, the probability of failure of some other external systems is minimal, despite the increase in the connectivity of system services. Each stage of implementation is easily tracked and logged. With the help of text search and attribute searches, it becomes possible to quickly request the necessary files in the file management system, which further reduces the time for solving tasks. All this can be considered as an advantage of the developed methodology and the solutions based on it.

5   Conclusion

The presented method of implementing a file management system allows you to significantly reduce labor costs for internal processes of the organization aimed at working with files, as well as increase the maturity of the processes themselves. It was based on the results of the study of modern approaches to the organization of object storage in microservice architecture, generalization of information about problem areas in the implementation of object storage in microservice architecture. The theoretical significance of the research results lies in the fact that data on technologies used in the processes of managing object storage files are structured. Using the example of a microservice architecture, the data is structured in such a way as to justify the developed methodology for implementing and implementing a file management system.

The indirect effect of the implementation of the system module is that when new services are added, the costs of implementing a new file management system will be significantly less than after implementation. It will also be more efficient to use the disk space of the file system, since it will be possible to create your own structure. In addition, the problem with duplicates of files disappears, which will entail saving memory.

The technique can be tested by dealer platforms, it is sufficiently developed so that end users can apply it. This is the applied significance of the research results.

References

1. Chevance, R.J.: Data storage. Serv. Archit., 377–472 (2005). https://doi.org/10.1016/B978-155558333-0/50011-0
2. Karakoyunlu, C., Chandy, J.A., Riska, A.: Adding data analytics capabilities to scaled-out object store. J. Syst. Softw. **121**, 16–27 (2016). https://doi.org/10.1016/J.JSS.2016.07.029
3. Bouaziz, S., Nabli, A., Gargouri, F.: Design a data warehouse schema from document-oriented database. Procedia Comput. Sci. **159**, 221–230 (2019). https://doi.org/10.1016/J.PROCS.2019.09.177
4. Dolk, D.R.: Integrated model management in the data warehouse era. Eur. J. Oper. Res. **122**, 199–218 (2000). https://doi.org/10.1016/S0377-2217(99)00229-5
5. Zezula, P., Rabitti, F.: Object store with navigation accelerator. Inf. Syst. **18**, 429–459 (1993). https://doi.org/10.1016/0306-4379(93)90002-I
6. Agarwal, A.K., Badal, N.: A novel approach for intelligent distribution of data warehouses. Egypt. Informatics J. **17**, 147–159 (2016). https://doi.org/10.1016/J.EIJ.2015.10.002
7. Karabey Aksakalli, I., Çelik, T., Can, A.B., Tekinerdoğan, B.: Deployment and communication patterns in microservice architectures: a systematic literature review. J. Syst. Softw. **180**, 111014 (2021). https://doi.org/10.1016/J.JSS.2021.111014
8. Hannousse, A., Yahiouche, S.: Securing microservices and microservice architectures: a systematic mapping study. Comput. Sci. Rev. **41**, 100415 (2021). https://doi.org/10.1016/J.COSREV.2021.100415
9. Zhao, H., Wang, S.: Data management trust system in pervasive environments. Procedia Environ. Sci. **11**, 334–338 (2011). https://doi.org/10.1016/J.PROENV.2011.12.053
10. Zhang, N., Yan, Y., Xu, S., Su, W.: A distributed data storage and processing framework for next-generation residential distribution systems. Electr. Power Syst. Res. **116**, 174–181 (2014). https://doi.org/10.1016/J.EPSR.2014.06.005
11. Chao, C.M.: Incremental maintenance of object-oriented data warehouses. Inf. Sci. (Ny) **160**, 91–110 (2004). https://doi.org/10.1016/J.INS.2003.07.014
12. Li, F., Du, J.: Mass data storage and management solution based on cloud computing. IERI Procedia **2**, 742–747 (2012). https://doi.org/10.1016/J.IERI.2012.06.164
13. Mateus-Coelho, N., Cruz-Cunha, M., Ferreira, L.G.: Security in microservices architectures. Procedia Comput. Sci. **181**, 1225–1236 (2021). https://doi.org/10.1016/J.PROCS.2021.01.320
14. Eichinger, F., Kramer, D., Böhm, K., Karl, W.: From source code to runtime behaviour: software metrics help to select the computer architecture. Knowl.-Based Syst. **23**, 343–349 (2010). https://doi.org/10.1016/J.KNOSYS.2009.11.014

Comparative Analysis of Traditional Machine Learning Approaches for Time Series Clustering Under Colored Noise

Petr Lukianchenko[ID] and Daniel Kopylov[✉][ID]

Higher School of Economics, 11 Pokrovskii bul., Moscow 119121, Russia
d.kopylov@centraluniversity.ru

Abstract. The work examines time series clustering using various machine learning approaches. The purpose of the study is to compare the performance of K-shape, K-means, and hierarchical density-based spatial clustering with noise (HDBSCAN) algorithms. Clusters were measured using the Rand Index, Adjusted Rand Index, Adjusted Mutual Information (AMI), and measures based on the electrocardiogram (ECG), ArrowHead, and SharePriceIncrease datasets. Noise was added to the time series data and clustering was performed on the noisy data. The resulting clusters were compared to the original clusters using Bcubed metrics to evaluate the robustness and accuracy of clustering algorithms in noise engineering. The results of the study will shed light on the effectiveness of these clustering algorithms in detecting anomalies in time series data. Additionally, the influence of colored noise on the accuracy and stability of the clustering algorithm will be determined.

Keywords: Time Series Clustering · K-shape · Noise Engineering

1 Introduction

Time series anomaly detection is an important area of research in several fields such as finance, healthcare, and cybersecurity. Cluster-based anomaly detection in time series data can help identify critical events or patterns that require immediate attention and manual decision making. Machine learning methods have shown effectiveness in clustering problems on complex time series data sets.

The purpose of the work is to compare the performance of four different clustering algorithms for detecting time series anomalies: K-shape, K-means with Euclidean distance metric, K-means with dynamic time warping (DTW) metric, and density-based hierar-chical spatial clustering. Applications with noise (HDBSCAN). These algorithms were selected based on their popularity and performance in research.

Three different data sets were selected to evaluate the clustering performance: electrocardiogram (ECG), arrowhead (ArrowHead), and stock price increase (Share-PriceIncrease). These datasets represent different time series fields: biology, physics, finance. Several metrics were used to assess the quality of clusters, including the Rand Index, Adjusted Rand Index, Adjusted Mutual Information (AMI), and Homogeneity.

© The Author(s), under exclusive license to Springer Nature Switzerland AG 2024
A. Gibadullin (Ed.): ITIDMS 2023, CCIS 2112, pp. 26–39, 2024.
https://doi.org/10.1007/978-3-031-60318-1_3

After evaluating the initial clusters, the effect of color noise on clustering performance is examined. Various types of color noise were added to the time series data to simulate real-world scenarios. The K-shape clustering algorithm was then applied to the noisy data, and the resulting clusters were compared with the original clusters using the Bcubed metric to evaluate reliability and accuracy.

The results of this study will provide valuable information about the performance of various algorithms. In addition, the influence of color noise on their accuracy and stability will be revealed.

2 Materials and Methods

Time series clustering is an important research area in machine learning and many authors have devoted their work to it.

Aghabozorgi, Shirkhorshidi, and Wah [1] present a comprehensive review of time-series clustering techniques over the past decade. They discuss different methods, such as hierarchical clustering, partitional clustering, grid-based clustering, and density-based clustering, and evaluate their strengths and weaknesses. The review also highlights the challenges and future directions in time-series clustering research.

Alqahtani, Ali, Xie, and Jones [2] focus on deep learning-based methods for time-series clustering. They explore various architectures, such as deep autoencoders, recurrent neural networks (RNNs), and long short-term memory (LSTM) networks, and discuss their applications in different domains. The review also discusses the challenges, limitations, and future research directions for deep time-series clustering.

Caiado, Maharaj, and D'Urso [3] provide an overview of time-series clustering, discussing both traditional and modern techniques. They cover distance measures, clustering algorithms, and evaluation metrics specific to time-series data. The chapter also discusses the challenges and open research questions in time-series clustering.

Ding, Wang, Dang, Fu, Zhang, and Zhang [4] introduce a fast and scalable time-series clustering algorithm called Yading. The algorithm utilizes a di-vide-and-conquer strategy to partition the data and employs an efficient indexing scheme based on the piecewise aggregate approximation (PAA) representation. The authors demonstrate the effectiveness and efficiency of Yading on large-scale time-series datasets.

Dose and Cincotti [5] focus on clustering financial time series data and its application in portfolio management. They propose a clustering approach based on the correlation matrix of the time series data and evaluate its performance by constructing index and enhanced index tracking portfolios.

Hautamaki, Nykanen, and Franti [6] present a time-series clustering algorithm called Time-Series Clustering with Approximate Prototypes (TSCAP). The algorithm approximates time series by a set of prototypes and uses the DTW distance measure and a modified k-means algorithm for clustering. Experimental results demonstrate the ef-fectiveness of TSCAP in capturing the patterns in time-series data.

Huang, Ye, Xiong, Lau, Jiang, and Wang [7] introduce a novel clustering algorithm called Time Series k-means (TSk-means) for time-series data. TSK-means considers each time series as a point in a multidimensional space and applies a smooth subspace clus-tering algorithm to identify clusters. The algorithm is evaluated on various datasets, demonstrating its effectiveness in capturing the similarities between time series.

Javed, Lee, and Rizzo [8] perform a benchmark study on different time-series clustering algorithms. They evaluate the performance of various algorithms, including k-means, hierarchical clustering, DBSCAN, and spectral clustering, on different types of time-series datasets. The evaluation includes metrics such as clustering accuracy, runtime, and stability, providing insights into the strengths and weaknesses of different algorithms.

Jokinen, Räty, and Lintonen [9] propose a density-based measure, called Cluster-ability Measure (CM), for analyzing the clustering structure in time-series data. CM assesses the clusterability of time-series data based on the density distribution of the data points. The authors perform experiments on various real-world datasets to evaluate the effectiveness of CM for analyzing the clustering structure in time-series data.

Kalpakis, Gada, and Puttagunta [10] focus on distance measures for clustering ARIMA time series data effectively. They propose two distance measures, Euclidian ARIMA (EARIMA) and dynamic time warping ARIMA (DTWARIMA), and compare their clustering performance on synthetic and real-world datasets.

Kotsakos, Trajcevski, Gunopulos, and Aggarwal [11] provide an overview of time-series data clustering, discussing various approaches, techniques, and challenges. They cover classical and modern time-series clustering algorithms, such as k-means, hierarchical clustering, density-based clustering, and subspace clustering. The chapter also discusses applications and future research directions in time-series data clustering.

Li and Prakash [12] introduce a time-series clustering algorithm called SaxDTW, which combines the symbolic aggregate approximation (SAX) representation with the dynamic time warping (DTW) distance measure. They argue that complexity in data representation can lead to simpler clustering algorithms. Experimental results demonstrate the effectiveness and efficiency of SaxDTW on various time-series datasets.

Liao [13] provides a comprehensive survey of time-series clustering algorithms. The author categorizes the algorithms into similarity-based methods, model-based methods, dimensionality reduction-based methods, and other methods. The survey discusses the strengths, weaknesses, and applications of different algorithms and provides insights into the challenges and future directions in time-series clustering research.

Ma, Zheng, Li, and Cottrell [14] focus on learning representations for time-series clustering. They propose a framework that leverages deep autoencoders to learn optimal representations for time series and introduce an unsupervised clustering loss that encourages the representations to capture the cluster structure. Experimental results demonstrate the superior performance of the proposed framework compared to traditional clustering algorithms.

Maharaj, D'Urso, and Caiado [15] provide a comprehensive overview of time-series clustering and classification techniques. They cover various methods, algorithms, and evaluation metrics specific to time-series data. The book also includes case studies and practical applications of time-series clustering and classification in different fields.

Montero and Vilar [16] introduce TSclust, an R package for time-series clustering. The package provides various clustering algorithms, distance measures, and visualization tools specifically designed for time-series data. The article provides an overview of the package's functionality, demonstrates its usage through examples, and discusses its advantages and limitations.

Paparrizos and Gravano [17] introduce k-Shape, a method for efficient and accurate clustering of time series. The method combines shapelets, representative subsequences that capture cluster shape.

Zotov and Lukianchenko [24] investigate bifurcation points in financial models by incorporating colored noise as a stochastic component in their study. Specifically, they examined the influence of colored noise on breakpoints and explored the feasibility of using neural networks to detect them. The Vasicek stochastic model, commonly employed in interest rate modeling, served as the research focus. A comprehensive literature review was conducted to explore existing studies on the utilization of colored noise in complex systems.

To evaluate the performance of clustering algorithms, three different datasets were selected: electrocardiogram (ECG), arrowhead (ArrowHead), and share price change (SharePriceIncrease). These datasets were selected to represent different areas of the time series and cover a wide range of anomalies.

Four different clustering algorithms were selected to detect time series anomalies: a) K-shape, b) K-means with Euclidean distance, c) K-means with dynamic time warping (DTW) metric, d) hierarchical spatial clustering based on application density with noise (HDBSCAN).

These algorithms were selected based on their popularity and performance reported in previous studies. Several metrics were used to assess the quality of clusters, including: a) Rand index, b) adjusted Rand index, c) adjusted mutual information (AMI), d) homogeneity measure. These metrics were calculated to compare the clustering performance of the four algorithms on the selected datasets.

To simulate real-world scenarios where time series data contains noise, various types of color noise were added to the original datasets. The introduction of color noise is aimed at assessing the stability and accuracy of clustering algorithms in the presence of noise. After introducing color noise, the K-shape clustering algorithm was applied to the noisy datasets.

The resulting clusters derived from the noisy data were compared with the original clusters using the B-cubed metric. This comparison allows us to evaluate the stability and accuracy of clustering algorithms in the presence of noise in time series data.

The performance of K-shape, K-means (with Euclidean distance and DTW metrics), and HDBSCAN clustering algorithms was compared based on the resulting clusters and evaluation measures. The impact of color noise on the accuracy and stability of these algorithms was analyzed and discussed.

3   Results

We focus on the analysis and clustering of various time series data sets obtained from the UCR Time Series Archive (Table 1), specifically from the website https://www.tim eseriesclassification.com/. Using these datasets allows research into a variety of fields, including healthcare, anthropology, and finance.

Table 1. Datasets.

Dataset name	ECG	ArrowHead	SharePriceIncrease
Dataset type	Biological	Physical	Financial
Number of time series	5000	211	1931
Time series length	140	251	60
Number of classes	5	3	2
Class 1	2919	81	1326
Class 2	1767	65	605
Class 3	194	65	–
Class 4	96	–	–
Class 5	24	–	–

The first dataset used in this study is the ECG5000 dataset, which contains a 20-h electrocardiography (ECG) signal. This signal was obtained from the Physionet database. To ensure consistency, the ECG signal was subjected to pre-processing steps such as extracting each individual heartbeat and standardizing their lengths using interpolation. As a result of random sampling, 5000 heart beats were selected for further analysis. The class labels associated with this dataset were obtained through automatic annotation and reflect the severity of congestive heart failure.

The normal class consists of ECG signals representing the standard electrical activity of a healthy heart, exhibiting regularity in waveform patterns with identifiable features. The abnormal class encompasses ECG signals that deviate from normal patterns due to various cardiac conditions or anomalies (see Fig. 1).

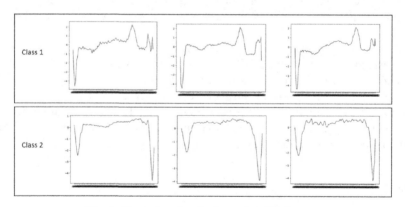

Fig. 1. Examples of main classes in ECG dataset.

The second dataset is the ArrowHead dataset, which contains the outlines of images representing arrowheads. To enable analysis, projectile point shapes were converted to time series using the angular method. The classification of these throwing points plays a crucial role in the field of anthropology. There are three distinct classes in this dataset: Avonlea, Clovis, and Mix. These classes represent unique differences in shape, including the presence and location of a notch on the frog (see Fig. 2).

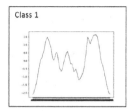
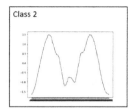
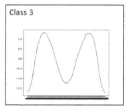

Fig. 2. Examples of main classes in Arrowhead dataset.

The third dataset examined in this study is the SharePriceIncrease dataset, a financial dataset designed to predict significant changes in a company's stock price following the announcement of quarterly earnings per share (EPS). The data in this set represents the percentage change in closing price for various NASDAQ 100 companies during the 60-day period before the company's report was released. The target class in this data set is defined as 0 if the price does not rise by more than 5 percent and 1 if the price rises by more than 5 percent. The SharePriceIncrease dataset was derived from daily price data obtained from the Kaggle dataset, and company reporting dates were obtained from NASDAQ.com (see Fig. 3).

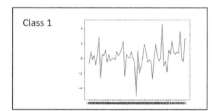
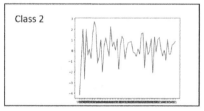

Fig. 3. Examples of main classes in SharePriceIncrease dataset.

Clustering metrics are used to evaluate the quality of the results of a clustering algorithm. They provide quantitative measures that can help determine the effectiveness of a clustering approach and compare different algorithms or parameter settings (Table 2).

Here are the formulas of the clustering metrics mentioned in Table 2:

Rand index (RI):

$$RI = (TP + TN) / (TP + FP + TN + FN) \tag{1}$$

where TP are true positives, FP are false positives, TN are true negatives and FN are false negatives;

Adjusted Rand index (ARI):

$$ARI = (RI - expected\_RI) / (max(RI) - expected\_RI) \tag{2}$$

Table 2. Clustering indices.

Clustering Metric	Strengths	Weaknesses
Rand index	Simple and easy to interpret	1. Sensitive to the number of clusters 2. Doesn't account for chance clustering
Adjusted Rand index	1. Handles chance clustering 2. Accounts for the number of clusters	1. Assumes independence between samples 2. Can produce negative values
Adjusted Mutual Information	1. Handles chance clustering 2. Accounts for the number of clusters 3. Doesn't assume independence between samples	1. Can be biased towards finding similar cluster sizes 2. Not suitable for large datasets
Homogeneity	1. Measures how pure clusters are 2. Insensitive to the number of clusters	1. Doesn't consider overlapping clusters 2. Ignores the actual content of cluster assignments
Bcubed	1. Measures precision and recall of each cluster 2. Considers overlapping clusters	1. Computationally expensive for large datasets 2. Requires ground truth cluster labels

where RI is Rand index, expected_RI is the expected value of Rand index given random assignment to clusters, max (RI) is the maximum value Rand index can take in the dataset. The adjusted Rand index is bounded below by -0.5 for especially discordant clustering

Adjusted Mutual Information (AMI):

$$AMI = (MI - expected\_MI) / (max(MI) - expected\_MI) \qquad (3)$$

where MI is unadjusted Mutual Information, expected_MI and max (MI) are achieved similarly to ARI above

Homogeneity:

$$Homogeneity = 1 - (H(C|K) / H(C)) \qquad (4)$$

where H is the measure of entropy, H(C|K) is conditional entropy of true labels given predictions and H(C)) is entropy of true labels

Bcubed:

$$B = (precision + recall + F1 - score) / 3 \qquad (5)$$

Among these metrics, Bcubed was specifically used in the last step where noise was added, and the rest were used in each dataset. Bcubed is useful for measuring the precision and recall of each cluster and also takes into account overlapping clusters.

K-shape Algorithm (KS): K-shape is a clustering algorithm specifically designed for time series data. It uses shape-based distances to measure the similarity between time series. This algorithm identifies time patterns and groups similar time series based on their shape. Kshape is effective at detecting complex patterns in time series data and is suitable for clustering time series of varying lengths.

K-means Euclidean (KME) algorithm: K-means is a widely used clustering algorithm that partitions data into K-clusters based on the Euclidean distance metric. In the context of time series data, Kmeans Euclidean calculates the similarity between time series using Euclidean distance. It aims to minimize the sum of squared distances within a cluster by grouping time series that are close to each other in terms of Euclidean distance.

Kmeans DTW (KMD) Algorithm: Kmeans DTW is an adaptation of the Kmeans algorithm for time series data that uses the dynamic time warp distance (DTW) metric. DTW measures the similarity between time series by considering the temporal alignment of their data points. Kmeans DTW performs clustering by minimizing the sum of DTW distances between time series within each cluster. This algorithm is effective when processing time series of different lengths and different time alignments.

HDBSCAN (H) Algorithm: HDBSCAN stands for density-based hierarchical spatial clustering of applications with noise. It is a density-based clustering algorithm that creates a hierarchy of clusters based on the density of data points. HDBSCAN identifies both clusters and outlier points in time series data. It assigns a density-based score to each data point, allowing it to flexibly identify clusters of different shapes and sizes. HDBSCAN is especially useful when working with noisy and high-dimensional time series data be-cause it does not require explicitly setting the number of clusters.

Table 3 presents the clustering results for three different datasets (ECG, ArrowHead and SharePriceIncrease). The metrics used to evaluate the results are the Rand index, adjusted Rand index, adjusted mutual information (AMI), and homogeneity. The best clustering algorithm for each data set is specified.

ECG Dataset: HDBSCAN (H) achieved the highest Rand Index, Adjusted Rand Index, AMI, and Homogeneity scores, indicating that it produced the most accurate clustering results.

ArrowHead Dataset: Kshape (KS) achieved the highest Rand Index, Adjusted Rand Index, AMI, and Homogeneity scores, indicating that it produced the most accurate clustering results.

SharePriceIncrease Dataset: Kmeans Euclidean (KME) achieved the highest Rand Index, Adjusted Rand Index, AMI, and Homogeneity scores, indicating that it produced the most accurate clustering results.

It is worth noting that the HDBSCAN algorithm did not produce results for the ArrowHead dataset, and the Kmeans DTW (KMD) algorithm performed poorly on the ArrowHead dataset compared to the other algorithms. Additionally, the SharePriceIn-crease dataset had relatively low scores for all metrics, indicating that the clustering performance for this dataset was poorer than the others.

Table 3. Unsupervised Clustering Results.

Metric/algorithm	Time	Rand Index	Adj. Rand	AMI	Homogeneity
ECG					
Kshape (KS) train	130 s	0.7827	0.5536	0.5303	0.666
Kshape (KS) test	130 s	0.7679	0.5232	0.5282	0.6793
Kmeans Euclidean (KME) train	717 s	0.769	0.5245	0.5125	0.6502
Kmeans Euclidean (KME) test	717 s	0.7674	0.5225	0.521	0.6667
Kmeans DTW (KMD) train	1002 s	0.7235	0.4286	0.4644	0.5993
Kmeans DTW (KMD) test	1002 s	0.7176	0.4178	0.453	0.5913
HDBSCAN (H) train	8 s	0.8873	0.7717	0.6544	0.7248
HDBSCAN (H) test	8 s	0.869	0.7343	0.6364	0.7208
Best	H	H	H	H	H
ArrowHead					
Kshape (KS) train	5 s	0.6181	0.259	0.3184	0.2699
Kshape (KS) test	5 s	0.5626	0.1764	0.2798	0.2324
Kmeans Euclidean (KME) train	14 s	0.6051	0.2351	0.2961	0.2544
Kmeans Euclidean (KME) test	14 s	0.5526	0.1507	0.2462	0.2344
Kmeans DTW (KMD) train	25 s	0.5135	0.0912	0.1514	0.1311
Kmeans DTW (KMD) test	25 s	0.5471	0.1484	0.3069	0.2861
HDBSCAN (H) train	instant	0.5513	0.0879	0.1238	0.1279
HDBSCAN (H) test	instant	0.5759	0.1487	0.1525	0.1433
Best	H	KS	KS	KS	KMD
SharePriceIncrease					
Kshape (KS) train	47 s	0.5004	−0.0001	0.0037	0.0044
Kshape (KS) test	47 s	0.4987	−0.0029	−0.0014	0.0007
Kmeans Euclidean (KME) train	140 s	0.5031	0.0061	0.0076	0.0085
Kmeans Euclidean (KME) test	140 s	0.5038	0.008	0.01	0.013
Kmeans DTW (KMD) train	104 s	0.5034	0.0069	0.0051	0.0059
Kmeans DTW (KMD) test	104 s	0.4988	−0.0025	−0.0019	0.0001
HDBSCAN (H) train	1 s	0.4892	−0.0017	0.0129	0.1053
HDBSCAN (H) test	1 s	0.5182	−0.003	−0.0025	0.1257
Best	H	H	KME	H	H

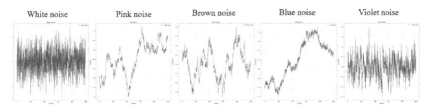

Fig. 4. Noise variations.

The idea of adding noise (see Fig. 4 above) to see if clusters break down involves introducing different types of noise into a data set and observing the effect on the existing clustering structure. The goal of this idea is to understand the robustness of the identified clusters and determine whether they are truly significant or sensitive to the presence of noise. Table 4 provides an overview of the different noise options in use, as well as their descriptions and potential applications in various fields (Table 4).

Table 4. Noise variations used.

Color	Description	Applications
White	White noise refers to a random signal with equal intensity across all frequencies, resulting in a flat spectrum. It contains all audible frequencies at equal power	Sleep Aid Studying and Concentration
Pink	Pink noise is a type of random noise where each octave carries an equal amount of energy, resulting in a decrease in power as the frequency increases	Sound Equalization Masking Background Noise (like white noise)
Brown	Brown noise, also known as red noise or random walk noise, has a power spectral density that decreases by 6 dB per octave as the frequency increases. It emphasizes lower frequencies	Sound masking Stress Relief Audio Testing
Blue	Blue noise, also known as azure noise, is a type of noise where the energy at higher frequencies is emphasized relative to lower frequencies. It has a more pronounced high-frequency content	Data Encoding Hearing Tests Relaxation and Focus
Violet	Violet noise, also known as purple or ultraviolet noise, emphasizes high frequencies even more than blue noise. It increases in intensity as the frequency rises	Sleep Improvement Neural Stimulation Tinnitus Management

Formulas:
White Noise:

$$x(t) = A * \xi(t) \tag{6}$$

where: x(t) - white noise signal at time t A - ampli-tude/scaling factor $\xi(t)$ - independent and identically distributed random variables at time t
Pink Noise:

$$PSD(f) = K/f \tag{7}$$

where: PSD(f) - power spectral density at frequency f K - constant f - frequency
Brown Noise:

$$PSD(f) = K/f^{\wedge 2} \tag{8}$$

where: PSD(f) - power spectral density at frequency f K - constant f - frequency
Blue Noise:

$$PSD(f) = K/f^{\wedge n} \tag{9}$$

where: PSD(f) - power spectral density at frequency f K - constant f - frequency n - exponent determining the rate of increase of spectral density with frequency
Violet Noise:

$$PSD(f) = K * f^{\wedge n} \tag{10}$$

where: PSD(f) - power spectral density at frequency f K - constant f - frequency n - exponent determining the rate of increase of spectral density with frequency

Based on Table 5 below, we can observe the Bcubed scores for noise addition to three datasets with different magnitudes.

For the ECG dataset, we see that as the noise magnitude increases, the Bcubed scores gradually decrease. This suggests that higher noise levels negatively affect the quality of clustering.

For the ArrowHead and SharePriceIncrease datasets, we see that B-cubed scores remain consistently high regardless of the amount of noise. This suggests that these datasets are more robust to noise and maintain clustering quality even with noisy data.

Overall, we can conclude that the impact of noise on clustering performance varies across datasets. While some datasets are more sensitive to noise, others exhibit higher levels of robustness. It is important to consider the characteristics of the dataset when analyzing the impact of noise on clustering performance.

Table 5. Noise addition results (Bcubed).

Dataset, Noise/Magnitude		−0.1	0	0.1	0.25	0.5
ECG	white	0.9814	1	0.9682	0.9496	0.8992
ECG	pink	0.9832	1	0.9198	0.8642	0.8518
ECG	brown	0.906	1	0.928	0.969	0.8464
ECG	blue	0.9848	1	0.974	0.9232	0.7248
ECG	violet	0.9612	1	0.991	0.8874	0.8714
ArrowHead	white	1	1	1	1	1
ArrowHead	pink	1	1	1	0.9905	0.9905
ArrowHead	brown	1	1	1	0.9953	0.9716
ArrowHead	blue	1	1	1	0.981	0.9384
ArrowHead	violet	1	1	1	0.9953	0.9479
SharePriceIncrease	white	1	1	1	1	1
SharePriceIncrease	pink	1	1	1	0.9905	0.9905
SharePriceIncrease	brown	1	1	1	0.9953	0.9716
SharePriceIncrease	blue	1	1	1	0.981	0.9384
SharePriceIncrease	violet	1	1	1	0.9953	0.9479
Dataset, Noise/Magnitude		1	10	100	1000	
ECG	white	0.8238	0.1408	0.3608	0.3608	
ECG	pink	0.777	0.0706	0.239	0.1856	
ECG	brown	0.62	0.2034	0.2198	0.1856	
ECG	blue	0.4888	0.0738	0.1856	0.1856	
ECG	violet	0.7588	0.199	0.144	0.1856	
ArrowHead	white	0.9716	0.1043	0.2227	0.2227	
ArrowHead	pink	0.9479	0.1706	0.2227	0.1043	
ArrowHead	brown	0.9431	0.1043	0.1043	0.2227	
ArrowHead	blue	0.9336	0.673	0.1043	0.1043	
ArrowHead	violet	0.9431	0.1137	0.1043	0.1043	
SharePriceIncrease	white	0.9716	0.1043	0.2227	0.2227	
SharePriceIncrease	pink	0.9479	0.1706	0.2227	0.1043	
SharePriceIncrease	brown	0.9431	0.1043	0.1043	0.2227	
SharePriceIncrease	blue	0.9336	0.673	0.1043	0.1043	
SharePriceIncrease	violet	0.9431	0.1137	0.1043	0.1043	

4   Discussion

The study analyzed three different datasets: ECG (biological time series data), ArrowHead (physical time series data), and SharePriceIncrease (financial time series data). The datasets varied in the number of time series, the length of the time series, and the number of classes.

The study used four clustering indices to evaluate the performance of clustering algorithms on data sets: Rand Index, Adjusted Rand Index, Adjusted Mutual Information, and Homogeneity. Each index had its own strengths and weaknesses.

The study then applied different clustering algorithms (K-shape, K-means Euclidean, Kmeans DTW and HDBSCAN) to the datasets and evaluated their performance using clustering indices. The best performing algorithm for each data set was determined based on the highest value for each index.

The study then examined the impact of adding noise on datasets and evaluated the performance of algorithms with added noise using the B-cubed clustering index. The noise magnitude ranged from -0.1 to 1000.

As for future research directions, cz suggests exploring other clustering algorithms and indices to further evaluate the performance of unsupervised clustering of time series data. Additionally, more research is needed into how different types and amounts of noise affect the performance of clustering algorithms.

5   Conclusion

Based on the results, the best clustering algorithm for each dataset is as follows:

1. ECG: HDBSCAN
2. ArrowHead: Kshape (KS)
3. SharePriceIncrease: HDBSCAN

The noise addition (B-cubed) results show that clustering performance decreases as the magnitude of noise increases for all datasets. This suggests that adding noise nega-tively affects clustering accuracy.

The usefulness of clustering algorithms for anomaly detection depends on the specific application and dataset. In general, clustering algorithms can be useful for detecting anomalies by identifying patterns or clusters that differ significantly from the majority of data points. However, the effectiveness of clustering for anomaly detection can vary depending on the characteristics of the data and the specific clustering algorithm used. It is important to carefully evaluate and validate the results of clustering algorithms for anomaly detection tasks.

References

1. Aghabozorgi, S.B., Shirkhorshidi, A.S., Wah, T.Y.: Time-series clustering–a decade review. Inf. Syst. **53**, 16–38 (2015)
2. Alqahtani, A., Ali, M., Xie, X., Jones, M.W.: Deep time-series clustering: a review. Electronics **10**(23), 3001 (2021)

3. Caiado, J., Maharaj, E.A., D'Urso, P.: Time-series clustering. In: Handbook of Cluster Analysis, pp. 262–285. Chapman and Hall/CRC (2015)
4. Ding, R., Wang, Q., Dang, Y., Fu, Q., Zhang, H., Zhang, D.: Yading: fast clustering of large-scale time series data. Proc. VLDB Endow. **8**(5), 473–484 (2015)
5. Dose, C., Cincotti, S.: Clustering of financial time series with application to index and enhanced index tracking portfolio. Physica A **355**(1), 145–151 (2005)
6. Hautamaki, V., Nykanen, P., Franti, P.: Time-series clustering by approximate prototypes. In: 19th International Conference on Pattern Recognition, pp. 1–4. IEEE (2008)
7. Huang, X., Ye, Y., Xiong, L., Lau, R.Y., Jiang, N., Wang, S.: Time series k-means: a new k-means type smooth subspace clustering for time series data. Inf. Sci. **367**, 1–13 (2016)
8. Javed, A., Lee, B.S., Rizzo, D.M.: A benchmark study on time series clustering. Mach. Learn. Appl. **1**, 100001 (2020)
9. Jokinen, J., Räty, T., Lintonen, T.: Clustering structure analysis in time-series data with density-based clusterability measure. IEEE/CAA J. Automatica Sinica **6**(6), 1332–1343 (2019)
10. Kalpakis, K., Gada, D., Puttagunta, V.: Distance measures for effective clustering of ARIMA time-series. In: Proceedings of the 2001 IEEE International Conference on Data Mining, pp. 273–280. IEEE (2001)
11. Kotsakos, D., Trajcevski, G., Gunopulos, D., Aggarwal, C.C.: Time-series data clustering. In: Data Clustering, pp. 357–380. Chapman and Hall/CRC (2018)
12. Li, L., Prakash, B.A.: Time series clustering: complex is simpler! In: Proceedings of the 28th International Conference on Machine Learning (ICML 2011), pp. 185–192 (2011)
13. Liao, T.W.: Clustering of time series data–a survey. Pattern Recogn. **38**(11), 1857–1874 (2005)
14. Ma, Q., Zheng, J., Li, S., Cottrell, G.W.: Learning representations for time series clustering. In: Advances in Neural Information Processing Systems, vol. 32 (2019)
15. Maharaj, E.A., D'Urso, P., Caiado, J.: Time Series Clustering and Classification. CRC Press, Boca Raton (2019)
16. Montero, P., Vilar, J.A.: TSclust: an R package for time series clustering. J. Stat. Softw. **62**, 1–43 (2015)
17. Paparrizos, J., Gravano, L. k-shape: efficient and accurate clustering of time series. In: Proceedings of the 2015 ACM SIGMOD International Conference on Management of Data, pp. 1855–1870 (2015)
18. Pedregosa, F., Varoquaux, G., Gramfort, A., Michel, V., Thirion, B., Grisel, O.: Scikit-learn: machine learning in Python. J. Mach. Learn. Res. **12**, 2825–2830 (2011)
19. Rani, S., Sikka, G.: Recent techniques of clustering of time series data: a survey. Int. J. Comput. Appl. **52**(15) (2012)
20. Sardá-Espinosa, A.: Comparing time-series clustering algorithms in R using the dtwclust package. R Package Vignette **12**, 41 (2017)
21. Singhal, A., Seborg, D.E.: Clustering multivariate time-series data. J. Chemom. J. Chemom. Soc. **19**(8), 427–438 (2005)
22. Wang, W., Lyu, G., Shi, Y., Liang, X.: Time series clustering based on dynamic time warping. In: 2018 IEEE 9th International Conference on Software Engineering and Service Science (ICSESS), pp. 487–490. IEEE (2018)
23. Wang, X., Smith, K., Hyndman, R.: Characteristic-based clustering for time series data. Data Min. Knowl. Disc. **13**, 335–364 (2006)
24. Zotov, G.A., Lukianchenko, P.P.: Neural network approach in the problem of predicting anomalies in interest rates under the influence of correlated noises. Reports of the Russian Academy of Sciences. Math. Inform. Control Processes **514**(2), 150–157 (2023)

On the Open Transport Data Analysis Platform

Mark Bulygin$^{(\boxtimes)}$ (iD) and Dmitry Namiot (iD)

Lomonosov Moscow State University, Moscow 119234, Russia
messimm@yandex.ru

Abstract. This article presents an open platform tailored for the analysis of transportation data. It provides an overview of the primary types of data involved, including individual transport mobility data and aggregated data organized by time intervals. The platform adopts a modular architecture. The first module is dedicated to data loading, storage, and sampling for practical problem-solving. Subsequently, the second module undertakes semantic data validation, ensuring the integrity of subsequent modules by identifying and rectifying errors encountered during data collection. The third, analytical, module allows experts to apply data analysis methods to solve problems of urban infrastructure management. A methodology grounded in the characterization of normality and the detection of anomalies is proposed for problem resolution. Furthermore, the fourth module specializes in visualizing analysis outcomes through diverse formats such as tables, graphs, and maps. The fifth module, an API component, extends the platform's accessibility and permits the integration of new functionalities into the analytical module, along with novel data management techniques. The operation of the platform is demonstrated by the example of searching for anomalies in traffic flows, clustering city districts, as well as visualizing the volume of passenger traffic at train stations in the Moscow region.

Keywords: Transport data · Software platform · Digital urbanism · Smart cities

1 Introduction

Presently, over half of the global population resides in urban areas, with United Nations projections indicating that this figure is expected to surpass two-thirds by 2050 [1]. The swift expansion of urban spaces poses challenges such as housing shortages, declining air quality, and a diminished quality of life. Addressing these issues necessitates timely and strategic urban infrastructure development. The concept of a smart city emerges as a solution, involving the efficient management of urban resources through extensive use of communication and information technologies.

Efforts to enhance urban infrastructure through data analytics are not novel. Previous approaches [2–5] relied on data analysis from surveys and censuses. It is crucial to note the difficulty in obtaining such data and the rapid obsolescence of information, leading to outdated research conclusions.

Modern scientists now have access to new data sources, including information from transport card validators and traffic flow data from cellular operators. These sources

A. Gibadullin (Ed.): ITIDMS 2023, CCIS 2112, pp. 40–52, 2024.
https://doi.org/10.1007/978-3-031-60318-1_4

enable the collection of accurate and timely data on city movements. To effectively address transport planning issues in a smart city, the development of a software platform becomes essential. This platform should facilitate the collection, storage, and analysis of data from various sources. Existing solutions like TIME [6] and Citadel [7], along with national-level initiatives [8], highlight the ongoing efforts in this direction. Notably, any intelligent transport system for a smart city, as discussed in the review [9], relies on historical data about transport system usage. Machine learning models for Smart City [10] also necessitate training on updated data.

However, there is no universal approach to data analysis [11], and platforms often present their own models. The desire to consolidate all data within one system can complicate the process, leaving room for proprietary systems built from the bottom up. Our approach emphasizes treating movement information as a set of metrics representing the behavior of city residents. This set of metrics enables the evaluation of socio-economic processes, urban planning outcomes, and the identification of problematic situations.

The subsequent sections of this article delve into available datasets and principles for populating them (Sect. 2). Section 3 outlines the proposed software platform architecture, detailing its structure, goals, and objectives for each module. Existing solutions that can be employed in implementing the platform are also discussed. Section 4 presents a discussion of results obtained from the framework, while Sect. 5 concludes the article.

2   Materials and Methods

The purpose of this work is to introduce an open platform developed for the analysis of transport data. The presented platform is specifically designed for the storage and analysis of two primary components of transport data that can be automatically collected. Firstly, these are the so-called correspondence matrices, which outline the number of movements from one point to another per unit of time. Geographically defined areas, as well as stations, bus stops, etc., can serve as such "points." Secondly, the platform focuses on travel document usage logs, such as passenger entrances to a subway station.

Below, we provide a detailed description of this data, the procedures for obtaining it, and potential limitations.

The data currently accessible to researchers can be categorized into two major groups: individual data and aggregated data. Individual data describe the movements of individual users within the city's transport network. A primary source of such data is the smart card validation data from public transport systems, commonly used for fare payment. The process of validating transport cards may vary across different transport systems. In the Moscow metro system, the fare between any two stations is consistent, with card validation occurring only at the entrance. Conversely, there are systems where the cost of a trip depends on the stations at the beginning and end of the journey. Card validation in such systems can occur at the entrance, exit, and during each transfer. Such data proves more convenient for research, providing not only the starting points of trips but also the destinations. In cases where the endpoint of a trip is unknown, heuristics can be employed to determine the destination. Table 1 illustrates an example of smart card data.

Table 1. Example of smart card validation data.

Timestamp	Card ID	Card Type	Validation Place
1652529600	0000050	Regular	Metro University1
1652529900	0000136	Student	Bus 4567

Source: compiled by the authors

GPS sensors serve as a crucial source of personal data, providing highly accurate readings for positioning through the Global Positioning System (GPS), a satellite-based system. These sensors, commonly found in smartphones and navigators, enable researchers to precisely track user trajectories with minimal spatial deviations. However, users often hesitate to share such trajectory data due to privacy concerns.

Historically, GPS data has been sourced from applications or tracking systems with business objectives, such as courier services, taxi services, and bus depots. Additionally, data can be obtained from smartphones through specialized applications that incentivize users with rewards for sharing their data.

These applications also facilitate the collection of data from the accelerometers of mobile devices, including smartphones and smartwatches. Numerous articles detail successful methods for analyzing such data, allowing for the identification of user activities and transportation modes.

Aggregated data, derived from individual data, is achieved through aggregation based on areas of origin/destination and time intervals. In the contemporary world, cellular operator data stands out as a primary source of aggregated data.

During the operation of cell phones, periodic updates of the cellular network involve the exchange of data on signal level (dB) and delay (ms) with multiple base stations. This information enables the determination of users' device locations. Figure 1 illustrates the interaction scheme between cell phones and base stations.

In Moscow, cellular operators have strategically placed base stations within the metro system, providing researchers with valuable data regarding the frequency of subway usage. The development of algorithms and heuristics for primary data analysis further enables the extraction of information on the duration of individuals staying in an area for more than one hour, as well as the count of people commuting from home to work and vice versa.

The primary advantage of utilizing cellular operator data lies in its mass availability. Globally, over 65% of people are subscribers of mobile operators, and in large cities, this figure can exceed 95%. It's worth emphasizing that this data is collected centrally on the operators' side, eliminating the need for additional participation from subscribers.

However, it's crucial to acknowledge the limitations of this type of data, primarily its low spatial and temporal accuracy. Consequently, researchers have access only to data aggregated by districts and half-hour intervals.

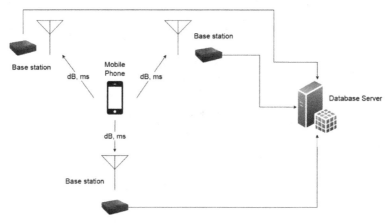

Fig. 1. The scheme of interaction between cell phones and base stations. *Source*: compiled by the authors.

3   Results

3.1   Software Platform Architecture

Every year, the field of transport data analysis witnesses the emergence of numerous new solutions working with both aggregated and individual mobility data. These solutions typically encompass a common set of operations: data reading and storage, verification, algorithmic analysis, and visualization of outcomes. The data pertinent to these solutions adhere to similar formats specific to their respective types.

We propose a modular architecture for a software solution designed to handle various types of transport data. The modules within this architecture can be utilized independently to construct novel solutions. The overall structure of the software platform is illustrated in Fig. 2.

It includes five modules: data loading and storage module, data validation module, data analysis module, visualization module.

This platform streamlines the process by obviating the need to redefine data handling and visualization operations for each new solution, focusing instead solely on defining new methods of data analysis through the API. This approach significantly accelerates the development cycle for new solutions and lowers the skill requirements for personnel involved in programming such solutions.

By leveraging this platform for solutions in the realm of digital urbanism, researchers can emphasize transitions from the technical intricacies of development to refining the algorithms and methodologies themselves. The change in the process of developing new solutions in the field of transport data analysis is shown in Fig. 3.

The primary user base for this platform consists of transport analysts. In selecting a programming language for platform implementation, it is advisable to opt for one that is easily learnable and boasts a vast global developer community. Python emerges as a prime candidate in this regard, given its abundance of libraries dedicated to tabular data analysis, such as Pandas. The intuitive nature of working with these libraries, reminiscent

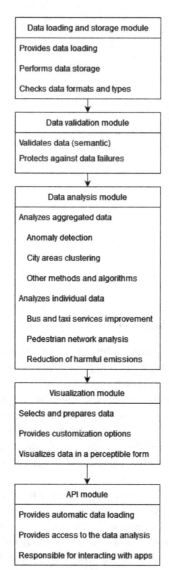

Fig. 2. The general structure of the proposed software platform. *Source*: compiled by the authors.

of using Excel, facilitates user adoption of the platform. The diagram illustrates the change in the development process when implementing an open transport data analysis platform.

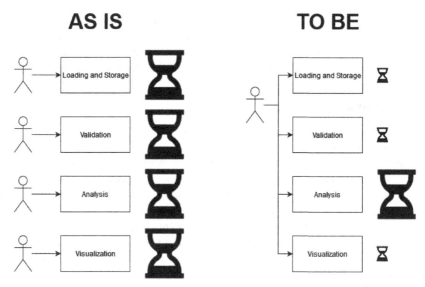

Fig. 3. The change in the process of new transport data analysis solution development. *Source:* compiled by the authors.

3.2 Data Load and Storage

Data intended for subsequent analysis should be downloaded and stored in a readily accessible format. A critical consideration in this process is the selection of tools for data storage and management. Transport data, both in aggregated and individual forms, can be effectively represented and processed using traditional relational Database Management Systems (DBMS), organized in tables.

Looking ahead, the emergence of new data sources, such as smart city sensors and potential access to raw data from cellular operator base stations, may become a reality with the advancement of Internet of Things (IoT) technologies. If this happens, vast volumes of new data will continuously emerge, potentially containing diverse formats like photos or videos. Such transport data will exhibit the characteristics of Big Data. To maximize the platform's potential in handling this influx, it's prudent to explore tools designed for processing big data, including NoSQL tools and those based on Hadoop (such as Spark, and Hive, among others).

Additionally, the first module of the system should incorporate checks to ensure the accuracy of incoming input files, verifying their compliance with data formats and field value boundaries.

3.3 Data Validation Module

In the realm of devices dedicated to collecting transport data, such as base stations and validators in the subway, glitches may arise during the data collection process. These malfunctions can significantly impact the functionality of the data analysis module.

In contrast to the initial module, which primarily scrutinizes data for format accuracy and the type of values, the second module specializes in semantic verification of correctness. For instance, it is designed to pinpoint situations where the subway flow surpasses the overall transport flow or when the transport flow to a workplace is unusually substantial. (After all, a sudden and significant shift in the workplace by a large number of city residents within a short timeframe is quite unexpected).

3.4 Data Analysis Module

The proposed architecture places the data analysis module at its core, encompassing a comprehensive array of data analysis methods.

To address challenges in a smart city using this platform, we propose our unique concept. The crux of this concept lies in calculating certain values, akin to metrics, for select transport data—be it aggregated or individual—that depict what is considered normal. These values, to some extent, portray the typical operations of city systems and services. When new data streams in, a comparison is made to gauge its alignment with the established normality. Any deviation from this norm can serve as a signal indicating specific processes within the city or disruptions in the operation of urban regulatory mechanisms.

The algorithm for the data analysis module operates as follows: initially, a model of normality is constructed using historical data. Subsequently, the deviation from this model is evaluated for incoming data, leading to a determination of its typicality. This determination can be made using predefined rules or heuristics, or through visual analysis by a subject area specialist.

In a previous work [12], we introduced an anomaly detection method tailored for aggregated data. Given the constancy of traffic flows in the city, anomalous or atypical values within the aggregated data from mobile operators serve as indicators of significant social events. Noteworthy is the fact that researchers need not predict these anomalies, as they either result from planned events, such as salutes and concerts or are unpredictable. The task lies in measuring and understanding the nature of these anomalies. While volunteer efforts and survey data have been employed in the past for this purpose, contemporary methods ensure precise measurements of these anomalies, offering valuable insights for city authorities to implement measures for improving the transport situation.

Within the framework of the proposed platform architecture, however, other tasks that do not fit the concept described above can be solved.

For example, another pivotal aspect of analyzing aggregated data is district clustering. Distinct city areas, whether industrial or residential, necessitate different infrastructure development. To classify city districts effectively, we propose an approach involving clustering city districts and their connections based on cellular operator data [12]. This method allows researchers to formally identify and justify the classification of city districts into specific types.

The identification of novelty in aggregated data is equally important, considering the regular construction of new residential buildings and infrastructure facilities in cities. The expansion of cities and their transport networks significantly impacts traffic flows. Detecting novelty in cellular operator data helps answer questions about the influence of new metro stations, stops, routes, and infrastructure objects on traffic flows and how the type of district changes with the appearance of new residential and social infrastructure.

Aggregated transport data can be represented as a fully connected weighted graph, with vertices being territorial units or public transport stops and edge weights indicating transport flow values between all vertices.

Utilizing algorithms to evaluate the centralities of graph vertices facilitates the identification of the most significant transport nodes within the city. General graph centralities, traditionally reliant on the topological structure of the graph, can be enhanced for traffic flow graphs by incorporating additional information, such as city population, the number of passengers, and time considerations. These centrality assessments are not only useful for identifying main transport hubs within the city but also for studying suburb-city interactions and analyzing the intercity transport network [13, 14].

The analysis of smart card validator data using algorithms for clustering stations, passengers, and routes empowers the city government to tailor transport services to the needs of its residents.

Addressing the challenge of detecting transfers becomes crucial, especially in cities where different transport systems (e.g., metro and bicycle) utilize separate smart cards. Several heuristics can be employed to identify transfers between these systems.

To harness GPS data within this platform, algorithms for analyzing the bus network's quality, optimizing and evaluating taxi services, and scrutinizing the GPS trajectories of pedestrians can be implemented. Such analyses not only identify issues in the city's pedestrian network but also highlight areas that attract a significant number of pedestrians.

3.5 Visualization Module

The envisioned software platform must incorporate robust methods for visualizing the outcomes of data analysis algorithms. Visualizing a large graph of traffic flows poses a non-trivial challenge, requiring the identification of key properties for displaying vertices.

The platform should offer visualization of algorithm results on maps, given that this format is the most convenient and natural for certain tasks, such as clustering areas. The visualization tool should come equipped with flexible scale settings. Users of the system should have the flexibility to examine method results at various levels, spanning the entirety of the city or region down to individual administrative districts and areas.

Various ready-made solutions are available for visualizing data on maps, including Kepler.gl, geopandas, and Folium.

For addressing different types of problems, solutions can be presented through tables, graphs, and text reports. These results can be conveniently accessed on interactive web pages across all platforms. Frameworks such as Django or Grad.io can be employed in the creation of such web pages.

The resulting reports can be shared with other city services to facilitate action-taking. It's essential to support the most common formats for such tasks:.xlsx for tabular data,.png for graphical data, and.doc for text reports.

3.6 API Module

The platform ought to empower prospective users to craft their algorithms for data analysis while facilitating seamless integration with other applications. To achieve this, the platform must offer a robust API, enabling users to fetch necessary data for specific periods and access the outcomes generated by the data analysis and visualization modules. Additionally, the platform should possess the capability to effortlessly retrieve data from external sources, streamlining the process of automating data transfers from their sources to the platform's central collection point.

The system's API module can be implemented through configuration files. For each problem, a dedicated configuration file is created wherein the system user specifies their preferences for the data storage and loading module, data validation module, analytical module, and visualization module.

Analytical modules can be seamlessly integrated into the platform by simply placing the corresponding files in the directories alongside the platform code. Similarly, new iterations of other system modules can be added, thereby enhancing the platform's capability to handle new data sources and formats, while also empowering users to define alternative methods for visualizing results as needed. To streamline the process of creating new modules for the platform, it's imperative to furnish its code with illustrative examples demonstrating the organization of these modules.

4 Discussion

The platform outlined in this article aims to streamline researchers' access to the outcomes derived from various data analysis techniques. Several methods within the data analysis module have already been developed and integrated.

The results obtained represent a novel approach compared to traditional forecasting methods commonly employed in transport problems [15]. The primary analytical model embedded in the proposed transport platform can be succinctly described as follows: 'determining the pattern of transport system utilization and identifying deviations.' When utilizing transport data as an indicator of urban processes, deviations from established usage patterns become indicative of changes. For instance, the active use of a new office complex or the occupancy of a residential complex manifests in alterations to public transport usage.

This suite of tools enables city administration personnel not only to oversee transport planning but also to assess the repercussions of various management decisions in the city, evaluate the impact of incidents, and more. The necessity for such decision-making tools has been highlighted in previous works [9, 16].

In Fig. 4, the results of the anomaly detection method applied to aggregated data from cellular operators are illustrated.

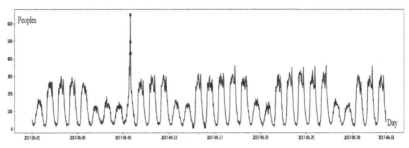

Fig. 4. The results of the anomaly detection method for aggregated cellular operator data (Transport flow from Begovoy to Tverskoy district), All of the anomalies are detected correctly. *Source*: [12].

The horizontal axis denotes time intervals spanning May 2017, while the vertical axis represents the total transport flow from the Begovoy district to the Tverskoy district in Moscow. The plotted dots signify anomalous values in the transport flow identified by the algorithm detailed in [12]. These anomalies correspond to the mass procession observed during the Immortal Regiment campaign. Notably, all anomalous values are accurately detected, and no false positives are observed in the algorithm's performance.

Figure 5 shows the example of configuration file for Open Transport Data Analysis Platform which can be used to obtaining results.

Figure 6 illustrates the outcomes of district clustering based on their transportation patterns, as per the methodology introduced in [17]. The vertical axis represents the average population count within each area during nighttime, while the horizontal axis depicts the average population count during working hours. To mitigate the influence of region size, the values are normalized accordingly.

The numerical annotations in Fig. 6 denote the clusters identified. Cluster 1 primarily comprises industrial and commercial zones, exhibiting peak occupancy during working hours. On the other hand, cluster 3 consists of residential areas where inhabitants reside at night but commute for work during the day. Clusters 0, 2, and 4 occupy an intermediary stance between these patterns.

In Fig. 7 provides visualization of input and output volumes through turnstiles at train stations in the Moscow region. This visualization is implemented using Kepler.gl, described earlier.

```
▼ {
    ▼ Data Loading : {
          Name : AggregatedData
        ▼ Parameters : {
              TimeStamp : ts
              Departure : departure_zid
              Arrival : arrival_zid
              Values : customers_cnt
          }
    }
    ▼ Data Validation : {
          Name : Dummy
    }
    ▼ Data Analysis : {
          Name : TransportFlowAnomalyDetection
        ▼ Parameters : {
              Values : customers_cnt
              Mode : Absolute_value
              Threshold : 250
          }
    }
    ▼ Data Visualization : {
          Name : TimeSeriesWithFlag
        ▼ Parameters : {
              TimeStamp : ts
              Values : customers_cnt
              Flag : Flag
          }
    }
}
```

Fig. 5. The example of configuration file for Open Transport Data Analysis Platform. *Source*: compiled by the authors.

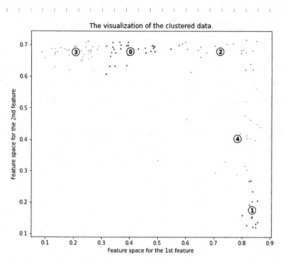

Fig. 6. The results of the city district clustering method for aggregated cellular operator data (Based on transport flows of Moscow Regions). *Source*: [17].

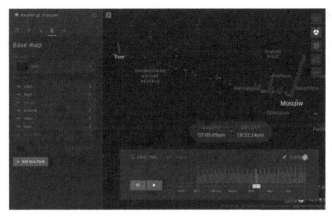

Fig. 7. The results of the visualization of input and output volumes through turnstiles at train stations in the Moscow region.

5   Conclusion

The essence of any software platform lies in providing optimal solutions for recurring operations. Our experience with transport data reveals that approaches to analyzing such data are largely standardized, given that the data itself is automatically gathered by telecommunication operators or transport companies. The pivotal aspect here is the term 'automatically,' indicating standardized presentation formats.

Consequently, a logical progression involves proposing and implementing standardized approaches for processing this data. The result is a straightforward and efficient tool built upon a relatively modest data model, encapsulating fundamental statistical information about transport system usage. A key attribute of this data lies in its automatic collection, a process seamlessly executed by telecommunication operators tracking subscriber locations for billing and maintenance, and transport companies recording passenger movements for billing purposes. The accumulation of such data doesn't necessitate expensive, separate technical solutions.

The primary model for analyzing this data centers on defining behavioral factors—ultimately constituting what we term 'transport behavior' [18]. We believe that behavioral factors are more easily comprehensible and, consequently, more verifiable. This implies a direct application of the derived insights for management decisions.

This approach aligns with current data analysis trends, such as AutoML [10], and is well-suited for potential Platform as a Service (PAAS) solutions [19], presenting transport data as a ready-made service.

References

1. Urbanization: Official site of UN. https://www.un.org/ru/youthink/urbanization.shtml. Accessed 22 Oct 2023
2. Richardson, A.J., Ampt, E.S., Meyburg, A.H.: Survey Methods for Transport Planning, pp. 75–145. Eucalyptus Press, Melbourne (1995)

3. Jones, P., Stopher, P.R.: Transport Survey Quality and Innovation. Emerald Group Publishing Limited, Bingley (2003)
4. Stopher, P.R., Jones, P.M.: Developing Standards of Transport Survey Quality. In: Transport Survey Quality and Innovation, pp. 1–38. Emerald Group Publishing Limited (2003)
5. Taaffe, E.J., Morrill, R.L., Gould, P.R.: Transport expansion in underdeveloped countries: a comparative analysis. In: Transport and Development London, pp. 32–49. Macmillan Education UK (1973)
6. Bacon, J., et al.: TIME: an open platform for capturing, processing and delivering transport-related data. In: 2008 5th IEEE Consumer Communications and Networking Conference. IEEE (2008)
7. Harding, M., Nigel, D.: Citadel: a community platform for archiving travel data. In: Proceedings of the 6th ACM Workshop on Next Generation Mobile Computing for Dynamic Personalised Travel Planning (2012)
8. Dong, X., et al.: A framework of future Innovative Urban Transport. In: 2016 IEEE 19th International Conference on Intelligent Transportation Systems (ITSC). IEEE (2016)
9. Kupriyanovsky, V.P., et al.: Digital economy – smart way to work. Int. J. Open Inf. Technol. 2(4), 26–32 (2016)
10. Kabir, M.H., et al.: Explainable artificial intelligence for smart city application: a secure and trusted platform. In: Ahmed, M., Islam, S.R., Anwar, A., Moustafa, N., Pathan, AS.K. (eds.) Explainable Artificial Intelligence for Cyber Security. Studies in Computational Intelligence, vol. 1025, pp. 241–263. Springer, Cham (2022). https://doi.org/10.1007/978-3-030-96630-0_11
11. An, S.H., Lee, B.H., Shin, D.R.: A survey of intelligent transportation systems. In: Proceedings - 3rd International Conference on Computational Intelligence, Communication Systems and Networks, CICSyN 2011, pp. 332–337 (2011)
12. Bulygin, M., Namiot, D.: Anomaly detection method for aggregated cellular operator data. In: 2021 28th Conference of Open Innovations Association (FRUCT). IEEE (2021)
13. Tsiotas, D., Polyzos, S.: Introducing a new centrality measure from the transportation network analysis in Greece. Ann. Oper. Res. 227(1), 93–117 (2015)
14. Cheng, Y.Y., Lee, R.K.W., Lim, E.P., Zhu, F.: DelayFlow centrality for identifying critical nodes in transportation networks. In: Proceedings of the 2013 IEEE/ACM International Conference on Advances in Social Networks Analysis and Mining (2013)
15. Medina-Salgado, B., et al.: Urban traffic flow prediction techniques: a review. Sustain. Comput. Inform. Syst. 35, 100739 (2022)
16. Akimov, A.V., et al.: Improving the methods of analysis and evaluation of the quality of the public transport system of the metropolis. In: Trends in the Economic Development of the Russian Transport Complex: Foresight, Forecasts and Strategies (2021)
17. Bulygin, M., Namiot, D.: A new approach to clustering districts and connections between them based on cellular operator data. In: 2021 29th Conference of Open Innovations Association (FRUCT). IEEE (2021)
18. Gohar, M., Muzammal, M., Rahman, A.U.: SMART TSS: defining transportation system behavior using big data analytics in smart cities. Sustain. Cities Soc. 41, 114–119 (2018)
19. Soomro, K., et al.: Smart city big data analytics: an advanced review. Wiley Interdisc. Rev. Data Mining Knowl. Discov. 9(5), e1319 (2019)

Investigation of the Characteristics
of a Frequency Diversity Array Antenna

Vladimir Volkov[1,2(✉)] ⓘ, Alexandr Avramenko[2], and Việt An Nguyễn[1,3]

[1] Saint-Petersburg State Electrotechnical University (LETI), Saint-Petersburg, Russia
vl_volk@mail.ru
[2] Saint-Petersburg State University of Aerospace Instrumentation, Saint-Petersburg, Russia
[3] Le Quy Don Technical University, Hanoi, Vietnam

Abstract. The transformations of signals and the properties of the radiation beam-pattern in a frequency-diversity antenna array are investigated. The effect of focusing and steering on the beampattern is being investigated. A conventional uniform coherent FDA antenna with a linear frequency plan is considered in detail, and its directional patterns with focus only on transmission, only on reception, and full focus are studied. FDA antennas with nonlinear and symmetrical frequency distributions over the elements are considered. The effect of matched filtering on the appearance of the radiation pattern has been studied.

Keywords: Radiation Beampattern · Frequency Diversity Array · Nonlinear Frequency Distribution · Focusing and Steering · Matched Filtering

1 Introduction

Intensive research on multi-element antennas with frequency diversity array (FDA) apparently began with the work of Antonik [1, 2] in 2006. However, back in 1997 in Russia, multi-frequency antenna arrays were used to generate pulse signals [3]. In the usual scheme of spaced equidistant antenna elements, each of them emits different frequencies, and initially the frequencies of neighboring elements differed by the same value Δf (FO – frequency offset), so that a linear frequency increase from one element to another was realized. Such a scheme of linear frequency plan is studied in detail in [4]. It was noticed that the phase shifts between the spaced antenna elements undergo changes depending on the range, and not only on the angular direction, and thus the radiation pattern turns out to depend on the angle, time and range [1]. The periodicity of the beam in angle, range and time was noted. The traditional separation of processing into spatial and temporal is no longer possible in such systems.

The implementation of the FDA radar generally includes flexible control of the frequencies, phases and amplitudes of the emitted signals from each element, as well as the possible dynamic movement of these elements (for example, in the case of a synthesized aperture). The time forms of the signals can vary from one radiation cycle to another, therefore, spatial, frequency and time changes are indicated in [1], and "fast" and "slow" time are highlighted.

© The Author(s), under exclusive license to Springer Nature Switzerland AG 2024
A. Gibadullin (Ed.): ITIDMS 2023, CCIS 2112, pp. 53–67, 2024.
https://doi.org/10.1007/978-3-031-60318-1_5

The spatial properties of the multi-frequency array radiation pattern are influenced by the location of the antenna elements and the values of the radiated carrier frequencies. For a uniform linear (equidistant) FDA with the same frequency increments, the range is related to the angle in the far-field radiation pattern, which leads to an S-shaped energy distribution in the angular plane [5].

The dependence of the radiation pattern on the angle, range and time allows for automatic scanning of space without the use of phase shifters, but this makes it difficult to focus the beam on selected areas of space. To overcome this dependence and achieve the point shape of the focusing beam, non-linearly increasing frequency increments were proposed, in particular, according to the logarithmic law [6], time-dependent [7], multi-carrier [8] and random [9, 10] frequency increments.

A genetic algorithm and a discrete spheroidal sequence were adopted to optimize frequency increments for focusing radiation patterns in [11] and [12], respectively. In addition, a mutually simple (coprime) array with mutually simple frequencies [13] and symmetric array geometry [14] was used to synthesize an uncoupled radiation pattern.

It should be noted that the characteristics of a multi-carrier radar are influenced by the modulation of the emitted signal and the type of processing. The idea of frequency separation of monochrome signals has been extended to modulated oscillations, in particular, to LFM oscillations [2] and to more complex types of modulation. Changing the modulation of time signals has opened up the possibility of controlling the spatial-temporal radiation pattern of the radar, including the possibility of building adaptive systems. Efforts to synthesize multi-frequency arrays were made in [14, 15], in which various particular problems were solved. The complexity of the problem does not currently allow us to obtain a universal solution for all reception and management tasks.

In order to obtain the required field distribution and beam control, it is necessary to understand the influence of each of the factors involved in beam formation, as well as the influence of the received signal processing algorithm. The article examines the transformations of the signals of a frequency-diversity antenna array using matched filters in comparison with the properties of the generated radiation pattern.

2   Materials and Methods

2.1   Signals in a Multi-carrier Antenna Array

Consider an M-element linear transmitting antenna array containing elements with coordinates d_m relative to the first element, so that $d_1 = 0$. We assume that the antenna elements have identical and isotropic radiation patterns and their sizes are small compared to the wavelength. Each transmitting element emits narrowband signals $s_m(t) = u_m(t)\exp(j2\pi f_m t)$ with the same initial phases and frequencies $f_m = f_0 + \Delta f_m$, $m = 0, \ldots, M-1$, where $u_m(t)$ are complex envelopes.

The total signal of the transmitting antenna at the point of the far zone at a distance R and at an angle θ to the normal (boresight direction) can (without taking into account amplitude attenuation) be written as:

$$x(t, R, \theta) = \sum_{m=0}^{M-1} w_{t,m} u_m(t) \exp(j2\pi f_m(t - R_m/c)) \tag{1}$$

where $R_m = R - d_m \sin\theta$, and θ is the angle relative to the normal to the array axis (boresight direction); $w_{t,m}$ – weights of mth transmitter channel. If there is no focusing and steering at the transmitting end all weights $w_{t,m} = 1$.

With the same time modulation of the signals of each element, the amplitude beampattern (BP) for transmission is equal to the modulus of the total signal $x(t)$. Compared to the phased array (PA) ($\Delta f_m = 0$) the BP turns out to depend on the angle, time, and distance to the point. Various attempts have been made to eliminate or weaken these dependencies and obtain static directional patterns necessary for detecting and estimating the coordinates of targets [16, 17]. How serious this disadvantage is depends on the focusing capabilities of the array.

The signals at the input of nth receiving element have the form:

$$y_n(t, R, \vartheta) = u(t - 2R/c) \sum_{m=0}^{M-1} \exp(j2\pi f_m(t - 2R/c) + j2\pi f_m(d_m + d_n)\vartheta/c), \tag{2}$$

where $\vartheta = \sin\theta$.

After focusing on the range by multiplying by $\exp(j2\pi f_m 2R/c)$ in each transmitting channel, we get:

$$y_n(t, \vartheta) = u(t) \sum_{m=0}^{M-1} \exp(j2\pi f_m t + j2\pi f_m(d_m + d_n)\vartheta/c).$$

The sum of the receiver signals is:

$$Y(t, R, \vartheta) = u(t) \sum_{m=0}^{M-1} w_{t,m} \exp(j2\pi f_m t) \sum_{n=0}^{N-1} w_{r,n} \exp(j2\pi f_m(d_m + d_n)\vartheta/c), \tag{3}$$

where $w_{r,n}$ are weights at the receiver end. A two-way beampattern is defined as the modulus of the sum signal Y (with two-way propagation).

2.2 Steering of Beampattern and Signal Processing

Steering by angle and range for the directional pattern to set values (R_0, α) is carried out by introducing phase multipliers for transmitting and receiving elements:

$$w_{t,m} = \exp(j2\pi f_m(R_0/c - d_m \sin\alpha/c))$$
$$w_{r,n} = \exp(j2\pi f_n(R_0/c - d_n \sin\alpha/c)) \quad,$$

This method is called in [18] non-adaptive formation of BP (non-adaptive beam-former).

A matched filter for the sum of the signals $Y(t, R, \vartheta)$ convolves this signal with the impulse response of the filter, which is a mirror image of this signal in time, as a result, its autocorrelation function is formed at the output for each value of the range and angle. This is the optimal processing, which is usually not divided into spatial and temporal parts. In many cases, this is too difficult to implement.

For signal processing various approaches are presented in the literature, such as the multichannel matched filtering structure presented in [5, 16, 17, 19], where each receiving antenna is accompanied by a group of carriers with matched filters. In a common variant, matched filtering is implemented in each receiving element for each carrier frequency of incoming signals, followed by summation of the results by receiving elements with the corresponding phase adjustment. In contrast to the matched filtering of the total signal, in this implementation, the receiver does not fully take into account the phase relationships between the summed signals, which may affect the processing efficiency.

This approach is justified for MIMO systems [20] but can also be used in the case of coherent FDA. Taking into account the narrowband of the signals, $\exp(j2\pi f_m d_n \vartheta/c) \approx \exp(j2\pi f_0 d_n \vartheta/c)$ can be considered, then the signal at the input of the nth receiving element is approximately:

$$y_n(t, \vartheta) \approx u(t) \exp(j2\pi f_0 d_n \vartheta/c) \sum_{m=0}^{M-1} \exp(j2\pi f_m t + j2\pi f_m d_m \vartheta/c).$$

As a result, filtering in each receiving channel can be made the same [5, 20] using a filter matched to the total signal of the transmitter. A matched filter for the total signal $Y(t, R, \vartheta)$ convolves this signal with an impulse response, which is a mirror image in time of this signal, as a result, its autocorrelation function is formed at the output for each range and angle value. In this case, the ideal focusing of the array is realized.

Further simplification can be obtained, which involves only matched filtering in each receiving channel with the signal $s_0(t) = \sum_{m=0}^{M-1} \exp(j2\pi f_m t)$. In this case, focusing in transmission channels is not used.

2.3 Problem Statement

In the literature on the FDA, it has been repeatedly noted that multi-frequency arrays have significant advantages over conventional PA. Specifically, FDA can provide *potential superiority* in precise target location, and range-dependent anti-jamming over conventional PA which can only perform the beamforming in an angle dimension [15].

However, there is still little concrete quantitative evidence of such benefits. At the same time, traditional FDA systems have their own problems related to changing characteristics in angle, range and time. In this regard, numerous attempts are being made to get rid of this periodicity and obtain characteristics that do not depend on range and time. The improvements mainly relate to frequency plans, the variants of which become non-linear and time-dependent, which significantly complicates the antenna system. Then spatio-temporal processing can no longer be divided into spatial and temporal, as in the cases of conventional FDA and PA. Obviously, the introduction of nonlinear and variable frequency plans affects BP by changing the width of the main lobe and generating a mass of side lobes. Quantitative analysis of these parameters is also poorly presented.

When calculating radiation patterns of multi-frequency antennas, phase relations are usually used, without considering the temporal nature of the signals involved in their formation. The influence of time parameters is taken into account by introducing time delays into the phase components [5, 19, 21–24]. A more subtle analysis is related to the modeling of time signals and their transformation processes.

To obtain the required field distribution and beam control, it is necessary to understand the influence of each of the factors involved in beam formation, as well as the influence of the received signal processing algorithm. The article examines the properties of the output signals of a FDA antenna when using matched filters in comparison with the properties of the constructed beampattern.

The following issues are discussed further:

– Signal transformations and the use of filters in conventional FDA with linear frequency plan;
– Using symmetrical linear frequency plans;
– Formation of beampattern in arrays with nonlinear symmetrical frequency plans.

3   Multi-carrier Antenna Array with Linear Frequency Plan

Consider a uniform linear array (ULA) comprising M transmitting and N receiving elements separated by a half-wave interval d. Often the transmitting and receiving elements turn out to be combined (collocated radar), so that $N = M$. We assume a linear increase in the radiation frequencies of each element (a linearly increasing frequency plan) $f_m = f_0 + m\Delta f$, $m = 0, ..., M-1$. Here Δf is a constant frequency offset. This option corresponds to the common "conventional" frequency diversity scheme (conventional FDA) [25].

3.1   Transmit Beamforming

Consider the case of the absence of angle focusing in transmitting elements emitting monochrome pulses of duration T. A total signal (1) is generated at each point in space. In fact, the radiation pattern turns out to be oriented normal to the lattice axis ($\theta = 0$, boresight direction). If the initial phases of the emitted pulses are the same, then the time form of the total signal for $M = 6$ is shown in Fig. 1a, where the direction normal to the antenna axis is selected ($\theta = 0$, boresight direction). A delay of 200 counts through $Ts = 0.01$ ns is also selected here, which corresponds to a range of 0.3 m.

The figure for comparison shows monochrome pulses from the first and sixth transmitting antenna elements. The maxima of the generated radiation are repeated after $T_f = 1/\Delta f = 25$ ns, which in this case corresponds to $\Delta R = 2.5$ m in range.

If the initial phases of the emitted pulses alternate from element to element, taking the values 0 and π, then the waveform changes so that the maxima are in the center of each initial T_f interval (Fig. 1b). The amplitude of the sum signal is shifted in time (range) when the target is moved along the angle in accordance with the directional pattern for transmission (Fig. 2a). The values of the angles of theta along the abscissa axis are increased by 90° compared to the values of the angle θ. At negative angles, the pulses move towards longer ranges, and at positive angles – towards smaller ones.

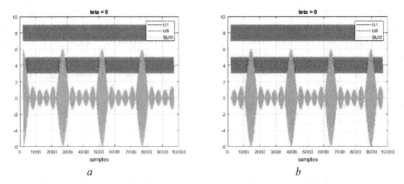

Fig. 1. The shapes of the total transmitter signals for $M = 6$: a – for identical zero initial phases in the transmitting elements; b – for alternating initial phases 0 and π.

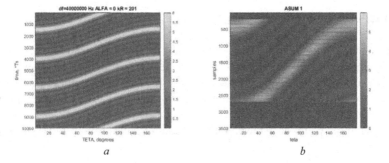

Fig. 2. Transmit beampatterns for $\alpha = 0$: a – for a long pulse; b – for a short pulse of Tf = 25 ns duration. Keep in mind the alternation of the initial phases across the elements.

The transmit BP exists in space only within the range limits associated with the duration of the emitted pulses. In particular, Fig. 2b shows the case of a short pulse $u(t)$ with a duration of $T = 25$ ns (2500 time samples). The pulse duration covers one period of the T_f. Figure 3 shows the trajectory of the maximum of the total signal $x(t)$ (lower curve IS) depending on the direction to the target. The time delay of the maximum of the total signal turns out to depend on the direction to the target, i.e. the angle and range to the target turn out to be coupled, which is usually undesirable.

If the sum signal $x(t)$ is subjected to matched filtering, then an autocorrelation function is formed at the filter output, the position of the maximum of which no longer depends on the angle of arrival of radiation. The corresponding horizontal line (IC) is shown in Fig. 3. Such filtering means focusing the transmitting BP by angle and range, which requires knowledge of these target parameters. In the case of using a filter tuned to a multi-frequency reference signal $s_0(t) = \sum_m \exp(j2\pi f_m t)$, , there is no focusing, and the dependence of the delay time of the maximum output signal of the filter on the angle is preserved (line IC0 in Fig. 3 for the case of a short pulse).

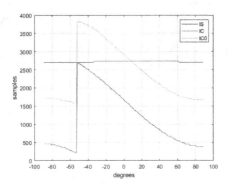

Fig. 3. Trajectories of the maxima of the pulses of the sum signal (IS) and the signals at the output of the filters (IC and IC0).

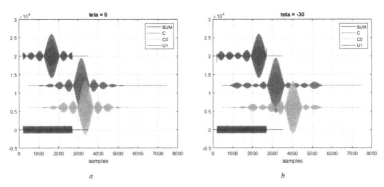

Fig. 4. The pulse shapes of the sum signal (IS) and the signals at the output of the filters (IC and IC0).

Figure 4 shows the time forms of the sum signal (SUM), its correlation function (C) and the shape of the result of unmatched filtering (C0) for the angular position of the target $\theta = 0$ (a) and $\theta = -30°$ (b). When this angle changes, the total pulse SUM and pulse C0 move along the range, and impulse C does not change its position. The transmit beampatterns are shown in Fig. 5. With matched filtering, we have a range-focused omnidirectional BP (Fig. 5a). Inconsistent filtering (C0) almost does not change the course of the radiation pattern compared to the total signal (SUM, Fig. 2a), although some focusing is noticeable in a narrow area of angles at a certain range (Fig. 5b).

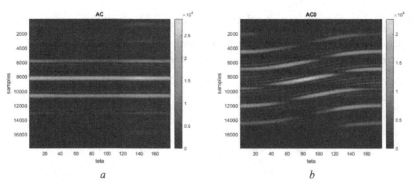

Fig. 5. Transmit beampatterns: *a* – with matched filtering (C); *b* – with unmatched filtering (C0).

3.2 Transmit-Receive Beamforming

Consider the case of a fixed point target in the far zone with coordinates (R, θ). Without considering the effect of attenuation during propagation, and assuming the reflection coefficients of the target are the same for each of the radiated frequencies, it is possible to investigate the behavior of the received signals depending on the range, angle of arrival and time. The received signal by the nth receiving element can be written by (2).

In the absence of focusing and tracking at the receiving end, the received signals are summed up:

$$Y(t, R, \vartheta) = \sum_{n=0}^{N-1} y_n(t, R, \vartheta), \qquad (4)$$

A two-way beampattern is defined as the modulus of the Y during two-way propagation. However, such a directional pattern does not take into account the processing in the receiving elements, which can be implemented in various ways. In the absence of directional interference, filtering can be matched with the sum signals (2) of the transmitter to ensure the best signal-to-noise ratio. For such filtering, it is necessary to set the values of the range and angle of the target.

In Fig. 6 the receiver beampatterns are presented with focusing at the angle α and range $R_0 = ct_0$, where t_0 is a one-way signal delay. In this example, $t_0 = kR\ Ts, kR = 201$.

The periodicity of the BP over the range can be eliminated by using short pulses. Full focus corresponds to matched filtering of the sum signal of the transmitter. In this case, the peak of the radiation pattern at the reception exactly corresponds to the set values of the range and angle. If focusing is applied only at the transmitting end (Fig. 7a), the maximum of BP is able to move only along the range. Focusing only on the receiving end (Fig. 7b) moves the peak to the desired angle, but the range is significantly distorted.

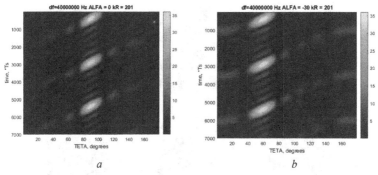

Fig. 6. Receiver beampatterns focusing at the range R0: *a* – focusing at an angle of α = 0°; *b* – focusing at an angle of α = –30°.

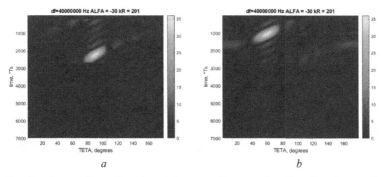

Fig. 7. Receiver beampatterns focusing at the range R_0: *a* – when focusing at an angle of α = –30° only in the transmitter; *b* – when focusing at an angle of α = –30° only in the receiver.

3.3 FDA Array with Symmetrical Linear Frequency Plan

The symmetric linear frequency plan is mentioned in [26] with reference to [27]. A further study of the symmetric frequency plan is given in [28].

With the simultaneous V-shaped implementation of the increasing and decreasing branches of the plan, it is necessary to avoid frequency overlap in various transmitting elements.

The transmit beampattern for a linearly increasing frequency plan (Fig. 8*a*) is not symmetrical in angle. In the case of a linearly decreasing set of frequencies (symmetrical to the original frequency plan) in GHz {3.20 3.16 3.12 3.08 3.04 3.00}, the directional BP develops in an angle in the opposite direction, as shown in Fig. 8*b*. If the two indicated directional patterns are used independently and the signals are stacked coherently, then as a result we have a symmetrical the picture shown in Fig. 8*c* and Fig. 9*a,b* with the preservation of periodicity in range, angle and time. The peaks of the diagram can move by angle and range by changing the phases of the signals of the transmitting and receiving elements (Fig. 9*c*).

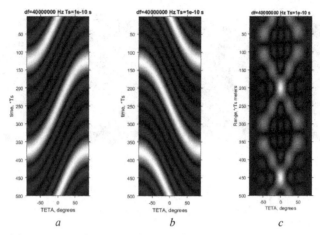

Fig. 8. Transmit beampatterns for symmetric linear frequency plans: a – increasing; b – decreasing; c – symmetrical.

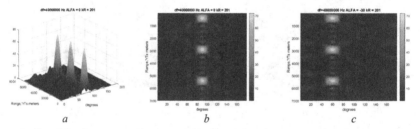

Fig. 9. Receive beampatterns for symmetrical linear frequency plan: a – peaks; b – focusing to $\alpha = 0°$; c – focusing to $\alpha = -30°$.

4 A Multi-carrier Array with a Nonlinear Frequency Plans

The disadvantage of the linear frequency plan for a homogeneous linear lattice is the periodicity of the main peaks in range and angle, which causes ambiguity in determining the coordinates of targets.

This phenomenon was combated by changing the frequency plan, introducing the dependence of the frequency offset on both the number of the radiated antenna element and on time, i.e. introducing frequency modulation. It quickly became clear that it is impossible to find an optimal solution by this method, especially if the elements are not equidistant [15, 21, 29]. Despite the significant complication of signal processing in the antenna array, the proposed solutions are of considerable theoretical and practical interest.

The results of recent publications indicate that it is not possible to completely stabilize the BP in time. However, it is possible to redistribute energy in space in such a way as to increase the exposure time of the target and reduce the exposure time of interference.

4.1 FDA Array with Logarithmic and Sinusoid Frequency Plans

Logarithmic frequency plan was first investigated in [6] for increasing offsets. There are many ways to use the logarithmical law. Jingwei Xu et al. [15] give formulas $\Delta f_m = -\Delta f\,(\ln(m))^{1.5}$ for decreasing plan. Increased version may be obtained as $\Delta f_m = \max(\Delta f_m) + \Delta f\,(\ln(m))^{1.5}$. For $M = 6$ and $\Delta f = 40$ MHz it gives non-overlapping curves (Fig. 10a). Previously [30], logarithmic offsets were offered in a simpler form: $\Delta f_m = -\delta\Delta f\,(\ln(m))$ for increased frequency plan. Then for decreased frequency plan we get $\Delta f_m = \max(\Delta f_m) + \delta\Delta f\,(\ln(m))$ and with $\delta = 2$ the two plans are overlapping (Fig. 10b).

Sinusoidal frequency plan may be taken from [15] $\Delta f_m = -9\Delta f\,\sin(m/38,8)$ which gives for $M = 6$ non-overlapping lines (Fig. 10c). Overlapping version is $\Delta f_m = 5.25\,\Delta f\,\sin((m/38,8)$ (Fig. 10d).

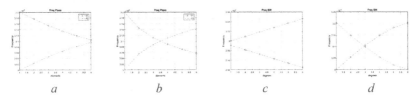

| a | b | c | d |

Fig. 10. Frequency plans: a – log non-overlapping [15]; b – log overlapping; c – sinusoidal non-overlapping; d – sinusoidal overlapping.

Here are the simulation results for the coherent accumulation of four symmetrical frequency plans shown in Fig. 10. Figure 11 presents results for non-overlapping log plan of Fig. 10a. Receive beampatterns focusing to $\alpha = 0°$ for symmetrical overlapping log frequency plan of Fig. 10b are presented in Fig. 12a,b. In Fig. 12c beampattern is focused to $\alpha = -30°$.

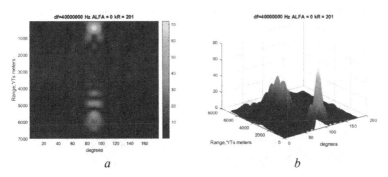

| a | b |

Fig. 11. Receive beampatterns for symmetric log non-overlapping frequency plan: a – intensity; b – peaks; c – cross-section over range for $\alpha = 0$.

A comparison of the results for the two log plans is shown in Fig. 13. It shows a significant reduction in the peaks of the ambiguity at long ranges in comparison with

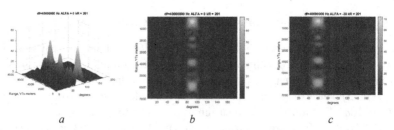

a   *b*   *c*

Fig. 12. Receiver beampatterns for symmetrical log frequency plan: a – peaks; b – focusing to α = 0°; c – focusing to α = –30°.

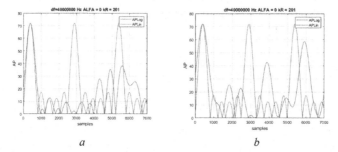

a   *b*

Fig. 13. Cross sections of the beampattern along the range focusing at α = 0°: *a* – symmetrical non-overlapping log frequency plan; *b* – symmetrical overlapping log frequency plan; APLog – for symmetrical log frequency plan; APLin – for symmetrical linear plan.

symmetrical linear plan (APLin). The overlapping version of the symmetrical log plan behaves somewhat worse (Fig. 13*b*).

Results for symmetrical sinusoidal plans are presented in Figs. 14 and 15. The sinusoidal version of the non-overlapping symmetrical plan appears to be the best for the case under consideration (Fig. 14). The overlapping variant is significantly inferior to all those already considered. Comparative analysis of cross-sections is presented in Fig. 15.

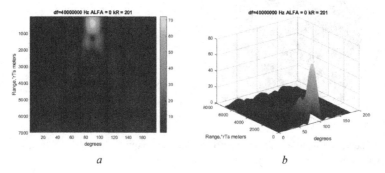

a   *b*

Fig.14. Receiver beampatterns for symmetrical non-overlapping sin frequency plan.

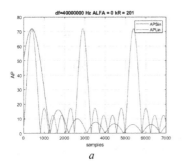 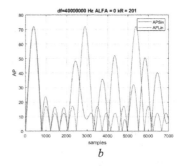

a   *b*

Fig. 15. Cross sections of the beampattern by range focusing at $\alpha = 0°$: a – symmetrical non-overlapping sin frequency plan; b – symmetrical overlapping sin frequency plan; APSin – for symmetrical sin frequency plan; APLin – for symmetrical linear plan.

5   Results and Discussion

FDA antennas have the valuable property of self-scanning space, however, the periodicity of the directional pattern in angle and range of a conventional FDA with a linear frequency plan and the coupling of these parameters makes it difficult to implement an unambiguous localization of the target. Greater stability and decoupling of angle and range can be achieved by focusing and controlling the array elements, as well as spatio-temporal signal processing. Matched filtering makes it possible to stabilize the resulting BP in range, which is not possible with multi-channel filtering followed by summation by receiving elements. The use of nonlinear frequency plans allows us to significantly reduce the influence of peaks of the BP ambiguity when using long pulses. Symmetrical frequency plans improve the properties of BP, providing better localization of the target, while non-overlapping options turned out to be more effective.

An urgent task is to study the influence of interference and interfering targets in the resolution of objects. In addition to the frequency plan, the location of the elements has a significant impact on the characteristics of the FDA antenna. Sparse structures in some cases have an advantage over equidistant ones, especially when resolving many goals. The general approach to optimization includes the search for the most successful geometric structures together with frequency plans and appropriate processing, which is the subject of further research.

In addition to the frequency plan, the location of the antenna elements has a significant impact on the characteristics of the FDA antenna. Sparse structures in some cases have an advantage over equidistant ones. The general approach to optimization includes the search for the most successful geometric structures together with frequency plans and appropriate processing, which is the subject of further research.

6   Conclusions

A number of characteristics of the FDA antenna with combined receiving and transmitting elements have been investigated. Signal conversion and the formation of a radiation pattern in a conventional FDA antenna with a linear frequency plan are considered, the possibilities of focusing and steering the beam and the effect of matched filtering are revealed. Variants of symmetric frequency plans for linear and nonlinear dependences of frequency increments on the element number are considered. The advantages of non-overlapping frequency plan for target localization are revealed.

References

1. Antonik, P., Wicks, M.C., Griffiths, H.D., Baker, C.J.: Frequency diverse array radars. In: Proceedings of the IEEE Radar Conference, Verona, NY, USA, pp. 215–217 (2006)
2. Antonik, P., Wicks, M., Griffiths, H., Baker, C.: Multi-mission multi-mode waveform diversity. In: Proceedings of the IEEE Radar Conference, Verona, NY, pp. 24–27 (2006)
3. Antonik, P.: An investigation of a frequency diverse array. Ph.D. thesis. University College London (2009)
4. Gui, R., Wang, W.-Q., Cui, C., So, H.: Coherent pulsed-FDA radar receiver design with time-variance consideration: SINR and CRB analysis. IEEE Trans. Sig. Process. 66(1), 200–214 (2018)
5. Khan, W., Qureshi, I., Saeed, S.: Frequency diverse array radar with logarithmically increasing frequency offset. IEEE Antennas Wirel. Propag. Lett. 14(1), 499–502 (2015)
6. Khan, W., Qureshi, I.: Frequency diverse array radar with time dependent frequency offset. IEEE Antennas Wirel. Propag. Lett. 13(1), 758–761 (2014)
7. Han, S., Fan, C., Huang, X.: Frequency diverse array with time dependent transmit weights. In: Proceedings of the 13th International Conference on Signal Process, Chengdu, China, pp. 448–451 (2016)
8. Liu, M., Hang, R., Wang, L., Nehorai, A.: The random frequency diverse array: a new antenna structure for uncoupled direction-range direction in active sensing. IEEE J. Sel. Topics Sig. Process. 11(2), 295–308 (2017)
9. Qin, S., Zhang, Y., Amin, M., Gini, F.: Frequency diverse coprime arrays with coprime frequency offsets for multitarget localization. IEEE J. Sel. Top. Sig. Process. 11(2), 321–335 (2017)
10. Xu, Y., Shi, X., Li, W., Xu, J.: Flat-top beampattern synthesis in range and angle domains for frequency diverse array via second-order cone programming. IEEE Antennas Wirel. Propag. Lett. 15(1), 1479–1482 (2016)
11. Tan, M., Wang, C., Li, Z.: Correction analysis of frequency diverse array radar about time. IEEE Trans. Antennas Propag. 69(2), 834–847 (2021)
12. Chen, B., Chen, X., Huang, Y., Guan, J.: Transmit beampattern synthesis for the FDA radar. IEEE Antennas Wirel. Propag. Lett. 17(1), 98–101 (2018)
13. Xu, Y., Huang, X., Wang, A.: Transmit-Receive sparse synthesis of linear frequency diverse array in range-angle space using genetic algorithm. Sensors 23(6), 3107 (2023)
14. Mu, T., Song, Y., Wang, Z.: Beampattern synthesis for frequency diverse array based on time-modulated double parameters approach. J. Microwaves Optoelectron. Electromagn. Appl. 17(3), 352–365 (2018)
15. Jia, W., Jakobsson, A., Wang, W.-Q.: Coherent FDA receiver and joint range-space-time processing, [eess.SP]. arXiv arXiv:2306.00688v (2023)
16. Wang, W.-Q., Shao, H., Cai, J.: Range-angle-dependent beamforming by frequency diverse array antenna. Int. J. Antennas Propag. 2012, 760489 (2012)
17. Jia, W., Wang, W.-Q., Zhang, Sh., Zheng, Zh.: FDA beampattern characteristics with considering time-range relations. arXiv arXiv:2204.07256v1 (2022)
18. Dong, Y.: Frequency diverse array radar signal and data processing. IET Radar Sonar Navig. 12(9), 954–963 (2018)

19. Tan, M., Bao, L., Zhu, H., Song, W., Wang, X.: Range-angle-dependent beamforming for FDA radar with Hamming interelement spacing and sinusoidal multicarrier approach. AIP Adv. **13**, 015003 (2023)
20. Zhao, Y., Tian, B., Wang, C., Gong, J., Tan, M., Zhou, C.: Analysis of multicarrier frequency diverse array radar over time. IET Sig. Process. **16**, 400–412 (2022)
21. Ahmad, Z., Chen, M., Bao, S.: Beampattern analysis of frequency diverse array radar: a review. EURASIP J. Wirel. Commun. Netw. **2021**, 189 (2021)
22. Xu., J, et al.: System design and signal processing for frequency diverse array radar. J. Beijing Inst. Technol. **30**(1), 1–19 (2021)
23. Ahmad, Z., Shi, Z., Zhou, C.: Time-variant focusing range-angle dependent beampattern synthesis by uniform circular frequency diverse array radar. IET Radar Sonar Navig. **15**, 62–74 (2021)
24. Zubair, M., Ahmed, S., Alouini, M.: Frequency diverse array radar: new results and discrete Fourier transform based beampattern. IEEE Trans. Sig. Process. **68**, 2670–2681 (2020)
25. Wang, W.-Q.: Overview of frequency diverse array in radar and navigation applications. IET Radar Sonar Navig. **10**(6), 1001–1012 (2016)
26. Sammartino, P., Baker, C., Griffiths, H.: Frequency diverse MIMO techniques for radar. IEEE Trans. Aerosp. Electron. Syst. **49**(1), 201–222 (2013)
27. Nusenu, S.: Transmit/received beamforming for frequency diverse array with symmetrical frequency offsets. Adv. Sci. Technol. Eng. Syst. J **2**(3), 1–6 (2017)
28. Shao, X., Hu, T., Zhang, J., Li, L., Xiao, M., Xiao, Z.: Efficient beampattern synthesis for sparse frequency diverse array via matrix pencil method. Sensors **22**, 1042 (2022)
29. Wang, W., Yan, S., Mao, L.: Time-domain frequency-invariant beampattern synthesis via alternating direction method of multipliers. J. Acoust. Soc. America **147**(5), 3372–3375 (2020)
30. Gao, K., Wang, W.-Q., Cai, J., Xiong, J.: Decoupled frequency diverse array range–angle-dependent beampattern synthesis using non-linearly increasing frequency offsets. IET Microw. Antennas Propag. **10**(8), 880–884 (2016)

Comparative Analysis of Fuzzy Controllers in a Truck Cruise Control System

A. Z. Asanov[1], D. N. Demyanov[2(✉)], and I. Yu. Myshkina[2]

[1] MIREA –Russian Technological University, 78, Vernadsky Street, Moscow, Russia
[2] Kazan Federal University, 18, Kremlyovskaya Street, Kazan, Russia
demyanovdn@mail.ru

Abstract. The paper considers the problem of improving the cruise control system used to control the speed of a truck. It is proposed to supplement the existing control system with a supervisor that adjusts the parameters of the classic PID controller in real time depending on the current state and driving modes of the vehicle. To ensure effective work of the supervisor in conditions of incompleteness and inaccuracy of incoming information, it is proposed to use fuzzy logic methods. Three most frequently used variants of the fuzzy supervisor implementation are considered: the PID controller coefficients are calculated by the supervisor based on the error signal, the PID controller coefficients are adjusted by the supervisor based on the error signal, the PID controller coefficients are calculated by the supervisor based on the difference between the output of the control system and the reference model. The parameters of the PID controller and the fuzzy supervisor are adjusted to ensure the minimum value of the transition process time. For each of the considered variants, the results of computer modeling of the processes of changing the speed of a truck are presented. The most effective algorithm for controlling the speed of a truck is proposed, as well as directions for further improvement of the cruise control system.

Keywords: Truck · Speed · Control System · Fuzzy Controller · Comparative Analysis

1 Introduction

One of the main trends at the current stage of development of automotive technology is the widespread introduction of various electronic systems for automating typical actions performed while driving [1]. At the same time, the effective functioning of the on-board information and control system of the vehicle involves solving various kinds of problems under conditions of significant uncertainty of parameters and external influences. The uncertainty in the source data and the algorithmic complexity of such problems, as well as the need to solve them in real time, require the use of intelligent information processing methods and control laws. Thus, ensuring the effective functioning of a modern vehicle with a high level of automation according to the SAE classification [2] is only possible if its on-board information and control system is an intelligent control system [3].

A. Gibadullin (Ed.): ITIDMS 2023, CCIS 2112, pp. 68–79, 2024.
https://doi.org/10.1007/978-3-031-60318-1_6

One of the elements of the vehicle's on-board information and control system is advanced driver-assistance systems (ADAS). ADAS is a set of software and hardware that assists the driver in making quick decisions to control the vehicle safely and easily [4]. Modern research devoted to the problems of managing transport and logistics systems and the development of algorithms for the functioning of individual ADAS modules actively uses artificial intelligence methods. For example, fuzzy logic and fuzzy cognitive models are used to predict the success of projects related to driving [5, 6]. Artificial neural networks are used in real-time driver status monitoring systems, to evaluate vehicles, etc. [7, 8]. The direction related to the use of the ontological approach in the design of ADAS is also actively developing [9, 10].

One of the important components of ADAS is the cruise control subsystem, which maintains the set vehicle speed. Traditional cruise control is a classic automatic control system, usually based on the use of a PID controller [11]. Despite the simplicity of setup and physical implementation, the classical PID controller has a significant limitation: in the case when the control object is of a nonlinear nature, the controller coefficients are guaranteed to provide control goals only in some neighborhood of a point in the state space [12]. To ensure the effective functioning of the system in all possible modes in the presence of uncertainties and external disturbances, intelligent methods and algorithms are currently used, such as artificial neural networks [13], fuzzy models and fuzzy controllers [14], including fuzzy PID controllers.

There are many variants for constructing control systems using fuzzy logic and PID controllers. One of the possible classifications of fuzzy PID controllers according to the principles of their construction is quite well known [15]:

- "Direct" fuzzy controller (PID-like fuzzy controller [16]), which is characterized by direct control of a given object: the controller in this case is a set of heuristic control rules, in which linguistic variables are used as input variables (in the conditions of the rules), corresponding to the error, derivative error and error integral;
- Adaptive PID controller (fuzzy supervisor [17]), in which a fuzzy controller is used to determine the coefficients of a conventional PID controller – such a controller automatically changes the coefficients of a classic PID controller at different stages of the transition process;
- Hybrid controller in which the control signal is the sum of the output signals of a conventional PID controller and a fuzzy controller (for example, a conventional PI controller and a fuzzy PI-like controller, or a fuzzy PD-like and I-controller [16]).

Currently, to impart adaptive properties to vehicle dynamics control algorithms, the table control method is most often used [18]. The closest to it in structure and principles of work organization is the variant with a fuzzy supervisor, the implementation of which will be discussed in this paper.

2 Problem Statement

Let's consider a model of a cruise control system with an adaptive fuzzy controller used to control the speed of the longitudinal movement of a truck. Its general block diagram is shown in the Fig. 1.

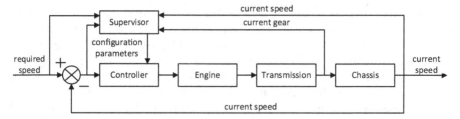

Fig. 1. Block diagram of the vehicle speed control system.

The model under consideration includes: a model of the operation of an internal combustion engine, a model of the dynamics of transmission units, a model of the longitudinal movement of a truck, and a controller model. To mathematically describe the main components of a truck, the equations set out in the work [13] are used. The numerical values of the parameters were chosen to be close to the real characteristics of the KAMAZ truck tractor of the K5 family [19, 20].

The adaptive controller used is a two-level system, in which a conventional PID controller is located at the lower level, and a supervisor implemented using fuzzy logic methods is located at the upper level [16, 17]. The supervisor analyzes the actual condition of the car and traffic conditions in real time, forming a vector of auxiliary coefficients used in the operation of the classic PID controller.

It is required to implement the most commonly used schemes for constructing a fuzzy supervisor, to configure parameters for each of the schemes that provide the best indicators of the quality of the transition process, to simulate the operation of the cruise control system and, based on its results, to give recommendations on the application of a particular law of truck speed control.

Within the framework of this work, it is planned to consider the three most commonly used implementation variants for a fuzzy supervisor: the coefficients of the PID controller are calculated by the supervisor based on the error signal, the coefficients of the PID controller are adjusted by the supervisor based on the error signal, the coefficients of the PID controller are calculated by the supervisor based on the difference between the output of the control systems and the reference model [17].

The main quality criterion used when setting the parameters of the controller is the acceleration time of the truck. It is required to ensure its minimum value, provided that the overshoot does not exceed 5%.

The cruise control system is used in trucks mainly when traveling on intercity routes. Therefore, this paper considers movement at speeds from 80 km/h to 100 km/h in the appropriate gear, the gearshift process is not taken into account.

3   Development and Research of the First Variant of the Fuzzy Controller Implementation

The first variant of a fuzzy controller implementation is shown in the Fig. 2.

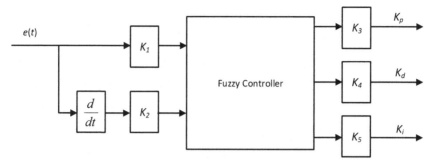

Fig. 2. Block diagram for the first implementation variant.

The input signals to the supervisor are the error (the difference between the desired and actual vehicle speed) and its increment/derivative. The output signals are the coefficients of the PID controller, which are then used at the lower level to generate a correction signal in the speed control system.

In Fig. 2 the amplifiers K_1, K_2 are the normalization coefficients of the input signals, K_3, K_4, K_5 are the denormalization coefficients of the output signals.

Graphs of the membership functions of the terms of the input and output linguistic variables are shown in the Figs. 3 and 4.

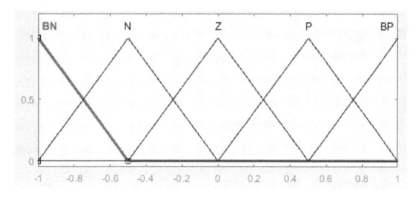

Fig. 3. Graph of the membership function of terms of input linguistic variables.

The rule bases used in the design of the fuzzy controller were formed based on the analysis of a typical transition process graph (Tables 1, 2 and 3).

The developed fuzzy PID controller was implemented in the computer mathematics system MATLAB. To determine the coefficients K_1, K_2, K_3, K_4, K_5 the tools of Simulink Response Optimization package were used. The minimum vehicle acceleration time from 80 km/h to 100 km/h is achieved with the following supervisor parameters: $K_1 = 0.010$; $K_2 = 0.005$; $K_3 = 6.667$; $K_4 = 0.315$; $K_5 = 6.961$.

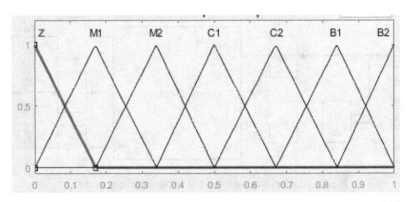

Fig. 4. Graph of the membership function of the terms of the output linguistic variables.

Table 1. Rule base for determining the coefficient K_p.

		Error derivative				
		BN	N	Z	P	BP
Error	BN	B2	B2	B2	B2	B2
	N	B1	B1	B1	C2	B2
	Z	Z	Z	M2	M1	M1
	P	B1	B1	B1	C2	B2
	BP	B2	B2	B2	B2	B2

Table 2. Rule base for determining the coefficient K_i.

		Error derivative				
		BN	N	Z	P	BP
Error	BN	C1	C1	C1	C1	C1
	N	M1	M1	M1	M1	M1
	Z	M2	M2	Z	M2	M2
	P	M1	M1	M1	M1	M1
	BP	C1	C1	C1	C1	C1

Table 3. Rule base for determining the coefficient K_d.

		Error derivative				
		BN	N	Z	P	BP
Error	BN	Z	M1	C1	C2	B2
	N	M1	B1	C2	B2	B2
	Z	C1	C2	C2	B2	B2
	P	B1	B2	B2	B2	B2
	BP	B2	B2	B2	B2	B2

4 Development and Research of the Second Variant of the Fuzzy Controller Implementation

The second variant of a fuzzy controller implementation is shown in the Fig. 5.

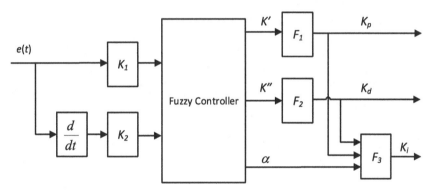

Fig. 5. Block diagram for the second implementation variant.

The input signals for the supervisor, as in the previous case, are the error and its increment/derivative. The output signals are auxiliary parameters K', K'', α. The obtained values are used to adjust the coefficients of the classical PID controller according to the formulas [21]:

$$\begin{cases} K_p = \left(K_{p\ max} - K_{p\ min}\right)K' + K_{p\ min} \\ K_d = (K_{d\ max} - K_{d\ min})K'' + K_{d\ min} \\ K_i = \frac{K_p^2}{\alpha K_d} \end{cases}$$

In Fig. 5 the amplifiers K_1 and K_2 represent the normalization coefficients of the input signals. Auxiliary parameters $K_{p\ min}$, $K_{p\ max}$, $K_{d\ min}$, $K_{d\ max}$ set the acceptable ranges for changing the coefficients of the lower-level PID controller.

Graphs of membership functions of terms of input and output linguistic variables are shown in the Figs. 6, 7 and 8.

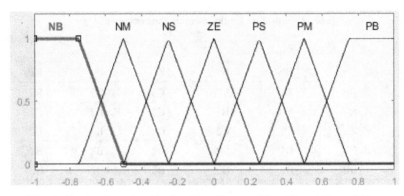

Fig. 6. Graph of membership function of terms of input linguistic variables.

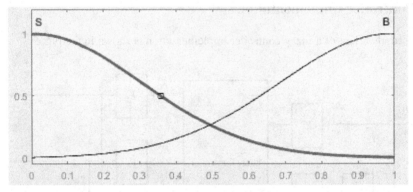

Fig. 7. Graph of membership function of terms of output linguistic variables K' and K''.

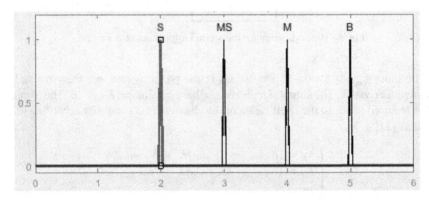

Fig. 8. Graph of membership function of terms of the output linguistic variable α.

The rule bases used in the design of the fuzzy controller were formed based on the analysis of a typical transition process graph (Tables 4, 5 and 6).

Table 4. Rule base for determining the coefficient K'.

		Error derivative						
		NB	NM	NS	ZE	PS	PM	PB
Error	NB	B	B	B	B	B	B	B
	NM	S	B	B	B	B	B	S
	NS	S	S	B	B	B	S	S
	ZE	S	S	S	B	S	S	S
	PS	S	S	B	B	B	S	S
	PM	S	B	B	B	B	B	S
	PB	B	B	B	B	B	B	B

Table 5. Rule base for determining the coefficient K''.

		Error derivative						
		NB	NM	NS	ZE	PS	PM	PB
Error	NB	S	S	S	S	S	S	S
	NM	B	B	S	S	S	B	B
	NS	B	B	B	S	B	B	B
	ZE	B	B	B	B	B	B	B
	PS	B	B	B	S	B	B	B
	PM	B	B	S	S	S	B	B
	PB	S	S	S	S	S	S	S

Table 6. Rule base for determining the parameter α.

		Error derivative						
		NB	NM	NS	ZE	PS	PM	PB
Error	NB	S	S	S	S	S	S	S
	NM	MS	MS	S	S	S	MS	MS
	NS	M	MS	MS	S	MS	MS	M
	ZE	B	M	MS	MS	MS	M	B
	PS	M	MS	MS	S	MS	MS	M
	PM	MS	MS	S	S	S	MS	MS
	PB	S	S	S	S	S	S	S

The developed fuzzy PID controller was implemented in the computer mathematics system MATLAB. The auxiliary parameters $K_{p\,min}$ and $K_{d\,min}$ were chosen constant, the values of the parameters K_1, K_2, $K_{p\,max}$, $K_{d\,max}$ varied. To determine the best values of these quantities, the tools of the Simulink Response Optimization package were used. The minimum vehicle acceleration time from 80 km/h to 100 km/h is achieved with the following supervisor parameters: $K_{p\,min} = 0.010$; $K_{d\,min} = 0.010$; $K_1 = 0.010$; $K_2 = 0.010$; $K_{p\,max} = 0.722$; $K_{d\,max} = 0.535$.

5   Development and Research of the Third Variant of the Fuzzy Controller Implementation

The third variant of a fuzzy controller implementation is shown in the Fig. 9.

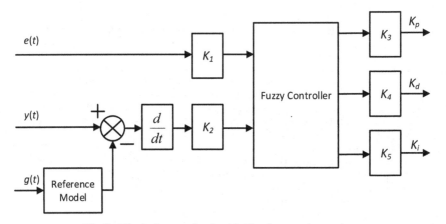

Fig. 9. Block diagram for the third implementation variant.

The input signals for the supervisor are the error, the actual and desired values of the vehicle speed (signals $e(t)$, $y(t)$, $g(t)$ respectively). The output signals are the coefficients of the PID controller, which are then used at the lower level to generate a correction signal in the speed control system.

Unlike the first variant of the supervisor implementation, in the case under consideration, the second input of the fuzzy logic output subsystem receives the increment/derivative not of the error, but of the difference in the reaction of the object and the reference model under the same input effect.

As in the first case, the adjustable parameters are K_1, K_2 (normalization coefficients of the input signals) and K_3, K_4, K_5 (denormalization coefficients of the output signals).

The graphs of the membership functions of the terms of the input and output linguistic variables are similar to the dependencies shown in Figs. 3 and 4. The rule bases used in the design of the fuzzy controller were formed based on the analysis of a typical graph of the transition process by analogy with the dependencies given in the Tables 1, 2 and 3.

An aperiodic link with the following transfer function was used as a reference model in this work:

$$W = \frac{1}{10s + 1}$$

The developed fuzzy PID controller was implemented in the computer mathematics system MATLAB. To determine the coefficients K_1, K_2, K_3, K_4, K_5 the tools of the Simulink Response Optimization package were used. The minimum vehicle acceleration time from 80 km/h to 100 km/h is achieved with the following supervisor parameters: $K_1 = 0.010$; $K_2 = 0.160$; $K_3 = 8.791$; $K_4 = 0.064$; $K_5 = 5.391$.

6 Comparative Analysis of Fuzzy Controller Implementation Variants

Figures 10, 11 and 12 show the results of modeling the acceleration of a truck from 80 km/h to 100 km/h for each of the implementation variants of the fuzzy controller. The values of the quality indicators of transition processes are presented in the Table 7.

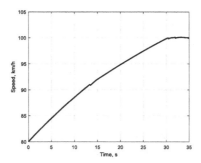

Fig. 10. Acceleration graph for the first implementation variant.

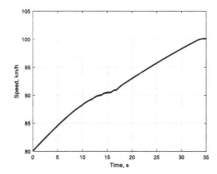

Fig. 11. Acceleration graph for the second implementation variant.

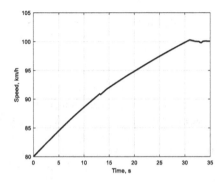

Fig. 12. Acceleration graph for the third implementation variant.

Table 7. Quality indicators of transition process.

Implementation variant	Acceleration time, s	Exceeding the set speed limit, %
Variant 1	31.12	0.11
Variant 2	33.86	0.14
Variant 3	30.37	0.28

The obtained simulation results indicate that fuzzy controllers work correctly in relation to the problem under consideration. The best results in terms of transition process time were obtained using an adaptive fuzzy controller with a reference model. The oscillatory nature of the obtained graphs in some areas is associated with the use as the controller input not of the derivative of the error, but of its increment.

It should be noted that the obtained indicators of the quality of the transition process can be improved by adjusting the parameters of the membership functions of the used linguistic variables.

7   Conclusion

The paper considers three typical schemes for constructing adaptive fuzzy controllers, and explores the possibility of their use in a cruise control system. The results of modeling the longitudinal motion of a truck in the Simulink environment of the MATLAB system using an adaptive fuzzy controller to control the speed are presented.

Computer modeling has shown that adaptive fuzzy controllers work correctly in relation to the problem under consideration. The quality of transition processes indicates the possibility of using fuzzy logic in a truck speed control system. The best dynamics are provided by an adaptive fuzzy controller with a reference model.

In the future, it is planned to study the possibility of applying hybrid approaches (for example, neuro-fuzzy models and algorithms) to the construction of adaptive control systems.

References

1. Kasai, S.A., Kolunina, Y., Ruzimov, A.O.: Modern on-board electronic control systems for trucks. Dual Technol. **4**, 17–20 (2022)
2. SAE J3016 2021: Taxonomy and Definitions for Terms Related to Driving Automation Systems for On-Road Motor Vehicles. SAE International 41 (2021)
3. Asanov, A.Z.: Architecture of on-board information and control systems of robotic heavy-duty mainline vehicles. Russ. Technol. J. **5**(3), 106–113 (2017)
4. Bakhmutov, S.V., Endachev, D.V., Mezentsev, N.P.: Development of intelligent driver assistance systems (ADAS) in the Russian Federation. Transp. Syst. **4**, 17–21 (2018)
5. Bağdatlı, M.E.C., Akbıyıklı, R., Papageorgiou, E.I.: A fuzzy cognitive map approach applied in cost–benefit analysis for highway projects. Int. J. Fuzzy Syst. **19**(5), 1512–1527 (2017)
6. Tsadiras, A., Zitopoulos, G.: Fuzzy cognitive maps as a decision support tool for container transport logistics. Evol. Syst. **8**(1), 19–33 (2017)
7. Akhmetvaleev, A.M., Katasev, A.S., Podolskaya, M.A.: A collective model of neural networks and a software package for determining the functional state of a person. Caspian J. Manage. High Technol. **1**(41), 69–85 (2018)
8. Akhmetvaleev, A.M., Katasev, A.S.: Neural network model of human intoxication functional state determining in some problems of transport safety solution. Comput. Res. Model. **10**(3), 285–293 (2018)
9. Davis, J., Goadrich, M.: The relationship between precision-recall and ROC curves. In: 23th International Conference on Machine Learning, vol. 148, pp. 233–240 (2006)
10. Asanov, A.Z, Myshkina, I.Yu.: The ontological approach in the design of the advanced driver assistance system. In: 7th International Conference on Industrial Engineering, vol. 2, pp. 463–472 (2022)
11. Ribbens, W.: Understanding Automotive Electronics, 8th edn. Elsevier, Burlington (2017)
12. Belodurin, A.D., Kharlashkin, K.E., Gartlieb, E.A., Litsin, K.V.: Analysis of an automatic control system based on linear controllers and MPC controllers. Proc. Tula State Univ. Tech. Sci. (7), 377–381 (2023)
13. Volkov, V.G., Demyanov, D.N.: Synthesis and neural network implementation of the PI controller of adaptive cruise control of a truck. Mekhatronika, Avtomatizatsiya, Upravlenie **19**(11), 707–713 (2018)
14. Pegat, A.: Fuzzy Modeling and Control, 2nd edn. BINOM. Laboratory of Knowledge, Moscow (2013)
15. Yesil, E., Güzelkaya, M., Eksin, I.: Fuzzy PID controllers: an overview. In: 3th Triennial ETAI International Conference on Applied Automatic Systems, pp. 105–112 (2003)
16. Demidova, G.L., Kuzin, A., Lukichev, D.V.: Features of the use of fuzzy controllers on the example of controlling the rotation speed of a DC electric motor. Sci. Tech. Bull. Inf. Technol. Mech. Opt. **16**(5), 872–878 (2016)
17. Burakov, M.V., Konovalov, A.S.: Fuzzy supervisor for PID controller. Inf. Control Syst. **5**, 13–21 (2018)
18. Solovyov, V.V., Nomerchuk, A.Ya.: Automatic cruise control model for a vehicle. Proc. YUFU Tech. Sci. **3**, 172–188 (2023)
19. Dem'yanov, D.N., Hazipov, I.M.: Estimation of the total road load coefficient for a road train. In: Radionov, A.A., Gasiyarov, V.R. (eds.) Proceedings of the 7th International Conference on Industrial Engineering, ICIE 2021. LNME, pp. 731–739. Springer, Cham (2022). https://doi.org/10.1007/978-3-030-85233-7_86
20. KAMAZ production vehicles. https://kamaz.ru/production/serial. Accessed 15 Nov 2023
21. Zhao, Z.-Y., Tomizuka, M., Isaka, S.: Fuzzy gain scheduling of PID controllers. IEEE Trans. Syst. Man Cybern. **23**(5), 1392–1398 (1993)

Implementation of a Blockchain-Based Software Tool to Verify the Authenticity of Paper Documents

Elizaveta Maksina⬤, Vladimir Shmakov⬤, Nikita Voinov$^{(\boxtimes)}$⬤,
Tatyana Leontyeva⬤, and Yury Yusupov⬤

Peter the Great St. Petersburg Polytechnic University,
29, Polytechnicheskaya, St. Petersburg 195251, Russia
`voinov@ics2.ecd.spbstu.ru`

Abstract. The paper describes the usage of blockchain technology to protect paper documents from forgery surpassing the characteristics of existing protection methods. Modern methods of paper documents protection and blockchain specifics regarding to this purpose are observed. A new approach to verifying the authenticity of paper documents using blockchain technology is proposed and a software tool that implements this approach is developed. Results of the tool application and its advantages in compare to existing methods are discussed.

Keywords: Blockchain · Authenticity of Paper Documents · Software Tool · Protection · Security

1 Introduction

Studies devoted to methods of documents forgery propose miscellaneous approaches to protect paper documents [1–9], for example:

- Technical protection – watermarks, protective fibers, optically changing paints, holographic protection.
- Physicochemical protection – magnetic protection, fluorescent protection, infrared protection.
- Printing protection – various printing techniques and methods that determine the properties of the image on the document: micro-printing or applying hidden images.

To apply protective equipment to authentic documents complex unique technologies are used which require the presence of specific equipment, materials, special knowledge and accordingly the presence of large monetary investments. Most organizations cannot afford the use of expensive technologies. Besides, an intruder can simulate the security methods described above so that without special equipment it will be impossible to determine the authenticity of the document.

Documents are often printed on plain paper with ordinary ink using a print impression. The seal gives the document its legal force – it confirms the authenticity of the

A. Gibadullin (Ed.): ITIDMS 2023, CCIS 2112, pp. 80–91, 2024.
https://doi.org/10.1007/978-3-031-60318-1_7

signature of the official. Such a document can be considered unprotected since forging a seal is not a difficult task as the production of a fake impression is inexpensive.

So today the degree of paper document security depends on the cost of implementing a security measure and ensuring a high level of security of a document with small investments is an unsolved task.

The problem is partially solved by switching to electronic document management. However a complete transition to electronic documents is not still possible [10].

To verify the authenticity of electronic documents there is an electronic digital signature technology. However, when printing documents such protection is removed and verification becomes impossible. A paper document becomes a copy of an electronic one. In order for a printed document with an electronic digital signature to be legally significant, it should be signed manually and stamped by the organization as «The copy is verified». It is quite easy to forge signatures and seals, so there is still a problem of authenticity of paper documents.

Some organizations use QR codes and information about the authenticity of the document can be obtained on their official website. Often a mobile application is used which automatically verifies the authenticity of the document when scanning. At the same time, the mobile application is distributed among the employees of the organization who regularly check documents. For example, a theater where the controllers have an application that allows you to quickly check the tickets of the audience. This is how electronic and printed electronic tickets are checked. At the same time, protection against creating a fake website with fake data is implemented.

This approach is convenient when verification is carried out inside an organization that stores data on the authenticity of documents. However, if it is necessary to issue a document and provide an opportunity for any interested person to verify the authenticity of this document, difficulties arise. The approaches described above may not always protect the authenticity of the document. It is physically impossible to install the application of every organization capable of issuing any document. It is also not advisable to attach QR codes leading to the organization's website since these sites are not well known and it is not difficult to create a fake website with a similar domain name without being noticed.

The approach and a software tool described in the paper make it possible to adapt the mechanism of protection of electronic documents to the protection of paper documents, specifically medical certificates, to solve the following problem. When applying for a job, it is often necessary to pass a number of medical tests and provide a certificate with tests results to the employer. Obtaining a certificate from a licensed medical organization has a certain cost. However, there are some shady organizations that provide services for forgery of certificates which does not require any equipment and consumables. Obtaining such a certificate has a lower price due to the low cost. Thus, consumers who want to hide the real test results or save money can buy fake documents, thereby endangering the health of other people. At the same time, an employer may accept such documents if checking their authenticity is not possible.

The proposed approach shall provide:

– Protection of a paper document from forgery which implies the impossibility of establishing the authenticity of a forged document.
– Verification of the authenticity of a paper document based on a paper document and a mobile device with Internet access.
– Protection of the personal data of the document owner.
– Impossibility to change the document owner.

The approach is based on blockchain technology [11–15]. Information about each document is recorded in the blockchain, so the information is available to everyone, but it cannot be changed. To access the data a QR code is used leading to a single Internet resource. If the QR code is replaced and a fake site is created, the verifier will notice a domain name that differs from the main one. To protect personal data the hashing function is used since it does not allow reverse conversion unlike encryption functions.

The software tool implementing the proposed approach is a set of desktop and mobile applications that allow automating the verification process and reducing it to scanning a QR code, followed by displaying the verification result on the screen.

2   Materials and Methods

2.1   Blockchain Technology

Blockchain is an innovative structure that allows storing data securely since it is impossible to delete or change existing information. The blockchain is a chain of blocks each of which contains information that links it to the previous block and transaction data. Due to the established links, any editing, modification or deletion of data in the blockchain leads to the invalidity of all the following blocks. Thus, it is possible to implement an immutable or perpetual registry.

The basis of this technology is the mechanism of linking blocks of information with each other. This is achieved by calculating the hash of the previous block and writing it to a new block. The hash sum of each block depends on two values: the contents of the block and the hash sum of the previous block. When making changes to a block, the hash sum of this block changes. In order for the chain to be correct, it is necessary to indicate the changes in the hash amount from the next block. Thus, changes to one block require changes to all the blocks following the changed one. The previous blocks are not affected. Thus, making changes to all blocks except the last one requires a lot of time and a lot of computing power as it is an extremely time-consuming process. Various functions can be used for hashing, for example, the SHA-256 function is used in bitcoin.

The hash of the block depends on all transactions contained in this block. If a block has been added to the blockchain, then canceling the operation or changing the information in the block is an extremely difficult task.

2.2   Implementation of the Proposed Approach

When issuing a new document on behalf of an organization, a new record is created in the transactions field in the block, which contains the following fields:

- Date and time (in plain text);
- Name of the organization (in plain text);
- Name of the document (in plain text);
- Client hash;
- Additional fields for mining implementation;
- Transaction ID for the search, identification and verification.

The block itself contains the following information:

- Index;
- Timestamp;
- Transaction list;
- The proof parameter for proof of work completion;
- Hash of the previous block.

Name of the organization (or ID of the organization) is indicated in plain text. Each organization has its own ID from a single registry. It is added automatically.

The client hash is a hash obtained from the following set of characters: <passport series> <passport number> <6-digit code>. For example, 1111222222Y3r67N.

When printing a document, a QR code is generated that contains a link and a code (1111222222xxxxxx) so that it does not have to be entered manually. The passport number and code are also printed on the paper document itself in plain text.

The software tool on the smartphone with the QR code scanning function allows to check whether the passport number and code are correct (whether the scanned one matches the printed one). Then the tool counts the hash, follows the link to the transaction, takes the user hash from the transaction summary and reports whether the document is valid or invalid.

Such approach of data storage provides additional protection of the document from forgery while confidentiality is not violated. The addition of a 6-digit one-time code increases the level of protection against disclosure of confidential data.

It is also worth noting the social component of the entire document authentication procedure. Verifiers tend to neglect the quality of verification in an effort to shorten the process, so any additional action, such as manual data entry or parallel use of a computer can greatly complicate the verification process. Thus, an important factor is the ease of use of this tool.

An intruder can forge not a complete document but just change some data in this document. To protect against this it is necessary to include in the blockchain not only the fact that the document was issued but also the information about what document was issued. So the name of the document and the result reflected in the document (if available) are also transferred to the blockchain.

Since the full name of the document may have a long length and in different organizations the same documents can be called differently, it is necessary to systematize this information. An unambiguous and simple name and corresponding numeric code shall be assigned. To do this a specific database is required to store all existing codes and decryptions of these codes.

Also most of the considered documents (medical certificates) contain a certain result. This may be one option out of a small number of possible outcomes (e.g., "detected/not detected") or a result in a certain range (e.g., 0% - 99.999%). To display this information it is necessary to specify in the database whether the document has a certain result and if so how exactly this result is presented.

2.3 Protection Functions

Each organization with required licenses and certificates must be registered in a special registry. Entries to the blockchain are added on behalf of the registered organization. To add records to the blockchain user needs to log in using a private key. Thus, only organizations that have passed state control will be able to issue confirmed documents. It also provides protection against issuing of forged documents on behalf of an official organization.

The passport number is used to log in so that it is not possible to find a person with the same hash of the client and provide document of another person. If a hash is received only based on passport data, then when the same person receives different documents, the hash will match. Also based on the passport data of a person the user can calculate the hash and find information about this person. Therefore, a one-time code is additionally used to protect against the disclosure of personal data.

A 6-digit code is a one-time randomly generated sequence of numbers and letters case-sensitive. 10 digits, 26 Latin lowercase letters, 26 uppercase, so the overall number of combinations is $62 \times 62 \times 62 \times 62 \times 62 \times 62$. Knowing the hash, it is unlikely to pick up the passport series and number which guarantees anonymity.

The use of a special application provides additional protection from the human factor. The application takes data about documents from a single resource which makes it impossible for an intruder to fake a website and get incorrect data from it.

It is possible that an intruder will issue one document after another. He will receive document A, transfer the QR code and a random code to the template of document B, and since the passport data will match, and the date of receipt will be up-to-date, then the fake document will be valid in this case. In order to provide protection in this case, it is necessary to specify the name of the document in the blockchain.

To ensure the protection of the document content, if there is a certain result reflected in the document, the content is also recorded in the blockchain.

The only available way to circumvent the protection for the intruder seeking to forge a document is to issue someone else's document as his own. In this case the intruder has:

- A list of hash values of users who received documents from a certain organization for a certain period $h_1, h_2, ...h_h$;
- Passport number N for which a document is going to be obtained.
- So the task is to find such a code X that:

$$h\,(N + X) = h_k \prime \tag{1}$$

The probability of collisions for data of the same size is extremely small, so given a limited list of hash values of users it is assumed that the probability of success for the intruder is negligible.

3   Results and Discussion

3.1   Blockchain Software Implementation

The blockchain is a chain of blocks where each block contains some array of transactions and additional information.

Each block contains:

- Index;
- Timestamp;
- The proof parameter obtained as a result of the PoW algorithm execution;
- Hash value of the previous block;
- List of transactions.

Each transaction contains:

- Transaction ID;
- Date;
- Organization code;
- Document code;
- Client hash;
- Number of coins;
- Address of the sender;
- Address of the recipient.

The following blockchain management functions were implemented:

- The function of creating a new block and adding this block to the chain. A new block is created, all fields are filled in, a list of transactions is added. The block is added to the blockchain. After the block is created, a new list of transactions is generated. The Proof-of-Work (PoW) algorithm is used as a consensus algorithm. If necessary, it can be replaced by another algorithm.
- A function that implements the Proof-of-Work algorithm. This algorithm is based on the problem of finding such a number p that the hash from the product of the number p by p' will have 4 leading zeros, where p' is the number p calculated by this algorithm in the previous block. The complexity of solving the problem can be adjusted by changing the hash value requirements. For example, if the condition specifies the need for not four, but five leading zeros, then the duration of the search for a solution will increase significantly. The solution of the problem is implemented by the only possible method – brute force, therefore it requires a lot of money, since it may require a huge number of iterations.
- The function of verifying the correctness of the Proof-of-Work calculation. Checks whether the hash(last_proof, proof) contains 4 leading zeros with known last_proof and proof. Unlike the solution of search function, it is fast and contains a single iteration with the calculation of the hash function value and checking for the presence of zeros in it.
- The function of verifying the correctness of the entire blockchain. It is implemented by successive checks of the correctness of the proof parameter and checking the correctness of the hash of the previous block specified in each block. If the blockchain has been changed, then this function will detect errors.

– The function of adding a new transaction to the list of transactions within a single block. The transaction fields are filled in. The transaction contains data fields for using the blockchain as a means of protecting paper documents. These are the date, organization code, document code, and client hash fields. There are also fields that are necessary for mining, so that the miner can receive a reward. The transaction ID is calculated as a hash of the transaction contents and timestamp. Then the generated transaction is added to the list of transactions, which will be added to the block in the future.
– Block hash calculation function. In this implementation, the SHA-256 function was used. If necessary, it can be replaced by another one.
– A function that returns the last block in the chain. It is necessary to calculate the proof parameter and hash when adding a new block to the blockchain.
– Transaction search function by the specified transaction ID.
– The function of adding a new node. The IP address and port of the new node are registered. A node is a computer (server) with Internet access, on which special software is installed and which is synchronized with other similar computers. A bunch of such nodes forms a blockchain. Using such a network makes it possible to quickly distribute large data streams.
– Conflict resolution function. Since there are many miners in the bitcoin network, it is possible that two miners will simultaneously add blocks to the chain. Thus, a branching of the chain will occur, and a conflict will arise. The next miner will add a new block to one of the two chains, and it will become longer. The conflict is resolved due to the fact that the longest chain will be saved, and the short ones will be cleared. Moreover, transactions from them will not be lost, they will be added to a new block.

HTTP requests are used to interact with the blockchain. In this implementation, the Flask framework was used. The following GET- and POST-methods were implemented:

– /mine – GET-method, starts the process of mining a new block, namely the PoW algorithm;
– /transactions/new – POST-method for adding a new transaction;
– /find – POST-method, to search for a specific transaction by transaction ID, returns the contents of this transaction;
– /chain – GET-method that returns a chain of blocks;
– /nodes/register – POST-method for registering a new node;
– /nodes/resolve – GET-method that implements a consensus algorithm that triggers a conflict resolution function.

3.2   Retrieving Data about Documents Types

To interact with the database it is necessary to implement a web server that will extract data from the database upon request and transmit it to the client.
   The following functions were implemented:

– The function of obtaining the name of the document by code. The input of the function is supplied with the document code in numerical form. Next, connections to the database are made and the name of the document corresponding to the code is extracted using the SELECT operator. The function returns the name of the document.

– The function of getting a list of document types and their transcripts by code. The input of the function is supplied with the document code in numerical form. Next, a connection to the database takes place and a list of all data about the types of the specified document is extracted.
– The function of obtaining a numeric type decryption, according to the specified code and type of documents. This function is needed to simplify obtaining information about the document, this information can also be obtained through the previous function, after converting the result.

To enable network interaction with this server, the following methods were added:

– /name – POST-method by which the full name of the document is obtained by the document code;
– /types – POST-method that allows to get a list of types for this code along with transcripts;
– /meaning – POST-method that allows to get a type decryption for a given code/type pair in numeric form.

A desktop application interacts with this server when creating documents, as well as a mobile application when checking documents.

3.3 Document Creation

A special desktop application was created to perform document creation, its main functionality is the following:

– Generating a new transaction;
– Generating a QR code required for further document authentication;
– Creation of a document for printing.

The following functions were implemented:

– Random numeric code generation function. The code is generated randomly. It consists of 6 characters, numbers, uppercase and lowercase Latin letters can be used. The code is necessary to protect against determining the passport series and number by hash using brute force. The series, passport number and code are needed to identify the client to whom the document was issued. The hash of these three values is recorded in the blockchain. The generated code is displayed on the application screen, and is indicated in the generated pdf file.
– QR code generation function. The QR code contains the date of issue of the document, the passport series and number, the generated random code, and the transaction ID. The first three are specified in the blockchain in order to facilitate the work of the inspectors and save them from having to enter this data manually. The transaction ID is needed to find the necessary transaction in the blockchain during verification. An example of a QR code and its contents is shown in Fig. 1.
– A function that creates a pdf file and writes the necessary data to it for further printing. This function is started after the transaction is added, since the QR code that will be located on the document depends on it. The document shall contain the series and passport number of the document owner, since this data is used in the

blockchain for verification. A random code is also indicated on the document and used for verification.

- A function that sends data to the blockchain to generate a new transaction. The code generation function is also called here, the hash of the passport data value and the random code is calculated. The code of the organization that issued the document and the date of issue of the document are indicated in plain text. The code and document type are written in one field in the transaction in plain text. If the result is quantitative, then it is written as well as non–quantitative, with a hyphen after the code, but when decrypting it is necessary to access the database and check whether the result is quantitative - whether the true flag is in the x_type column for this document. An example of the transaction content is shown in Fig. 2.

- A function that receives information from the database web server about the possible types of the specified document. For convenience, when specifying the document code, the possible types of the specified document are automatically pulled from the database, so one can select the desired type without using auxiliary resources. The result can be specified separately if it is provided by the document type.

1111222222
Tyl6jx
27892ac84fd37e89ef732fe2e759785f562e9b
7f02fcc24de5e4664330630c35

Fig. 1. Contents of a QR code.

```
"transactions": [
    {
        "amount": 0,
        "client": "000d68c5254c5f8d26ead05d5bb37490b428f039ae41711e6d24f9edf047899b",
        "code_of_doc": "1000-3",
        "code_of_org": "123",
        "date": "01.05.2023",
        "recipient": "addr 2",
        "sender": "addr 1",
        "txid": "27892ac84fd37e89ef732fe2e759785f562e9b7f02fcc24de5e4664330630c35"
    },
```

Fig. 2. Example of transaction contents.

3.4 Document Authenticity Verification

A mobile application was developed providing the function of scanning a QR code and subsequent search and verification of the transaction.

The QR code contains the series, passport number and code so that the inspector does not have to manually enter these data. A hash is calculated from this data, and in the future this hash is compared with the hash value in the blockchain. The passport series and number from the QR code are displayed on the screen and shall be checked by the inspector. Since an intruder can forge a QR code by specifying the wrong series and passport number in it, the inspector shall make sure that the series and passport number of the person being checked are entered in the QR code by checking the passport data displayed on the screen with the original ones. Also, the QR code contains the transaction ID, with its help the mobile application automatically receives information on a specific transaction. A date is taken from the blockchain and displayed on the screen, it shall be checked by the verifier, since an intruder may try to issue a previously received document for a fresh one by changing the date in a paper document. Also, the code and document type are displayed on the screen from the blockchain.

If the verifier needs to check a large number of identical documents, then it is possible to automate the verification of the code and document type. To do this, one can specify the expected type and choose which result is acceptable and which is not. For example, when checking tests for viruses, the result «NOT DETECTED» will be acceptable and it will be highlighted in green, while the result «DETECTED» will be selected as unacceptable and highlighted in red. Also, if the document code specified in the blockchain does not match the code specified by the verifier, then a corresponding message is displayed. To implement this tool, there is interaction with a public database via a web server.

Scanning was tested with different input data. The message that the document is valid, highlighted in green, is displayed if the hash calculated from the passport data matches the hash specified in the transaction. Otherwise, the message «The document is invalid» is displayed and highlighted in red for easier visual perception. If the document code specified on the first page as the code of the document being checked does not match the code specified in the blockchain, a message highlighted in red is displayed on the screen.

The scan results are shown below.

1. Input data: the verifier specified the code of the document being checked and the type that is acceptable. Output data: the document is valid, the document code and type matched the expected ones.

   Required actions:

– Check if the date shown on the screen is up to date;
– Check whether the passport series and number displayed on the screen are correct.

   If one of two requirements is not met, the document is considered invalid.

2. Input data: the verifier specified the code of the document being checked and the type that is acceptable. Output data: the document is valid, the document code did not match the expected one.

   Required actions:

– Check if the date shown on the screen is up to date;
– Check whether the passport series and number displayed on the screen are correct.
– Additionally check whether the code and type displayed on the screen are correct, as there may be an error on the part of the verifier.

If one of the three requirements is not met, the document is considered invalid.

3. Input data: the verifier specified the code of the document being checked and the type that is acceptable. Output data: the document is valid, the document code matched the expected one, the document type did not match the expected one.

Required actions:

– Check if the date shown on the screen is up to date;
– Check whether the passport series and number displayed on the screen are correct;
– Additionally check whether the type displayed on the screen is satisfactory, since there may be an error on the part of the inspector.

If one of requirements is not met, the document is considered invalid.

As a result, the developed tool, consisting of several software applications, allows to verify the authenticity of documents in accordance with the proposed approach. It is impossible to fully automate the process, the verifier shall manually check the correspondence of the passport data indicated on the application screen with the real passport data of the document owner. It is important to notice that this tool will not protect the entire contents of the document. It can confirm the fact that a specific organization has issued a specific document to a specific person and confirm the result, if it is specified. But other information that is also specified in the document is not still protected. Nevertheless, this method is more secure than, for example, using a seal impression for protection. When using combined protection by writing to the blockchain and affixing a seal, the security of the document will increase significantly.

4   Conclusion

A new approach and a software tool implementing this approach were developed that allow to increase the level of security of paper documents. This is achieved by registering each issued paper document in a single, change-proof database. Due to the fact that the system is decentralized, it does not incur large expenses for maintaining the operation of this system.

The proposed approach has significant advantages over other methods of protection in terms of the price-quality ratio. Many types of document protection that provide a high level of security require financial investments in special equipment. At the same time, there are cheap methods of protection, for example, affixing a seal, but a document protected by a seal cannot be called fully protected, since forgery of a seal is a cheap and simple task.

A mobile application for document verification has been developed taking into account the specifics of the inspector's work. The effort required to validate a document using the application is comparable to the effort required for a simple visual verification of the document. Thus, the introduction of this system will not complicate the work of inspectors and will not cause a sharply negative reaction.

The developed prototype demonstrates the idea of protecting paper documents using blockchain technology. For commercial use some organizational and juridical activities shall be performed such as communications with companies to compile a single database of existing documents, register organizations that have the right to issue certain types of documents, make changes to corporate programs for the formation and printing of documents and so on.

References

1. Khadim, U., Iqbal, M.M., Azam, M.A.: An intelligent three-level digital watermarking method for document protection. Mehran Univ. Res. J. Eng. Technol. **40**(2), 323–334 (2021)
2. Taşcıoğlu, D., Ünlütürk, S.S., Özçelik, S.: An anticounterfeiting technology combining an InP nanoparticle ink and a versatile optical device for authentication. Mater. Adv. **2**(18), 5967–5976 (2021)
3. Wellem, T., Nataliani, Y., Iriani, A.: Academic document authentication using elliptic curve digital signature algorithm and QR code. JOIV : Int. J. Inf. Vis. **6**(3), 667 (2022). https://doi.org/10.30630/joiv.6.2.872
4. Kanika, G.K., Singh, S., Gupta, B.K.: A novel approach to design luminomagnetic pigment formulated security ink for manifold protection to bank cheques against counterfeiting. Adv. Mater. Technol. **6**(2), 2000973 (2021). https://doi.org/10.1002/admt.202000973
5. Abou-Melha, K.: Preparation of photoluminescent nanocomposite ink toward dual-mode secure anti-counterfeiting stamps. Arab. J. Chem. **15**(2), 103604 (2022)
6. Muthamma, K., Gouda, B.M., Sunil, D., Kulkarni, S.D., Anand, P.J.: Water-based fluorescent flexo-ink for security applications. Chem. Pap. **77**(7), 4033–4040 (2023)
7. Abdelhameed, M.M., Attia, Y.A., Abdelrahman, M.S., Khattab, T.A.: Photochromic and fluorescent ink using photoluminescent strontium aluminate pigment and screen printing towards anticounterfeiting documents. Luminescence **36**(4), 865–874 (2021)
8. Singh, A.K.: Data hiding: current trends, innovation and potential challenges. ACM Trans. Multimedia Comput. Commun. Appl. **16**(3s), 1–16 (2020)
9. Mohanarathinam, A., Kamalraj, S., Prasanna Venkatesan, G.K.D., Ravi, R.V., Manikandababu, C.S.: Digital watermarking techniques for image security: a review. J. Ambient. Intell. Humaniz. Comput. **11**, 3221–3229 (2020)
10. Sardor, Z.: Integration of electronic document circulation into the healthcare system. Pedagogical Sci. Teach. Methods **2**(22), 73–76 (2023)
11. Das, M., Tao, X., Liu, Y., Cheng, J.C.: A blockchain-based integrated document management framework for construction applications. Autom. Constr. **133**, 104001 (2022)
12. Pathak, S., Gupta, V., Malsa, N., Ghosh, A., Shaw, R.N.: Blockchain-based academic certificate verification system—a review. In: Shaw, R.N., Das, S., Piuri, V., Bianchini, M. (eds.) Advanced Computing and Intelligent Technologies: Proceedings of ICACIT 2022, pp. 527–539. Springer Nature Singapore, Singapore (2022). https://doi.org/10.1007/978-981-19-2980-9_42
13. Meirobie, I., Irawan, A.P., Sukmana, H.T., Lazirkha, D.P., Santoso, N.P.L.: Framework authentication e-document using blockchain technology on the government system. Int. J. Artif. Intell. Res. **6**(2) (2022)
14. Dewangan, N.K., Chandrakar, P., Kumari, S., Rodrigues, J.J.: Enhanced privacy-preserving in student certificate management in blockchain and interplanetary file system. Multimedia Tools Appl. **82**(8), 12595–12614 (2023)
15. Sharma, P., Namasudra, S., Crespo, R.G., Parra-Fuente, J., Trivedi, M.C.: EHDHE: enhancing security of healthcare documents in IoT-enabled digital healthcare ecosystems using blockchain. Inf. Sci. **629**, 703–718 (2023)

Development of Methods and Algorithms for Dimension Reduction of Space Description for Pattern Recognition Problem

D. Z. Narzullaev$^{(\boxtimes)}$ ⓘ, A. S. Baydullaev ⓘ, B. A. Abdurakhmanov ⓘ,
A. T. Tursunov ⓘ, and Kh. Sh. Ilhamov ⓘ

Tashkent Pharmaceutical Institute, 45, Oybek Street, Tashkent 100015, Uzbekistan
`davr1960@mail.ru`

Abstract. The essence of the dimensionality reduction process is the transition to a more concise set of indicators in such a way that the associated loss of information present in the source data is minimized. This article proposes methods and algorithms for reducing the dimension of the original feature description space for the problem of pattern recognition. Four types of applied problems of reducing the dimension of the analyzed feature space are defined. The mathematical model underlying the construction of one or another dimension reduction method has been determined. For each method discussed below, a step-by-step algorithm is given that allows you to quickly and efficiently translate these methods into programming languages for various types of computers.

Keywords: Pattern Recognition · Classification · Experimental Data Table · Dimensionality Reduction · Informative Indicator

1 Introduction

We can distinguish four types of applied problems of reducing the dimension of the analyzed feature space [1].

The first type includes the class of problems for selecting the most informative indicators. Here, from the initial set of features $X = \left(x^{(1)}, x^{(2)}, \ldots, x^{(\rho)}\right)$, $\rho' < \rho$ features are selected, or a combination of relatively initial features of a small number of ρ' variables $Z(X) = \left(z^{(1)}(X), \ldots, z^{(\rho')}(X)\right)$, is built that would have the property of being the most informative in the sense of optimizing a certain $I_{\rho'}(Z)$ informativeness criterion. This criterion is "customized" to a specific data analysis task: classification, pattern recognition, regression analysis, etc. For example, if the $I_{\rho'}(Z)$ criterion is aimed at maximum auto-informativeness of the new system of indicators Z for the most accurate reproduction of all initial characteristics $X^{(1)}, X^{(2)}, \ldots, X^{(\rho)}$ for a relatively small number of auxiliary variables, then in this case they turn to models and methods of factor analysis and principal component methods [1–4].

The second type includes the task of compressing arrays of processed and stored information. Such tasks arise when analyzing large amounts of information in order to

A. Gibadullin (Ed.): ITIDMS 2023, CCIS 2112, pp. 92–102, 2024.
https://doi.org/10.1007/978-3-031-60318-1_8

save computer memory and are relevant in terms of the need to minimize the capacity of the media on which archival information is stored. In this case, a combination of classification and dimensionality reduction methods is used.

Using classification methods, you can move from an array containing information on all N statistically examined objects to the corresponding information only on K reference samples (K ≤ N). The most typical representatives of classes obtained as a result of various cluster procedures are taken as reference samples. The use of methods for reducing the dimension of the original description space allows us to move on to the most informative features $\rho'(\rho' < \rho)$. .. Thus, from the original table of experimental data (TED) with the dimension $N \times \rho$ they move to the TED with the dimension $K \times \rho'$ and, taking into account that K and ρ' are usually an order of magnitude smaller, respectively, N and ρ, the dimension of the original array is reduced tens of times.

The third type includes data visualization tasks. In this case, the problem arises of reducing the dimension of the original description space to ρ', and $\rho' \le 3$. .. If such a representation of the original features distorts the structure of the data minimally, then it becomes possible to visually ("actually tangible") represent the data on a straight line, plane or in three-dimensional space, and thus it is possible to determine whether the studied set of points breaks up into clearly defined clumps in these spaces and what is the approximate number of these clots.

The apparatus [1] for solving such problems is called "targeted projection" of multidimensional data.

The fourth type of applied problems of dimensionality reduction includes problems of constructing conditional coordinate axes. As is known, the original TED can be presented not only in the form of "object-feature", but also in the form of "object-object", i.e. in the form of a matrix A of pairwise relationships $a_{ij}(i, j = 1, 2, ..., N)$ between objects. In this case, the problem arises of determining for a given ρ' dimension of auxiliary conditional coordinate axes $Oz^{(1)}, ..., Oz^{(\rho')}$, and a method for matching each object O_i with its coordinates $\left(z_i^{(1)}, ..., z_i^{(\rho')} \right)$ in such a way that the pairwise relations $\hat{a}_{ij}(\mathbb{Z})$, in a certain sense, are minimally different from the original a_{ij} values. Dimension reduction occurs here in the sense that we move from the $N \times N$ matrix to the $N \times \rho'$ matrix, where $\rho' \ll N$. These problems are solved by multidimensional scaling methods [1, 2].

Let us consider in more detail the problems of the first and second types, as well as, in the case of $\rho' \le 3$, the problem of the third type. The expediency and effectiveness of dimensionality reduction methods are determined by the mathematical formulation of the problem, the defining moment of which is the answer to the question on what initial information the model is based on. Initial information about the phenomenon being studied consists of a priori information about the classes under study and selective information, i.e. so-called training samples.

A priori information about the classes under study is obtained, as a rule, either from theoretical considerations about the nature of the phenomena under study, or as a result of preliminary research. To obtain selective information, it is necessary to carry out a special preliminary stage devoted to solving the problem of simple typology of objects in the space of resulting indicators.

This problem of dividing objects into homogeneous groups is solved by various classification methods [1, 5, 6].

The mathematical model underlying the construction of one or another dimension reduction method includes three components: the form of specifying the initial information; type of optimized criterion $I_{\rho'}(\mathbb{Z})$ for the information content of the required set of $\mathbb{Z} = \left(z^{(1)}, ..., z^{(\rho')}\right)$ features; $L(X)$ class of admissible transformations of original features X.

The first component includes the method of specifying the initial information (a table of the "object- feature" or "object-object" type), the presence or absence of training information, and the form of presentation of training samples. Training samples can be presented, for example, in the form of belonging of some objects from a set M to a limited number of groups, or in the form of values of a quantitative resulting variable in regression models.

The information content criterion can be focused on achieving different goals. In particular, criteria optimization of which leads to a set of auxiliary $\mathbb{Z} = \left(z^{(1)}, ..., z^{(\rho')}\right)$ variables that allow the original information to be reproduced as accurately as possible are called auto-informativeness criteria.

In addition, the last component is the $L(X)$ class of admissible transformations of original X features. Solving an $I_{\rho'}(\mathbb{Z}(X)) \rightarrow extr$ optimization problem presupposes the presence of restrictions on feasible $L(X)$ solutions.

This class can represent a variety of linear or nonlinear transformations of the original $x^{(1)}, ..., x^{(\rho)}$ features. It should be noted here that the vast majority of dimensionality reduction methods are based on linear models [6–8], i.e. $L(X)$ is a class of linear transformations of $x^{(1)}, ..., x^{(\rho)}$ features.

The entire process of solving dimensionality reduction problems can be divided into the following stages [1]:

- Installation;
- Staged;
- Informational;
- A priori mathematical-staged;
- Exploratory analysis;
- A posteriori mathematical production;
- Computing;
- Final.

Thus, the essence of the dimensionality reduction process is the transition to a more concise set of indicators in such a way that the associated loss of information present in the source data is minimized. In this case, new $z^{(1)}, ..., z^{(\rho')}$ features can be selected from among the original ones or determined according to some rule based on the totality of the original characteristics. At the same time, certain requirements are imposed on the new system of features: the greatest information content, mutual uncorrelation, the least distortion of the geometric structure of the data, etc. Depending on the version of these requirements, one or another dimensionality reduction algorithm can be obtained. The main prerequisites that determine the transition to a smaller number of features, the most informative in a certain sense, are: duplication of information in the presence of highly interrelated features; uninformative features that change little when moving from one object to another; the possibility of simple or "weighted" summation according to certain criteria.

2 Materials and Methods

The following methods were used in this study: 1) theoretical: analysis of the literature to study approaches to reducing the dimension of the description space for the problem of pattern recognition; 2) empirical: comparison of the results of developed algorithms for converting feature types using the example of solving a pattern recognition problem.

As a result, we have developed new algorithms for reducing the dimensionality of the description space for the problem of pattern recognition.

3 Results

Formally, the problem of dimensionality reduction can be described as follows. Let $Z = Z(X)$ be some ρ-dimensional vector - a function of the original $x^{(1)}, x^{(2)}, ..., x^{(\rho)}$ features, $I_{\rho'}(Z(X))$- a measure of the information content of the ρ'-dimensional system of $Z(X) = \left(z^{(1)}(X), ..., z^{(\rho')}(X)\right)$, $\rho' < \rho$ features. The task is to determine the set of $\tilde{Z}$ features found in the F class of admissible transformations of the original $x^{(1)}, ..., x^{(p)}$ variables, such that the relation is satisfied:

$$I_{\rho'}\left(\tilde{Z}(X)\right) = \max\left\{I_{\rho'}(Z(X))\right\} \qquad (1)$$

Accordingly, the selected $I_{\rho'}(Z)$ information content criterion and the F class of admissible transformations lead to specific methods for reducing the dimensionality of the description.

Below are methods for reducing the dimension of the initial feature description space for the problem of pattern recognition, focused on selecting the most informative indicators, solving the problem of compressing arrays of processed and stored information, and, finally, data visualization (at $\rho' \leq 3$). Let us first present a rigorous mathematical formulation of the problem of pattern recognition (classification in the presence of training samples), a detailed description of which can be found in [1, 6].

Let us introduce the necessary definitions. Let an initial set of E objects be given, each of which is described by E characteristics $x = \left(x^{(1)}, ..., x^{(\rho)}\right)$. Let us introduce $A_i \bigcup\limits_{i=1}^{m} A_i = E$ subsets as a subjective assessment by the researcher of the number of m parts of the $|A_i|$ volume into which the E set should be classified. Let us also introduce a B_κ, $k = \overline{1, m_1}$ subset, where m_1 is the objective number of parts of $|B_\kappa|$ volume, into which the E set can be classified using a certain H set of mathematical rules for a given description space.

Definition. By the class we mean the combination of research objects into a B_κ subset using one or another selected method.

Definition. By the A_i image we mean the combination of many E objects into m groups corresponding to the subjective assessment of the researcher.

Let the researcher indicate that the N_1 objects included in the N set belong to the t $A_i, i = \overline{1, t}$ images. The number of objects belonging to each A_i image is known, $|A_i|$, and $\sum_{i=1}^{t} |A_i| = N_1$. The recognition task is to determine whether the remaining $M = N - N_1$ objects E belong to one of the specified images. The A_i set is called training samples (TS), and E objects not included in the TS are recognized.

The most general way to solve the problem of pattern recognition is the population hypothesis, according to which the E set is a representative sample from a certain population, and all the properties inherent in this population can be assessed based on E research. Bayesian decision-making theory, based on minimizing the overall decision risk [4], is applied provided that the type of distributions of random variables corresponding to each of the images is known. However, such a case is rare in practice, and to find a classification rule, one tries to estimate in one way or another the unknown probability of the appearance of objects of each image at each point in the description space. Let us denote by $\hat{f}(x/A_i), x \in R^\rho$, the estimate of the distribution density function for the A_i image. Then, under the condition of equally probable appearance of images, the classified object with x^* coordinates should be attributed to the image for which $\hat{f}(x^*/A_i)$ is maximum. Thus, in all cases, the description space, using a system of certain functions, is divided into non-overlapping subregions, and the classified object belongs to the image in which subregion it falls.

Of particular note is a group of local pattern recognition methods in which the assignment of an x^* object to one of the images depends on the TS points closest to it. These methods use the $\hat{f}(x^*/A_i) = k_i/|A_i|V$ estimate where V is the volume of a certain neighborhood of a point; $x^* \in R^\rho$, k_i- the number of A_i image objects included in this volume. The simplest of the local methods is the "nearest neighbor" rule - the classified object belongs to the image to which the nearest object from the TS belongs. In this case, in the description space, a distance function between objects must be selected that satisfies the following conditions:

- $\varrho(x_i, x_j) \geq = \varrho(x_i, x_i)$;
- $\varrho(x_i, x_j) = \varrho(x_j, x_i)$;
- $\varrho(x_i, x_j) \leq \varrho(x_i, x_\ell) + \varrho(x_\ell, x_j)$.

In the case of small volumes of TS, the decision-making procedure can be modified depending on the shape of the A_i images, using the average connection classification rule, or the "distant neighbor" rule. These rules are heuristic and reflect the experience of researchers; they do not serve to estimate the density of distribution of objects by A_i images.

Let us now move on to presenting methods for constructing an informative subsystem of features. Let us describe the first method for solving this problem and present its algorithmic implementation.

Formulation of the problem. Let a training set of $X = \{x\}$ objects be given, which is divided into disjoint $X_1, X_2, ..., X_m$ subsets (classes). Each object x is specified by a set of characteristics $\left(x^{(1)}, x^{(2)}, ..., x^{(\rho)}\right)$. Let each x_q class contain m_q objects $x_{q_1}, x_{q_2}, ..., x_{q_{m_q}}$, where $x_{qi} = \left(x_{qi}^{(1)}, x_{qi}^{(2)}, ..., x_{qi}^{(\rho)}\right)$, $i = 1, ..., m_q$. A certain $l < \rho$. Number is specified.

It is required in the original system from the ρ features to select a subsystem from the l features that is the most informative (providing the best quality of separation) among all power l subsystems.

To solve the problem, we first introduce some definitions and notations.

We will consider the $\left\{x=\left(x^{(1)}, x^{(2)}, ..., x^{(\rho)}\right)\right\}$ feature space to be Euclidean and denote it by R^ρ. Let's introduce a Boolean vector $\lambda = (\lambda^1, \lambda^2, ..., \lambda^p)$, where λ^k either zero or one and the following holds:

$\sum_{\kappa=1}^{\rho} \lambda^\kappa = p$. Let's call λ l an -informative vector.

Definition. Truncation of space $R^\rho = \{x = (x^{(1)}, x^{(2)}, ..., x^{(\rho)})\}$ by λ let's call the space $R^\rho|_\lambda = \{x|_\lambda = (\lambda^1 x^{(1)}, ..., \lambda^\rho x^{(\rho)})\}$.

Under the truncated distance between two objects $x, y \in R^\rho$ we will understand the Euclidean distance between $x|_\lambda$ and $y|_\lambda$ in space $R^\rho|_\lambda$, i.e.:

$$\|x - y\|_\lambda = \sqrt{\sum_{k=1}^{\rho} \lambda^k (x^{(k)} - y^{(k)})} \tag{2}$$

Let's denote:

$$S_q|_\lambda = \sqrt{\frac{1}{m_q} \sum_{i=1}^{m_q} (\|\bar{x}_q - x_{qi}\|_\lambda)^2} \tag{3}$$

where $\bar{x}_q = \frac{1}{m_q} \sum_{i=1}^{m_q} x_{qi}$;

$S_q|_\lambda$ - root mean square spread of objects in a class X_q regarding truncation by λ.

Let us determine the measure of proximity between classes X_q, X_t regarding truncation by λ:

$$R_{qt}|_\lambda = \sqrt{\frac{1}{m_q m_t} \sum_{i=1}^{m_q} \|\bar{x}_t - x_{qi}\|_\lambda^2 \sum_{i=1}^{m_t} \|\bar{x}_q - x_{ti}\|_\lambda^2} \tag{4}$$

As a measure of separation between classes X_q, X_t regarding truncation by λ we will understand the value:

$$L_{qt}|_\lambda = \frac{R_{qt}|_\lambda}{S_q|_\lambda S_t|_\lambda}. \tag{5}$$

The information content of truncation by λ is determined by the formula:

$$\mathrm{I}(\lambda) = \min_{\substack{q, t \\ q \neq t}} L_{qt}|_\lambda. \tag{6}$$

The method is to find l - informative vector λ, on which information content $\mathrm{I}(\lambda)$ reaches maximum.

We will look for the maximum of the function $I(\lambda)$ by brute force method $\lambda = (\lambda^1, \lambda^2, ..., \lambda^k)$, $\lambda^k \in \{0, 1\}$, for which $\sum\limits_{k=1}^{\rho} \lambda^k = l..$

Let's denote:

$$\overline{x}_q^{(k)} = \frac{1}{m_q} \sum_{i=1}^{m_q} x_{qi}^{(k)}, \quad q = \overline{1, m}, \tag{7}$$

$$S_q^k = \sqrt{\frac{1}{m_q} \sum_{i=1}^{m_q} (\overline{x}_q^{(k)} - x_{qi}^{(k)})^2}, \tag{8}$$

$$R_{qt}^k = \sqrt{\frac{1}{m_q m_t} \sum_{i=1}^{m_q} (\overline{x}_t^{(k)} - x_{qi}^{(k)})^2 \sum_{i=1}^{m_t} (\overline{x}_q^{(k)} - x_{ti}^{(k)})^2}. \tag{9}$$

From (2) – (9) it follows that:

$$S_q|_\lambda = \sum_{k=1}^{\rho} \lambda^k S_q^k, \tag{10}$$

$$R_{qt}|_\lambda = \sum_{k=1}^{\rho} \lambda^k R_{qt}^k. \tag{11}$$

Function Maximization $I(\lambda)$ requires search of C_ρ^l options. To make the search more efficient, let us strictly order all possible l - informative vectors λ. The first vector in this order will be considered the vector the last l component of which is equal to one, the rest are equal to zero. The last one will be the vector, the first l component of which is equal to one, the rest are equal to zero. Let some l - informative vector $\lambda_r = (\lambda_r^1, ..., \lambda_r^\rho)$, located in a certain place of a given order. Let us define a rule for choosing the vector immediately following it

$$\lambda_{r+1} = (\lambda_{r+1}^1, \lambda_{r+1}^2, ..., \lambda_{r+1}^\rho).$$

If:

$$\lambda_r^1 = 0, \ \lambda_r^2 = 0, ..., \lambda_r^k = 0, \ \lambda_r^{k+1} = 1,$$

then:

$$\lambda_{r+1}^1 = 0, ..., \lambda_{r+1}^{k-1} = 0, \ \lambda_{r+1}^k = 1, \ \lambda_{r+1}^{k+1} = 0, \ \lambda_{r+1}^{k+2} = \lambda_r^{k+2}, ..., \lambda_{r+1}^\rho = \lambda_r^\rho.$$

If:

$$\lambda_r^1 = 1, ..., \lambda_r^k = 1, \lambda_r^{k+1} = 0, ..., \lambda_r^j = 0, \lambda_r^{j+1} = 1, ..., \lambda_r^\rho = 1,$$

then:

$\lambda^1_{r+1} = 0, ..., \lambda^{j-k-1}_{r+1} = 0, ..., \lambda^{j-1}_{r+1} = 0, \lambda^j_{r+1} = 1, \lambda^{j+1}_{r+1} = 0, \lambda^{j+2}_{r+1} = \lambda^{j+2}_r, ..., \lambda^\rho_{r+1} = \lambda^\rho_r.$

Schematically, this rule can be represented in the form $(0, ..., 0, 0, 1*, ..., *), (1, ..., 1, 0, ..., 0, 0, 1, *, ..., *)$.

Let us show that the described rule guarantees enumeration of all possible options.

Let us denote by Λ the set of all vectors of the form $\lambda = (\lambda^1, ..., \lambda^\rho), \lambda^k \in \{0, 1\}, k = \overline{1, p}$ (no limit on l - information content). Number Λ is ultimate and consists of elements. Let us denote by Λ^l the set of all l informative vectors, i.e.:

$$\Lambda^l = \left\{ \lambda = \left(\lambda^1, ..., \lambda^\rho \right) \in \Lambda; \sum_{\kappa=1}^\rho \lambda^\kappa = l \right\}.$$

Let's introduce the function $K(\lambda), \lambda \in \Lambda, \lambda = \left(\lambda^1, ..., \lambda^\rho \right)$:

$$K(\lambda) = 2^{\rho-1}\lambda^1 + 2^{\rho-2}\lambda^2 + ... + 2\lambda^{\rho-1} + \lambda^\rho.$$

It is obvious that when $\lambda, r \in \Lambda, \lambda \neq r \Rightarrow K(\lambda) \neq K(r)$.

It is possible to prove Statement 1 that for any integer M, $0 \leq M \leq 2^\rho$, there is $\lambda \in \Lambda$ such as $K(\lambda) = M$.

Let $\lambda_1 = \left(\underbrace{1, ..., 1}_{l}, 0, ..., 0 \right)$. Let us define the following rule Q:

$$\lambda = \left(*, *, ..., *, 1, 0, \underbrace{0, ..., 0}, \underbrace{1, ..., 1} \right), \mathbb{Q}(\lambda) = \left(*, *, ..., *, 0, 1, \overbrace{1, ..., 1}, \overbrace{0, ..., 0} \right)$$

And also prove statement 2, that if $\lambda_2 = \mathbb{Q}(\lambda_1), \lambda_3 = \mathbb{Q}(\lambda_2), ...$ Then $\{\lambda_i\} = \Lambda^l$.

Let us now describe step by step the algorithm for determining the informative subsystem of l features.

Step 1. Calculating Values $\bar{x}^{(k)}_q, k = \overline{1, \rho}, q = \overline{1, m}; S^k_q, k = \overline{1, \rho}, q = \overline{1, m}; R^k_{qt}, k = \overline{1, \rho}, q, t = \overline{1, m}(q \neq t)$ according to formulas (7)–(9).

Step 2. $\lambda = (0, ..., 0, 1, ...1), I_* = 0, \lambda_* = \lambda$.

Step 3. Calculating Values $S_q|_\lambda, q = \overline{1, m}; R_{qt}|_\lambda, q, t = \overline{1, m} (q \neq t); L_{qt}|_\lambda, q, t = \overline{1, m} (q \neq t); I(\lambda)$ according to formulas (10), (11), (5), (6).

Step 4. If $I(\lambda) > I_*$, then $I_* = I(\lambda), \lambda_* = \lambda$.

Otherwise, go to the next step.

Step 5. If $\lambda \neq (1, ..., 1, 0, ..., 0)$, then the next λ is selected and proceed to step 3. Otherwise, the procedure ends and the result of the calculations is l- informative vector λ_*.

Thus, the method described above allows us to identify the most informative subsystem, consisting of l features. In this case, the number l is specified by the user in advance and is fixed.

Let us now outline a method for selecting in the original system of features the smallest subsystem of features that is maximally informative in the sense of a given criterion for the quality of recognition of objects in the control sample.

Formulation of the problem. The training set of objects is specified $X = (x)$, which is divided into disjoint subsets (classes) $X_1, X_2, ..., X_m$. Each object is specified by a set of ρ features $x = (x^{(1)}, x^{(2)}, ..., x^{(\rho)})$. Let every class X_q consists of m_q objects $x_{q1}, x_{q2}, ..., x_{m_q}$, where $x_{qi} = (x_{qi}^{(1)}, x_{qi}^{(2)}, ..., x_{qi}^{(\rho)})$, $i = \overline{1, m_q}$.

It is required to determine the smallest subsystem of features that is the most informative in the sense of the pattern recognition problem.

As before, the feature space $(x = (x^{(1)}, ..., x^{(\rho)}))$ we will assume that it is Euclidean and denote $R^{\rho(x=(x^{(1)}, ..., x^{(\rho)}))}$.

Let some vector be given $\lambda = (\lambda^1, ..., \lambda^\rho)$, where λ^k- either zero or one and $\sum\limits_{i=1}^{\rho} \lambda^k = l.$

Distance between $x|_\lambda$ and $y|_\lambda$, and $S_q|_\lambda$ is determined in accordance with the formulas (2), (3).

Let $x = (x^{(1)}, ..., x^{(\rho)})$ - some recognizable object.

Let's denote:

$$d_q(x)|_\lambda = \frac{\|x - \overline{x_q}\|_\lambda}{S_q|_\lambda}, q = \overline{1, m} \tag{12}$$

By $d_q(x)|_\lambda$ is understood as a measure of the distance of x object from X_q class relative to truncation by λ.

Let us define the recognition principle for truncation by λ. We will assume that x object most likely belongs to X_t class if:

$$d_q(x)|_\lambda = \left. \min_{q=\overline{1,m}} d_q(x) \right|_\lambda . \tag{13}$$

We denote this relationship as $x \xrightarrow{\lambda} x_t.$.

Let us introduce a measure of recognition for l - informative vector λ Every class X_q contains m_q objects, the total number of objects is equal to $\sum\limits_{q=1}^{m} m_q$.

Let $M(\lambda)$ - the total number of such objects for which two relations are simultaneously satisfied.

$x \xrightarrow{\lambda} x_t$, $x \in X_t$, i.e. $M(\lambda)$ - the number of correctly recognized objects out of the total number of objects. As a measure of recognition reliability we use the value:

$$\mathbb{Q}(\lambda) = M(\lambda)/\sum\limits_{q=1}^{m} m_q \cdot 100\%. \tag{14}$$

Above, a method was proposed for determining the most informative combination of l features for a given $l \leq \rho$, i.e. for each $l \leq \rho$ fixed, an informative $\lambda = (\lambda^1, ..., \lambda^\rho)$ vector is determined such that the combination of l features corresponding to non-zero λ^i values is the best in the sense of reliably distinguishing classes among all other combinations of the l properties being studied.

Thus, for each $l \in \{1, 2, ..., \rho\}$, an informative l vector is defined:

$$\lambda(l) = \left(\lambda^1, ..., \lambda^\rho\right), \ \sum_{k=1}^{\rho} \lambda^k = l, \ \lambda^k \in \{0; 1\} \tag{15}$$

The least of these l is proposed to be selected according to the following criterion:
$$\mathbb{Q}(\lambda(l)) = \max_{1 \le n \le \rho} \mathbb{Q}(\lambda(n)).$$

Let us now describe the algorithm for solving the problem.

Step 1. Calculating Values $\overline{x}_q^{(k)}$, $k = \overline{1, \rho}$, $q = \overline{1, m}$; $S_q^k, k = \overline{1, \rho}, q = \overline{1, m}$ according to the formulas (7), (8); $l = 0$.

Step 2. For $l = l + 1$ we find the vector λ using the formulas (12), (13).

Step 3. Determination of $\mathbb{Q}(\lambda)$ using the formula (14).

Step 4. If $l = \rho$, then go to step 5. Otherwise, go to step 2.

Step 5. Determination of the smallest l by criterion (15).

The result of this algorithm is the smallest l- informative vector satisfying the condition (15).

4 Discussion

The methods described above for reducing the dimension of the initial feature description space were successfully applied in determining the most important risk factors for the health of highly qualified athletes [7], and were also included in the curriculum for the course "Information technologies and mathematical modeling of processes" at the Tashkent Pharmaceutical Institute [8].

5 Conclusion

Thus, for a certain class of recognition problems in the presence of a large number of properties under study, the above methods can be used to reduce the dimension of the original feature description space. In this case, the result of the solution is the exact value of the optimal number l of the most informative features.

References

1. Ayvazyan, S.A., Bukhstaber, V.M., Enyukov, I.S., Meshalkin, L.D.: Classification and Dimensionality Reduction. Finance and Statistics, Moscow (1989)
2. Teryokhina, A.: Data Analysis using Multidimensional Scaling Methods. The Science, Moscow (1986)
3. Ayvazyan, S.A., Bezhaeva, Z.I., Staroverov, O.V.: Classification of Multivariate Observations. Statistics, Moscow (1974)
4. Duda, R., Hart, P.: Pattern Recognition and Scene Analysis. World, Moscow (1976)
5. Nishanov, A.X., Ruzibaev, O.B., Tran, N.H.: On one method for solving the multi-class classification problem. In: 2016 International Conference on Information Science and Communications Technologies, ICISCT 2016, p. 7777382 (2016)

6. Nishanov, A.H., Akbaraliev, B.B., Tajibaev, ShKh.: About one feature selection algorithm in pattern recognition. In: Aliev, R.A., Yusupbekov, N.R., Kacprzyk, J., Pedrycz, W., Sadikoglu, F.M. (eds.) 11th World Conference "Intelligent System for Industrial Automation" (WCIS-2020). AISC, vol. 1323, pp. 103–112. Springer, Cham (2020). https://doi.org/10.1007/978-3-030-68004-6_13

7. Narzullaev, D., Tursunov, A., Samigova, N., Tursunov, U., Shadmanov, K.: Methods for assessing risk factors to the health of highly qualified athletes. E3S Web Conf. **284**, 01010 (2021)

8. Baydullaev, A.S., Mamatkulov, Z.U., Samigova, N.H., Shadmanov, K.K., Narzullaev, D.Z.: Principles of internet education for students on the subject information technology and mathematical modeling of processes on the basis of moodle distance learning system. J. Phys. Conf. Ser. **2001**, 012024 (2021)

Service for Checking Students' Written Work Using a Neural Network

Galina B. Barskaya⬤, Tatiana Y. Chernysheva⁽✉⁾⬤, Ludmila N. Bakanovskaya⬤,
Stanislav O. Sbrodov⬤, and Anastasiya O. Shestakova⬤

University of Tyumen, 6, Volodarskogo Street, Tyumen 625003, Russia
`t.y.chernysheva@utmn.ru`

Abstract. The article discusses the necessity of automating the process for checking and evaluating students' written work in educational institutions. It proposes the recognition of handwritten texts through computer vision methods, specifically by considering the application of convolutional neural networks (CNNs). An architecture for a CNN capable of recognizing letters from both the English and Russian alphabets is developed. The network is trained on extended datasets to enhance recognition accuracy and prevent overfitting. The authors have designed a conceptual model for an information system that processes students' tests via an adaptive website. This includes various user scenarios, context diagrams for uploading test answers, and procedures for text recognition in images. The article also deconstructs the contextual structure of the written work assessment process. Automating the checking of written work promises to expedite and simplify the assessment process for students' assignments.

Keywords: Automation of Written Work Verification · Handwritten Character Recognition · Letters of the Russian Alphabet · Convolutional Neural Network · Image Segmentation · Computer Vision · Adaptive Website

1 Introduction

Due to the development of digital technologies and the increasing use of computers and mobile devices, the need for efficient methods of image analysis and processing has increased. One of the key tasks in these methods is to recognize text in images. This technology has a wide range of applications in areas such as computer vision, image processing, workflow automation, and information accessibility for people with disabilities.

There is a need to automate the processes of analysing and processing huge amounts of digital data. Text-to-image recognition can extract information from photographs, document scans, videos and other types of images making this information available for further processing and analysis. Such technology will automate the process of checking handwritten assignments in various educational institutions with large flows of students [1].

A. Gibadullin (Ed.): ITIDMS 2023, CCIS 2112, pp. 103–116, 2024.
https://doi.org/10.1007/978-3-031-60318-1_9

With the development of cloud technologies, it becomes possible to implement real-time text recognition on images using computing resources of remote servers. This opens up new opportunities for wide application of this technology in various fields, including mobile applications, security systems, medical information systems and others. Technology of text recognition on images has a huge potential for solving a wide range of problems in various spheres of human activity [2].

Therefore, the relevance of this technology is due to the increasing amount of digital data and the development of cloud computing. Development prospects include improved recognition accuracy, enhanced functionality, and integration with other technologies, making this an interesting area for research and innovation.

2 Materials and Methods

2.1 Conceptual Design

The purpose of this paper is to develop an information system designed as a service aimed at reducing the workload faced by teachers in checking academic papers. The anticipated effects of utilizing this service include:

– Accelerating the process of checking academic work;
– Minimizing the risk of errors during the paper checking process;
– Analyzing papers and generating reports on the educational activities undertaken;
– Ensuring user convenience by making the service accessible from any device, thereby necessitating a cloud-based solution.

The core concept of the service involves utilizing a computer vision model to recognize photos of students' answers and convert them into an easily readable format. Subsequently, the service displays the answers on the screen, offering the option to edit them. Upon verification of the answer accuracy, the service saves the answers in a database for analysis. Therefore, the service functions as an adaptive website that facilitates the uploading of photos containing handwritten answers, which are then transformed into a digital text format through a neural network. The data thus obtained are leveraged for statistical analysis and to track the progress in material mastery. The website's functionalities include:

– Managing information about student groups;
– Supporting test administration;
– Analyzing test answers;
– Site administration;
– Data hashing.

Data hashing represents a concealed website feature, not accessible to users, intended for the secure storage of confidential information (such as passwords and banking details). This method displays data as a short, fixed-size string, regardless of the original information volume, ensuring its integrity and rendering the original data irrecoverable.

One of the key design principles of the developed system is the differentiation of access rights between the administrator (Fig. 1) and the user (Fig. 2). The system administrator is endowed with the authority to delete or add users and possesses the capability to modify the status and type of user subscriptions. In the event of system expansion, the administrator is empowered to implement modifications by incorporating details regarding new service functionalities.

Conversely, the user is granted access to features such as managing groups, conducting tests, and analyzing answers. A personal user account is made available, within which the user can modify personal information and review test outcomes.

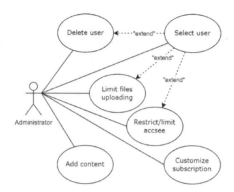

Fig. 1. Precedent diagram for the administrator.

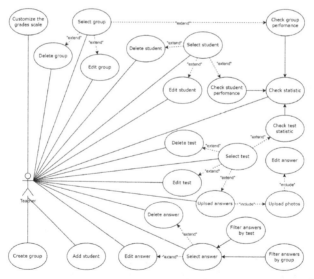

Fig. 2. Diagram of service use options.

The process of uploading answers for test work, as depicted in the context diagram, is examined. The external entity in this model is the user, who submits test images to the system. The system then returns the test results to the user. Upon decomposing the process, a model emerges that comprises three functions: text recognition from images, evaluation of the papers, and storage of the results. These functions are detailed in the decomposition of the context diagram (Fig. 3).

The process begins with the recognition of text from images, which is then applied to the test papers. Test data and a list of students are retrieved from the database, following which the results are stored in the database and presented to the user. To delineate the work evaluation process with greater precision, a functional process diagram in IDEF0 notation is employed. This facilitates the definition of mechanisms essential for task realization and the identification of controlling factors.

The contextual structure of the control work assessment process undergoes decomposition, revealing four subprocesses: text recognition, identification of the learner by name and surname as the author of the work, comparison of answers, and determination of the grade [3].

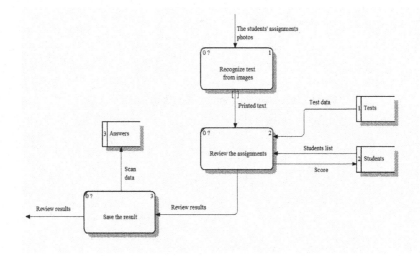

Fig. 3. Decomposition of the context diagram for uploading test answers.

Further decomposition is performed on the process of image text recognition, yielding four subprocesses: converting the image into a simplified form, selecting characters, recognizing characters, and combining characters into text. The procedure for converting an image to a simplified view initiates with capturing a photograph of the learner's work, followed by its preparation for neural network processing. This involves applying various filters to enhance contrast and eliminate unnecessary elements from the image using computer vision libraries. The outcome is a contrast-enhanced image ready for the character extraction stage. Through computer vision techniques, individual characters are identified and isolated in the image, then saved as separate images.

The qualitative criteria for evaluating the site's performance include the time cost and the error rate for verification. The site's target function aims to minimize these indicators. The reduction in the error rate for work verification is directly proportional to the success rate of neural network recognition and the efficacy of site verification algorithms. The anticipated reduction in time spent on paper checking by a single teacher, facilitated by the application, is calculated to be 9.8 h per month.

2.2 Technical Solution

The architectural design of an application represents a high-level outline of its structure, highlighting the interactions among its various components. This perspective enables an assessment of the autonomy of each component group and the system's scalability potential. The conceptual architecture of the application is delineated into three main blocks (Fig. 4).

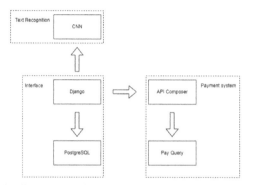

Fig. 4. Conceptual architecture.

The Text Recognition block is tasked with identifying handwritten characters in images. For this purpose, a convolutional neural network (CNN) specialized in efficient pattern recognition is recommended for scanning images. This method is identified as the most optimal approach for fulfilling the system's requirements.

The Payment System block encompasses a payment aggregator and an interface for interactions. The primary criteria for the payment service include the reliability of the aggregator, ease of integration, and the contracting process for connection. Yukassa and Robokassa are evaluated as potential payment aggregators for the service. Yukassa offers two main tariffs for legal entities, varying by the company's turnover, which includes same-day payments and individual rates for substantial turnovers. Conversely, Robokassa features a tiered tariff system with a gradual commission reduction and next-day payment processing. After reviewing the terms and services, Yukassa is preferred as the payment provider.

The user interaction interface is realized through a website integrated with a database. Selecting the primary development platform is crucial for defining the software system's architecture. The Django framework is selected for its robustness and ease of use, with PostgreSQL chosen as the database for the developed service, due to its reliability and performance.

The project employs the MVC (Model-View-Controller) design pattern, a widely recognized architectural pattern that organizes the system into three primary components: the data model, the view, and the controller. This separation facilitates the independence of each component and minimizes their interdependence, thereby simplifying maintenance and scalability when modifications are made to any single component (Fig. 5).

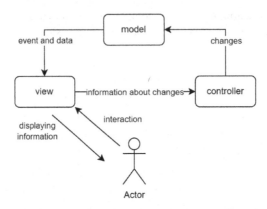

Fig. 5. Interaction of service components and user.

The Model component encapsulates the domain model of the application, comprising data and the methods required to process this data. It abstracts the information from its visual representation, effectively hiding it from the end user. Controllers interact with the Model to fetch or modify data, ensuring a separation of concerns.

The role of the View component is to render data visually in various formats. It is responsible for presenting information to the user, enabling the display of objects in multiple visual formats such as tables or lists. Additionally, the View component is capable of exporting data to several formats, including JSON, XML, XLSX, among others, providing versatility in data presentation.

The Controller component serves as the intermediary that manages interactions between the user and the system. It leverages Models and Views to formulate the system's responses to user inputs. The Controller is tasked with filtering data, verifying user rights, and fetching the necessary information, thus orchestrating the flow of data within the system.

The delineation of components within the MVC framework significantly simplifies the maintenance of software code. Modifications to the user interface have no impact on the underlying business logic, and alterations to the business logic do not necessitate changes in the visualization. This separation of concerns maintains the clarity and independence of each component, thereby streamlining both the development and subsequent maintenance processes of the system [5].

3   Result

3.1   Interface Implementation

The project leverages the React.js JavaScript library for the development of its user interface, necessitating the preliminary installation of Node.js. Node.js serves as a platform that enables JavaScript execution both on the client side and server side by compiling JavaScript into machine code. Following the installation of Node.js, the creation of a React project is the next step. For server communication the axios library is employed to facilitate data retrieval through HTTP requests. Specifically, to interface with the Django API and fetch data via GET requests, the componentDidMount function is utilized, initializing a data variable to store the incoming information.

React.js adopts a component-based architecture, which represents website objects as modular components, thereby easing system maintenance. These components, whether functions or classes, are tasked with rendering information to the user.

The structure of the main pages is composed of three key components: the top navigation bar (header), the content block (main body of the page), and the bottom information bar (footer). The homepage provides an overview of the site's features. An illustration of the homepage layout can be found in Fig. 6.

Fig. 6.   View of the main page.

The tests page is designed to showcase the tests created by the user. It achieves this by querying the specified host address and then displaying a list of the user's tests (Fig. 7). This consistent approach is extended to all other pages of the site, ensuring uniformity and enhancing usability in the interface design.

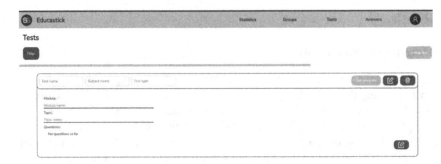

Fig. 7. Test page output.

3.2 Neural Network Training

Survey results indicate the necessity of training neural networks for both English and Russian, due to the overlap in the alphabets of these languages. To address this requirement, two neural network models will be trained, each designed to recognize digits and symbols. The convolutional neural network (CNN) model, renowned for its object classification efficacy, has been selected as the primary tool for this task. The training process for each model is estimated to take between 2 to 2.5 h, aiming to achieve an accuracy rate of 97–99%. The implementation of model training utilizes the following Python libraries:

- Numpy: for supporting multidimensional arrays and performing mathematical operations on these arrays;
- Os: for accessing operating system functions;
- PIL: a library for image processing in Python;
- Tensorflow: a library for machine learning used to train artificial intelligence for a variety of tasks;
- Keras: a library for deep machine learning;
- Sklearn: an open-source machine learning library for partitioning datasets, calculating metrics, and performing cross-validation [8].

    The neural network training process is segmented into four distinct stages:

- Data Loading and Expansion: This initial stage involves generating datasets for both training and testing the neural network, ensuring a robust foundation for effective learning.
- Model Architecture Creation: At this stage, the structure of the neural network is meticulously defined, laying out the framework within which the model will operate.
- Training the Model: During this critical phase, the model undergoes training with the prepared data, learning and adjusting its parameters to improve performance.
- Model Preservation: The final stage involves saving the trained model, making it readily available for future application and further analysis.

3.3 Data Loading and Expansion

Data expansion takes place in several steps:

- 'original': saving the image in its original form;
- 'rotate + ' and 'rotate-': create a new image with clockwise and anti-clockwise rotation;
- 'blur': blur the image;
- 'blur&rotate': combine blur and rotate the image;
- 'shift': shift the image along x and y axes.

Following these transformations, the images are categorized into two groups for the purposes of training and testing the model. Each transformation step, including rotation, blurring, and shifting, is implemented to introduce a wide range of variations in the dataset (Figs. 8, 9 and 10) [9].

Fig. 8. Image rotation.

Fig. 9. Image blurring.

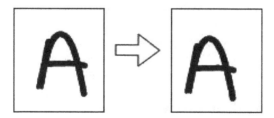

Fig. 10. Image Shift.

After data expansion the augmented image dataset is partitioned into two groups: 85% allocated for training and 15% reserved for testing. The neural networks initiate the process by taking an input vector, which is then propagated through a series of hidden layers. These layers are comprised of independent neurons, with each neuron interconnected within its layer and to the neurons of the preceding layer. In a conventional three-layer neural network, the final layer serves as the output layer, categorizing the distribution of scores into classes for classification tasks. The architecture of a general convolutional neural network (CNN) typically involves a sequence of CONV-RELU layers followed by a POOL layer. This arrangement is repeated until the representation size of the original image is reduced to a predetermined threshold. Subsequently, the network transitions to a fully connected layer, which holds the output data. The CONV (convolutional) layer conducts computations between its weights and a specific segment of the input image to which it is linked. The RELU (Rectified Linear Unit) layer introduces the max(0, x) activation function to the data, preserving its dimensionality without alteration. Lastly, the POOL (pooling) layer undertakes a downsampling operation across two dimensions-height and width of the image-effectively reducing its size while retaining essential information.

3.4 Building the Neural Network Architecture

The Sequential class from the Keras library is employed to construct a linear stack of layers, forming a sequential neural network architecture. The configuration of the Sequential model begins with specifying the dimensionality of the input data to the input layer. This foundational step ensures that subsequent layers in the model are capable of automatically determining their dimensions, thereby obviating the need for manual specification by the user.

The dimensionality of the input layer can be defined in several ways:

– Passing the input_shape argument to the first layer;
– Passing the input_dim argument to the 2D layers;
– Specifying a fixed data batch size (batch_size).

In this architecture, the input layer is implemented as a 2D convolutional layer utilizing the Conv2D class. This class constructs a convolution kernel that is convolved with the layer input to produce a tensor of outputs. The use of Conv2D as the initial layer facilitates the processing of images by extracting features through convolution operations. To construct and optimize the neural network model, various layers are employed, each tasked with specific data transformations. The Conv2D convolution layer is initialized with several parameters:

– Filters is the number of output filters in the convolution;
– Kernel_size are dimensions of the 2D convolution window;
– Padding are specifies the padding applied to the input;
– Input_shape are dimensions of the input layer;
– Activation is the activation function used.

Pooling layers, such as MaxPooling2D, are utilized for subsampling, effectively reducing data size. They are configured with parameters including:

– Pool_size are factors by which to downscale (in both vertical and horizontal directions);
– Strides is the stride lengths of the pooling operation;
– Padding are specifies the padding applied to the input;
– Data_format is the ordering of dimensions in the input.
– The Dropout layer aims to reduce overfitting by randomly setting a proportion of input units to 0 at each update during training time, determined by a specified rate.

To prepare for the creation of a fully connected layer, the Flatten class is used to flatten the input while maintaining the batch size. The Dense class is employed to create a fully connected layer, executing the operation output = activation(dot(input, kernel) + bias), with parameters:

- Units is the number of neurons in the layer.
- Activation is the activation function.

The learning process is configured using the.compile() method which accepts:

- Optimizer is the optimization method, such as Adam, a variant of stochastic gradient descent;
- Loss is the function to minimize during training;
- Metrics is the performance evaluation metrics for the model.

To ensure orderly training and evaluation, the parameter run_eagerly = True is set before model training begins. The outcomes of the training are documented in Fig. 11, displaying an evaluation of the model's training process. Upon completion of training, the neural network is saved, selecting an appropriate path and filename for the model.

```
Epoch 17/200
972/972 [==============================] - 2015s 2s/step - loss: 0.0712 - accuracy: 0.9776 - val_loss: 0.4465 - val_accuracy: 0.9147
Epoch 18/200
972/972 [==============================] - 67s 69ms/step - loss: 0.0675 - accuracy: 0.9787 - val_loss: 0.4395 - val_accuracy: 0.9105
Epoch 19/200
972/972 [==============================] - 67s 69ms/step - loss: 0.0695 - accuracy: 0.9780 - val_loss: 0.3928 - val_accuracy: 0.9191
Epoch 20/200
972/972 [==============================] - 68s 70ms/step - loss: 0.0610 - accuracy: 0.9813 - val_loss: 0.3819 - val_accuracy: 0.9250
Epoch 21/200
972/972 [==============================] - 67s 69ms/step - loss: 0.0587 - accuracy: 0.9820 - val_loss: 0.4049 - val_accuracy: 0.9242
```

Fig. 11. Training evaluation of the model.

4 Discussion

To accurately recognize letters with the trained neural network model, the input image must undergo specific preprocessing steps. Given that the training dataset comprises black and white images, the input image must be adjusted to match this format, and the text contained within it should be segmented into individual letters.

The segmentation process is facilitated by the OpenCV library. Initially, the source image is loaded using the cv2.imread(path_to_image) function, followed by its conversion to black and white. This conversion employs the following functions:

- cv2.cvtColor(image, cv2.COLOR_BGR2GRAY);
- cv2.threshold(image, threshold_value = 100, max_value_below_threshold = 255, threshold_type = cv2.THRESH_BINARY).

The thresholding procedure assumes the use of different threshold types:

- cv.THRESH_BINARY;
- cv.THRESH_BINARY_INV;

– cv.THRESH_TRUNC;
– cv.THRESH_TOZERO;
– cv.THRESH_TOZERO_INV.

Figure 12 demonstrates the outcomes of applying these different threshold types. To facilitate contour detection, image dimensionality is increased using the cv2.erode function. Contours are then identified with cv2.findContours. The resulting hierarchical tree of image contours has an order of importance:

– Letter contour;
– Internal contour.

The challenge lies in isolating only the letter contours, necessitating an examination of their relationship to the overall contour [10].

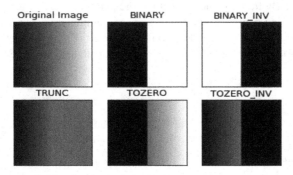

Fig. 12. Threshold types.

For subsequent training, it is essential to standardize the size of the letters to a 32x32 square. This process includes several steps, starting with the delineation of letter outlines using cv2.boundingRect, and resizing the letters to 32x32 with cv2.resize. Prepared letters are then ordered by their X-coordinate and stored in a tuple format (x, w, letter), facilitating the identification of spaces between letters. To proceed with letter recognition the saved model is loaded using keras.models.load_model and the predict_classes function is called for prediction. If dataset images are rotated, they must be corrected to their proper orientation prior to recognition.

The pre-determined character width assists in inserting spaces between letters, applying a threshold of more than 1/4 of a character width to denote a space [11].

5   Conclusion

The automation of assessing students' work marks a pivotal advancement in contemporary educational practices. This discussion delves into the significance, benefits, and prospective enhancements of the developed service, underscoring its principal advantages and potential for further development. The automation streamlines and simplifies the assessment process, thereby liberating teachers from time-consuming tasks. Moreover, it promotes a more equitable evaluation of students' work by minimizing the human element and potential biases. The proposed service is an innovative tool for benchmarking students' progress. It has several key advantages:

– Efficiency: The service's automated verification significantly diminishes the time required for assessments, relieving teachers of repetitive tasks;
– Accuracy: Leveraging neural networks for text recognition, the service achieves high accuracy levels, even with handwritten inputs;
– Usability: With smartphone compatibility, the service offers convenience and accessibility to a broad user base.

A crucial aspect of deploying the service involves managing data exchange between client and server components, necessitating custom adjustments due to varying standards. Despite these challenges, such an approach facilitates the creation of a scalable and efficiently optimized project. The cornerstone of the service is the automatic verification of test submissions, enabled by a convolutional neural network adept at precise handwritten text recognition. This network undergoes training on extensive datasets to enhance accuracy and prevent overfitting. Despite its significant advantages, the service requires further improvement:

– Improved neural network training: Enhancing the service's handwriting recognition capabilities through further algorithm training and optimization;
– Expansion of functionality: Introducing additional features, such as varied assignment checks, paper commenting, and report generation could render the service more beneficial for educators.

A critical phase in service implementation is the processing of images, using filters to generate contrasting, black and white images that accentuate words and letters for recognition. Smartphones emerge as the primary access tool for their ease in uploading images, supported by an adaptive website that ensures functionality across both desktop and mobile platforms.

In conclusion, the developed service represents a significant leap forward in automating the educational process. While its current advantages are notable, ongoing refinement and expansion could transform it into an even more potent and valuable tool for assessing student work and enriching the educational experience.

References

1. Alexeyev, A., Malandii, T., Moshna, A.: Mobile application for test control of knowledge among mechanical engineering students. In: Ivanov, V., Trojanowska, J., Pavlenko, I., Zajac, J., Peraković, D. (eds.) DSMIE 2021. LNME, pp. 289–300. Springer, Cham (2021). https://doi.org/10.1007/978-3-030-77719-7_29
2. Skrypnikov, A.V., Denisenko, V.V., Hitrov, E.G., Evteeva, K.S., Savchenko, I.I.: Handwritten text recognition using neural networks. Sovremennye naukoemkie tehnologii **6–1**, 91–95 (2021)
3. Glukhikh, I., Chernysheva, T., Glukhikh, D.: Neural network models for situation similarity assessment in hybrid-CBR. J. Intell. Fuzzy Syst. **44**(15), 7669–7682 (2023)
4. Ngaogate, W.: Integrating flyweight design pattern and MVC in development of web application. In: Proceedings of the 2020 2nd International Conference on Information Technology and

Computer Communications, ITCC 2020. ACM International Conference Proceeding Series, pp. 27–31 (2020)

5. Węgrzecki, K.S., Dzieńkowski, M.: Performance analysis of LARAVEL and YII2 frameworks based on the MVC architectural pattern and PHP language. J. Comput. Sci. Inst. **24**, 265–272 (2022)

6. Dolgushin, M., Ismakova, D., Bidulya, Y., Krupkin, I., Barskaya, G., Lesiv, A.: Toxic comment classification service in social network. Lect. Notes Comput. Sci. **12997**, 157–165 (2021)

7. Deng, J., Dong, W., Socher, R., Li, L.-J., Li, K., Fei-Fei, L.: ImageNet: a large-scale hierarchical image database. In: IEEE Conference on Computer Vision and Pattern Recognition, pp. 248–255 (2009)

8. Gafarov, F.M., Galimjanov, A.F.: Artificial Neural Networks and Applications. Izd-vo Kazan. un-ta, Kazan' (2018)

9. A new convolutional neural network for recognizing handwritten letters of the Russian alphabet. https://github.com/ansafo/CNN_RusAlph.git. Accessed 23 Apr 2023

10. Alam, M.S., Rahman, M.S., Hosen, M.I., Mubin, K.A., Hossen, S., Mridha, M.F.: Comparison of different CNN model used as encoders for image captioning. In: 2021 International Conference on Data Analytics for Business and Industry, pp. 523–526 (2021)

11. Calik, R.C., Demirci, M.F.: CIFAR-10 image classification with convolutional neural networks for embedded systems. In: 2018 IEEE/ACS 15th International Conference on Computer Systems and Applications, p. 8612873 (2019)

Implementing a Jenkins Plugin to Visualize Continuous Integration Pipelines

Nikita Kubov⬤, Vladimir Shmakov⬤, Nikita Voinov$^{(\boxtimes)}$⬤, Anton Tyshkevich⬤, and Yury Yusupov⬤

Peter the Great St.Petersburg Polytechnic University, 29, Polytechnicheskaya, St. Petersburg 195251, Russia
voinov@ics2.ecd.spbstu.ru

Abstract. The paper is devoted to visualization of continuous integration pipelines of the Jenkins system. When working with the Jenkins system additional tools are needed to automate the process by visualizing pipelines. There are a number of existing Jenkins plugins for pipelines visualization, however all of them have specific shortcomings. Based on the analysis of existing solutions requirements for a new plugin were formulated. Also presented in the paper are the architecture and implementation details of the developed plugin which allows to visualize pipelines both in the form of a graph and a Gantt chart as well as provides the user with metadata, crash and restart information. Results of the plugin integration into Jenkins pipeline prove its effectiveness due to reduction of efforts on integration pipeline analysis.

Keywords: Jenkins · Plugin · Continuous Integration Pipeline · Visualization · Graph

1 Introduction

Modern software development approaches include the practice of continuous integration [1–4]. This approach consists of compilation, building and testing processes as well as other routine project-specific tasks. Tasks of building and testing often increase in execution time with the growth of the code base and can often end up with errors, therefore these tasks and their corresponding processes shall be automated using special tools.

Jenkins tool [5, 6] is one of the support systems for continuous integration and allows to automate routine operations. Despite the rich functionality of the technology and the large set of tools available by default, users need additional plugins [7, 8] to visualize assembly chains to analyze the performance of the continuous integration process and simplify their work. There are several popular plugins for pipeline visualization, but none of them provides sufficient functionality as shown below.

So the purpose of this work is to develop a software tool for visualizing assembly chains as a plugin for Jenkins continuous integration system. The proposed tool shall provide an intuitive graphical interface embedded into the Jenkins base interface. It shall

A. Gibadullin (Ed.): ITIDMS 2023, CCIS 2112, pp. 117–129, 2024.
https://doi.org/10.1007/978-3-031-60318-1_10

also implement the functionality to visualize all kinds of Jenkins continuous integration system pipeline structures in stacked-parallel form and in the form of Gantt charts. Finally, the tool shall provide the user with metadata, failure and restart information for individual sections of the assembly chain.

2 Overview of Existing Solutions

Blue Ocean [9] is a software tool with a redesigned Jenkins user interface to improve the understandability of Jenkins pipeline. This tool performs visualization of continuous integration pipelines, which is represented as a graph. When errors occur during the pipeline execution process, the vertices of the graph are marked with a color corresponding to the status. Also the tool allows integration with GitHub [10] and Bitbucket [11] for automatic integration of version control systems.

Pro:

- Visual editor of continuous integration pipelines. It allows to create and edit a continuous integration process using individual user interface elements without writing code.
- Displays the execution of the assembly chain in the form of a graph.
- Displays metadata. It allows to set up and resolve problems using log mapping.

Cons:

- Assembly chains in the form of a graph are not always displayed correctly. There are situations when one of the stages of the continuous integration process has completed with an error, but the plugin displays information that the process has completed without errors.
- Insufficient granularity of visualization tools in the form of a graph. The current implementation does not allow the engineer to quickly view the status of child elements of the continuous integration process in the graph.
- Other visualization methods (Gantt charts) are not available.

Pipline Graph View [12] performs visualization of the continuous integration process in the form of a graph in a stacked-parallel form. The status of the stages completed successfully is colored green. It also provides UI elements for viewing the status of the entire continuous integration process and its individual steps.

Pro:

- A small extension without excess functionality.
- A graph representation of the continuous integration process in a stacked-parallel form.
- Displays the progress status of the individual stages of the assembly chain in the form of a specific color and icon.

Cons:

- Logs are not available.
- Inorrect visualization of assembly chains. Concurrent branches of the continuous integration process can be displayed sequentially.

– Other visualization methods (Gantt charts) are not available.

Yet Another Build Visualizer [13] performs a visualization of the continuous integration process in the form of a graph. The tool is compatible with all types of assemblies in Jenkins. Provides visualization without adding actions or tagging assemblies in Jenkins with additional metadata. Displays the execution time of an individual assembly and child assemblies.

Pro:

– Displays the status of the child job of the assembly chain.
– Compatible with all types of Jenkins builds.

Cons:

– Not detailed visual representation of the graph.
– Other visualization methods (Gantt charts) are not available.
– Metadata and logs are not available in quick access. User shall use other software tools for additional research to find out the problems.

Stage View [9] is designed to visualize the execution history of a continuous integration process in the form of a table. The visualization shows the status, stage number and its execution time, as well as the number of commits for the whole continuous integration process.

Pro:

– Provides information in the following form: run time, status and conveyor assembly step.
– Displays tags and commits from the Git repository of the project.

Cons:

– Graph visualization is not available.
– Visualization of conveyor assembly in the form of diagrams is not available.
– Visualization of metadata and logs is not available.

The analysis of existing tools for visualization of continuous integration processes revealed that current implementations do not provide the necessary functionality for visualization of continuous integration process in the form of Gantt charts. In the Pipline-GraphView software tool visualization of assembly chains in the form of a graph does not work correctly. Also existing solutions have limitations in visualization of detail information about child jobs. PiplineGraphView and Stage View plugins do not display metadata about the stages of assembly chain execution. Overall results of the analysis are presented in Table 1.

So it can be concluded that existing software tools do not satisfy the requirements either completely or partially and a new Jenkins plugin shall be developed to implement all the required functionality to visualize continuous integration pipelines.

Table 1. Analysis of existing solutions.

Tool name	Gantt charts	Displays assembly chains as a graph	Displays metadata	Displays failures and restarts
Blue Ocean	–	+/–	+	+
Pipeline Graph View	–	+/–	–	Failures only
Yet Another Build Visualizer	–	+/–	–	Failures only
Stage View	–	–	–	Failures only

3   Materials and Methods

3.1   Architecture of the Proposed Solution

The proposed tool is implemented as a separate module embedded into the Jenkins system. Operation of the developed plugin after integration into Jenkins system is based on the principle of web application in terms of client-server architecture.

The client interacting with the user initiates requests to the web server via HyperText Transfer Protocol (HTTP). Depending on the processed request from the client, the web application creates a new Hypertext Markup Language document and sends it back to the client. All computations take place on the web server, the web client only provides user interaction and sending requests.

In the developed plugin it is necessary to visualize the result of the execution of the continuous integration process. With the help of visualization tools, the web client should display status, structure, and metadata about the assembly chain and provide the user with the ability to switch between visualization tools and retain the ability to use the basic user interface of the Jenkins system. The web server should respond to commands from the user and provide the modified state of the user interface upon request.

Figure 1 shows the flowchart of the developed software tool. When the user calls the Jenkins interface, the client sends a request to the web server. To get the data for visualization of the required components the code on the web server side is launched, which uses an algorithm to convert the data of the internal Jenkins chain representation into a suitable data format for visualization. The web server then sends a response to the web client, after which the page in the browser is refreshed.

When using the described interaction scheme, the following approach is implemented: the web server supplies an HTML document, including markup, Cascading Style Sheets (CSS) and JavaScript templates. JavaScript scripts are responsible for handling user interaction with the page and used only by the browser.

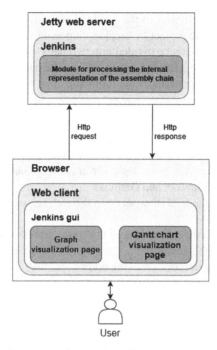

Fig. 1. Components interaction within the developed plugin.

3.2   Implementation of the Client Side

The Feature Sliced Design (FSD) approach was used to organize the code of the client side of the developed tool. FSD is an architectural methodology for developing client-side web applications. This approach focuses on designing a modular, extensible and easily maintainable application architecture.

This approach includes the following basic principles:

– Separation by functionality. An application is divided into separate modules, each of which is responsible for a specific function. Each module can have its own structure containing components, business logic and data required to implement this functionality.
– Organization of code around business logic. The application architecture is built around business logic rather than technical layers, which allows to create modules that integrate all the components necessary for their own implementation: interfaces, services, data models, etc.
– Independence of modules. Each module (slice) should have minimal dependencies on other modules. This aspect allows new functionality to be developed, tested, and deployed in isolation, simplifying the support and scaling of the application.
– Reuse. The FSD architecture encourages code and component reuse. Common components and methods needed to implement multiple entities that provide different functionality can be moved to separate modules to avoid code duplication and to facilitate code maintenance.

This approach lends itself well to the needs of the software being developed and makes it easy to structure the project by breaking it down into smaller layers.

Schematically, the client can be divided into two parts which are separate one-page applications embedded in the basic Jenkins interface. The part responsible for the Gantt chart is shown in Fig. 2 and consists of the following main files:

- App.tsx - launches a single-page application.
- GanttPage.tsx - contains the basic logic of the application. It implements the logic of displaying all page content. This file displays internal components and uses React-hooks to redraw components when data is updated asynchronously.
- GanttChart.tsx - contains the basic logic for drawing a Gantt chart and consists of two components: TreeView.tsx and Gantt.tsx.
- ganttModel.ts - stores the URL that accesses the web server to download data to the Gantt chart page.
- TreeView.tsx - contains the description of the component that visualizes elements of the chain as a nested tree structure.
- Gantt.tsx - contains the description of the component that visualizes timelines of the Gantt chart.
- GanttStage.ts - contains a description of the model for displaying timelines.

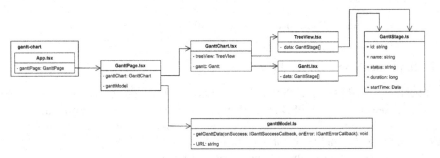

Fig. 2. Scheme of the client side implementing Gantt chart functionality.

The scheme of the part responsible for handling the graphical representation of the assembly chain is shown in Fig. 3 and consists of the following main files:

- App.tsx - launches a single-page application.
- GraphPage.tsx - contains the basic logic of the application. It implements the logic of displaying the entire page content. This file displays internal components and uses React-hooks to redraw components when data is updated asynchronously.
- Dag.tsx - contains the basic logic for drawing a directed acyclic graph diagram with a stacked-parallel form.
- graphModel.ts - stores the URL that accesses a web server to load data into a graph page.
- Stage.ts - contains the description of the model for displaying the stages of the assembly chain in the form of graph vertices.

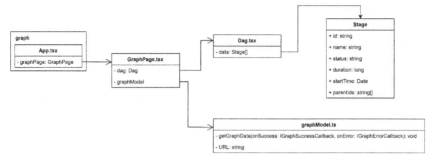

Fig. 3. Scheme of the client side implementing graph drawing functionality.

3.3 Implementation of the Server Side

The main technology for implementing the module running on the web server is the Java programming language. The Jenkins Pipeline: API tool [14] was used to interact with the Jenkins continuous integration system. The capabilities of the Stapler tool were used to process the client's request and send the response.

Figure 4 shows a scheme of the module running on a web server. The files PipelineGraphVisualizerAction.java and PipelineGanttVisualizerAction.java implement the Action interface which is used in the Jenkins system to create an additional URL subspace under the parent model object for user interaction. These two files contain the getGraph and getGantt methods, which are labeled with @WebMethod annotations. These methods are called as soon as the web server receives a request from the client for the corresponding URL. The methods run the code responsible for generating the continuous integration pipeline data.

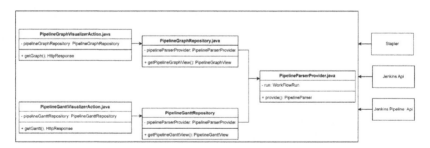

Fig. 4. Scheme of the server side implementation.

The files PipelineGraphRepositroy.java and PipelineGanttRepository.java provide data for the graph and Gantt chart respectively. In these files the PipelineParser entity, which handles the internal representation of the assembly chain, is accessed through a call chain.

The Jenkins system stores information about the build chain as a collection of objects corresponding to each line of a script describing the entire continuous integration process.

Jenkins Pipeline: API provides a workaround to the internal representation in the form of callback methods.

An algorithm based on grammar recognition was developed to work with Jenkins Pipeline API. Figures 5, 6 and 7 show the rules for processing the internal representation of the assembly chain.

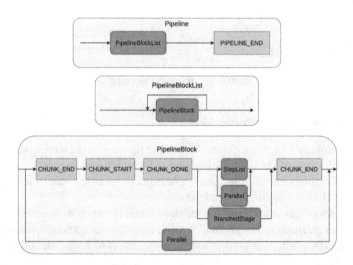

Fig. 5. Processing Pipeline, PipelineBlockList and PipelineBlock entities.

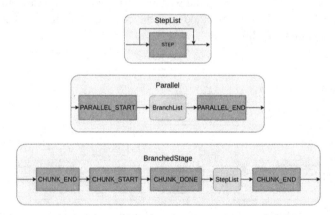

Fig. 6. Processing StepList, Parallel and BranchedStage entities.

The processing of the internal representation of the assembly chain in Jenkins is based on the principle of token recognition. Each token corresponds to an execution of the Jenkins Pipeline API callback method. The algorithm uses the following set of tokens:

– CHUNK_START - corresponds to the call of the chunkStart method. It signals that the object of internal representation refers to the beginning of the chunk.

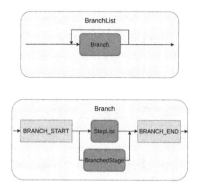

Fig. 7. Processing BranchList and Branch entities.

- CHUNK_END - corresponds to the call of the chunkEnd method. It signals that the object of the internal representation belongs to the end of the chunk.
- CHUNK_DONE - corresponds to the call of the handleChunkDone method. It signals that the execution of a chunk has finished. The object marked with this token can get information about the status, start time of execution, amount of execution time.
- PARALLEL_START - corresponds to the call of the parallelStart method. It signals that the object of internal representation refers to the beginning of the concurrent part of the assembly chain execution.
- PARALLEL_END - corresponds to the call of the parallelEnd method. It signals that the object of internal representation belongs to the end of the concurrent section of the assembly chain execution.
- BRANCH_START - corresponds to the call of the parallelBranchStart method. It signals that the object of internal representation refers to the beginning of the branch inside the concurrent block.
- BRANCH_END - corresponds to the call of the parallelBranchEnd method. It signals that the object of internal representation refers to the beginning of the branch inside the concurrent block.
- STEP - corresponds to the call of the atomNode method if the internal view object is a separate step.
- PIPELINE_END - corresponds to the call of the atomNode method if the internal view object is the end of the assembly chain.

After processing the internal representation of the assembly chain, the web server sends a JSON object to the client, the structure of the object is shown in Fig. 8.

The main class of the data model is PipelineGraphView with the following fields:

- pipelineName - assembly name and number;
- totalTime - execution time;
- endTime - time elapsed since the end of the assembly;
- stageContainers - list of concurrent elements.

The StageContainer class is a wrapper over the concurrent section of the assembly chain and has the following structure:

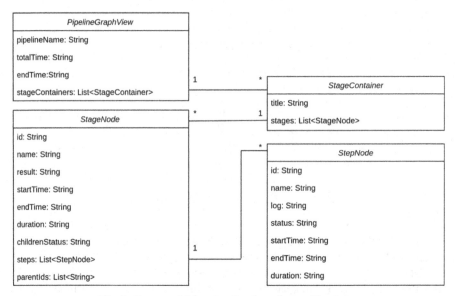

Fig. 8. Data model for visualization of assembly chain.

– title - the name of the concurrent node, if the node is wrapped in a stage in the Jenkins internal view;
– stages.

The StageNode class is a description of the stage of the assembly chain and has the following structure:

– id - stage identifier;
– name - stage name;
– result - stage execution status;
– startTime - execution start time;
– endTime - end time of execution
– duration - execution time;
– childStatus - execution status of the child assembly chain;
– steps;
– parentIds - list of identifiers referring to the preceding stages.

The StepNode class is a description of a step within a stage and has the following structure:

– id - step identifier;
– name - step name;
– log - logs with metadata;
– status - status of step execution;
– startTime - execution start time;
– endTime - end time of execution;
– duration - execution time.

4   Results and Discussion

Interface of the developed plugin was tested manually while JUnit [15] и Jenkins Unit Test Harness [16] tools were used for unit testing of the main algorithms and logic of the plugin. As input test data miscellaneous assembly chains were used which contain:

- 3 executed stages;
- 2 executed stages and 1 unstable stage;
- 2 executed stages and 1 failed stage;
- 1 missed stage;
- 1 concurrent block and 8 stages;
- 1 concurrent block and 1 unstable stage;
- 1 concurrent block and 1 failed stage;
- 1 concurrent block and 1 missed stage;
- "when"-expression;
- "timeout"-expression;
- 2 concurrent blocks;
- executed parent assembly chain;
- parent assembly chain with failed child assembly chain;
- parent assembly chain with failed stage within child assembly chain;
- parent assembly chain with concurrent child assembly chains.

60 unit tests overall were prepared and run, all of them passed successfully.

To assess the effectiveness of the implemented plugin the following experiment was held. For a standard task of continuous integration required time efforts on its analysis were estimated and then compared with actual time efforts spent.

The task includes the following process of building and deploying a template web application:

- Download the source code from the repository.
- Assemble the project.
- Build the project into a container image.
- Check the code with a static analyzer.
- Check the code with a dynamic analyzer.
- Vulnerability check of the container image.

The script used to implement the above chain in Jenkins is shown in Fig. 9.

Results of the experiment are presented in Table 2. Actual time efforts on assembly chain analysis while using the implemented plugin is 40% less than estimated efforts and 33% less than actual efforts without usage of the plugin.

```
pipeline {
    agent any
    stages {
        stage('Clone Git repository') {
            steps {
                checkout scm
            }
        }
        stage('Build project') {
            steps {
                sh 'mvn clean package'
            }
        }
        stage('Build image') {
            steps {
                sh 'echo Build application image'
                sh 'mkdir -p pkg'
                sh 'mv target/demo.war pkg/demo.war'
            }
        }
        stage('Run container') {
            steps {
                sh 'echo Run container'
                sh 'docker run -h demoapp --network sonar_jenkins_default --rm -p 80:80 -d roundkubik/docker_id'
            }
        }
        stage('SonarQube analysis') {
            steps {
                sh 'echo Run SAST - SonarQube analysis'
            }
        }
        stage('OWASP ZAP analysis') {
            steps {
                sh 'echo Run DAST - OWASP ZAP analysis'
                sh "docker run --network sonar_jenkins_default -t owasp/zap2docker-stable \
            }
        }
        stage('Trivy analysis') {
            steps {
                sh 'echo Trivy check'
                sh 'trivy image --exit-code 1 --severity CRITICAL,HIGH roundkubik/docker_id:latest '
            }
        }
    }
}
```

Fig. 9. The script running the experimental assembly chain in Jenkins.

Table 2. Time efforts on assembly chain analysis.

	Using the implemented plugin	Without usage of the plugin
Estimated (man-hour)	0.8	1
Actual (man-hour)	0.6	0.9

5   Conclusion

The paper describes the implementation of a Jenkins plugin for visualizing assembly chains within the Jenkins continuous integration system. Analysis of existing tools of the similar functionality revealed that all of them have specific shortcomings which shall be eliminated for more convenient and reliable process of visualization of continuous integration pipelines. The implemented plugin provides an intuitive graphical interface embedded into the Jenkins base interface, the functionality to visualize all kinds of Jenkins continuous integration system pipeline structures in stacked-parallel form and in the form of Gantt charts. It also provides the user with metadata, failure and restart information for individual sections of the assembly chain. Results of the plugin integration into

Jenkins pipeline prove its effectiveness due to reduction of time efforts on integration pipeline analysis.

References

1. Soares, E., Sizilio, G., Santos, J., da Costa, D.A., Kulesza, U.: The effects of continuous integration on software development: a systematic literature review. Empir. Softw. Eng. **27**(3), 78 (2022)
2. Elazhary, O., Werner, C., Li, Z.S., Lowlind, D., Ernst, N.A., Storey, M.A.: Uncovering the benefits and challenges of continuous integration practices. IEEE Trans. Softw. Eng. **48**(7), 2570–2583 (2022)
3. Shahin, M., Babar, M.A., Zhu, L.: Continuous integration, delivery and deployment: a systematic review on approaches, tools, challenges and practices. IEEE Access **5**, 3909–3943 (2017)
4. Ståhl, D., Mårtensson, T., Bosch, J.: The continuity of continuous integration: correlations and consequences. J. Syst. Softw. **127**, 150–167 (2017)
5. Rakshith, M.N., Shivaprasad, N.: Build optimization using Jenkins. In: Hemanth, D.J., Shakya, S., Baig, Z. (eds.) ICICI 2019. LNDECT, vol. 38, pp. 401–409. Springer, Cham (2020). https://doi.org/10.1007/978-3-030-34080-3_45
6. Narang, P., Mittal, P.: Implementation of DevOps based hybrid model for project management and deployment using Jenkins automation tool with plugins. Int. J. Comput. Sci. Netw. Secur.: IJCSNS **22**(8), 249–259 (2022)
7. Révész, Á., Pataki, N.: Visualisation of Jenkins pipelines. Acta Cybernet. **25**(4), 877–895 (2022)
8. Dingare, P.: Managing plugins in Jenkins. In CI/CD Pipeline Using Jenkins Unleashed: Solutions While Setting Up CI/CD Processes, pp. 33–44. Apress, Berkeley (2022)
9. Labouardy, M.: Pipeline as Code: Continuous Delivery with Jenkins, Kubernetes, and Terraform. Simon and Schuster, New York (2021)
10. Voinov, N., Garzon, K.R., Nikiforov, I., Drobintsev, P.: Big data processing system for analysis of GitHub events. In 2019 XXII International Conference on Soft Computing and Measurements (SCM)), pp. 187–190. IEEE (2019)
11. Chakraborty, S., Aithal, P.S.: A practical approach to GIT using bitbucket, GitHub and SourceTree. Int. J. Appl. Eng. Manag. Lett. (IJAEML) **6**(2), 254–263 (2022)
12. Pipline Graph View. https://plugins.jenkins.io/pipeline-graph-view/. Accessed 26 Nov 2023
13. Yet Another Build Visualizer. https://plugins.jenkins.io/yet-another-build-visualizer/. Accessed 26 Nov 2023
14. Cepuc, A., Botez, R., Craciun, O., Ivanciu, I. A., Dobrota, V.: Implementation of a continuous integration and deployment pipeline for containerized applications in amazon web services using jenkins, ansible and kubernetes. In: 2020 19th RoEduNet Conference: Networking in Education and Research (RoEduNet), pp. 1–6. IEEE (2020)
15. Tudose, C.: JUnit in Action. Simon and Schuster, New York (2020)
16. Straubinger, P., Fraser, G.: Gamekins: gamifying software testing in jenkins. In Proceedings of the ACM/IEEE 44th International Conference on Software Engineering: Companion Proceedings, pp. 85–89 (2022)

Elimination of Optical Distortions Arising from In Vivo Investigation of the Mouse Brain

Timur Bikbulatov[1], Violetta Sitdikova[2] (ID), and Dmitrii Tumakov[1][(✉)] (ID)

[1] Institute of Computational Mathematics and Information Technologies,
Kazan Federal University, Kazan, Russia
dtumakov@kpfu.ru

[2] Laboratory "New Engineering Solutions for Modern Laboratory Research",
Kazan Federal University, Kazan, Russia

Abstract. An algorithm is proposed for eliminating refractive distortions caused by the oscillating surface of a liquid when studying the brain of a live mouse. Studies like this in mice allow monitoring neuronal activity in a living organism, and the fluid is needed to ensure that the brain remains in its natural environment. However, the presence of fluid flow causes distortions that significantly complicate tracking waves of neuronal activity. The goal of the present work is to remove effects that displace and distort images of individual parts of the brain, and, in fact, bring the entire image to a static picture. The proposed algorithm, based on tracking individual parts of images, gives a 10% improvement in approximation to a static picture compared to the original recording.

Keywords: Tracking · Optical Distortion · Image Restoration of Video Sequences

1 Introduction

Scientific methods in biology and medicine are quite advanced and have been allowing carrying out in vitro research for a long time. There exist many ways to obtain accurate data with this approach to research. These methods are usually more affordable and allow for tighter control over the experimental conditions. Despite this, the in vivo approach is still practiced these days [1]. This approach helps to model the experiment more realistically. Its main problem is the observation of the subject. An animal in such experiments can behave in a completely unpredictable way, which makes it difficult to maintain the conditions of the experiment itself. In such cases, the animal is put under anesthesia and fixated with the aid of special devices, as minimal blurring can lead to image distortions [2].

In addition to distortions caused by the movements of the animal, distortions can also be introduced by the elements involved in the experiment. For example, in [3], research was conducted on the open brain of a mouse. In this experiment, changes occurring in the open part of the animal's brain were recorded on camera. In order to keep the brain from drying out, a liquid, which is almost the same density and consistency as water, is

A. Gibadullin (Ed.): ITIDMS 2023, CCIS 2112, pp. 130–142, 2024.
https://doi.org/10.1007/978-3-031-60318-1_11

flowed over its surface. This flow introduces distortions and artifacts associated with the appearance of glare and refractive phenomena on the surface.

Similar problems can be found in other fields of science and engineering. For example, such distortions occur when imaging objects that are in denser environments; the simplest example of such an environment is water. Such interference occurs in underwater archaeology [4] or maintenance of underwater infrastructure [5]. Various techniques have been applied to reduce the interference. For example, neural networks trained on specialized datasets have been considered in [6–8]. Such an approach is not suitable for our case due to the complexity of data partitioning. In [9], methods for modeling refractive distortions using geometric approaches were applied. Moreover, a specially assembled setup was used to generate the dataset. The advantage of this approach is the interpretability of the model. However, in contrast to our data, the above work uses high-definition images and rather large distortion angles. In [5], a similar problem was solved using 3-D point cloud modeling.

The approach proposed in this paper is based on object and zone tracking algorithm. Tracking is a rather widespread problem that has different ways of solution [10]. There exist classical approaches to solving the problem. One of the approaches is the optical flow [11, 12]. Neural network approaches are also widely used [13, 14]. However, these approaches are difficult to apply to the current problem and they are most often applied to higher definition images.

In the present paper, to eliminate refractive distortions, we propose an algorithm based on tracking the displacement of individual frame elements in the entire recording, with their subsequent return to their (undistorted) place. In fact, the problem of removing side effects from fluid motion is solved. Images demonstrating the algorithm operation are presented and the efficiency of the algorithm at different parameters is evaluated.

2 Materials and Methods

2.1 Data Description

The data is a set of images combined into a video sequence. The images are snapshots of a specific part of the mice's brain, which are obtained by examining their brain activity. The immobility of the brain and the stability of the images is achieved by keeping the mice under anesthesia with a trepanized skull. To avoid swelling, the brain is held down with the aid of an almost transparent holder. Figure 1 shows an example of such an image. One can distinguish the holes and the surface of this holder. It is also possible to distinguish elements such as brain tissue, brain vessels, skull bones, hair, legs of the holder, electrodes and bright yellow glare.

LEDs of three colors are used to illuminate the area to be imaged: green (~850 nm), red (~620 nm) and infrared (~520 nm). They are usually located above the holder near the microscope lens (i.e. near the camera, since the camera is connected to the microscope lens).

On the green color one can see blood, bleeding and oxygen-enriched vessels clearly. Several LEDs of each color can be used if there is a lack of light. A camera (QICAM Fast 1394, Qimaging) with a CCD sensor that captures more light and a short focal length is used for imaging. The lens is positioned perpendicular to the surface of the brain. The

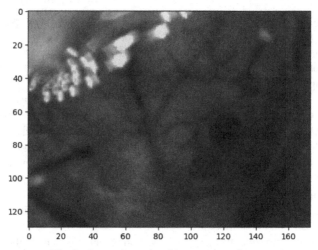

Fig. 1. Image from the video sequence image.

frame resolution is 130 × 174 pixels. A pixel is ~35 μm, thus yielding a rectangle of 4.55 × 5.95 square mm. That is roughly the same as cutting out a rectangle in the entire circle. The focus with the aid of the microscope is aimed just below the surface of the brain, specifically at the vessels running under the surface of the brain. Approximately 24 frames per second are taken, which includes 8 frames for each color replacing each other. First an LED, such as green, lights up, reaches its operating brightness. The camera turns on and records usually 8 frames. Then it turns off and stores the frames in memory, then the LED turns off. The next LED, such as red, turns on and the process repeats. It goes round and round with each color. The glow of each LED lasts about 25 ms. The whole cycle with three colors takes one second. For the duration of the experiment, the chamber with the subject is covered with a screen so that a minimum of light from the outside gets in (but it still comes in a little at the edges of the screen, as if curtains covered a larger window), so that it becomes quite dark inside. The lighting is done by the above mentioned LEDs only. The emphasis is on the image quality (more light enters due to the shutter speed) rather than the frequency of the image. Figure 2 shows a schematic of the experiment.

In Fig. 3, one can see one of the raw frames from the camera during the experiment. The needle inlet through which the drug is delivered is labeled in yellow. The electrodes that read the voltage changes during the experiment are labeled in blue and red. When the setup is ready for the experiment, the recording of the electrophysiology of the animal's brain and the video recording on the camera is started. First, control recordings are made in the amount of 10 pieces for further comparison. Recording one such fragment takes about 105 s. Then the epilepsy-inducing drug is administered. It can be administered repeatedly as needed during the experiment. After that, the recording begins.

In order to avoid drying out the surface of the brain, a water-like solution is constantly flowing through the bathtub. The drugs are also delivered with this flow. Due to this flow, the surface tension of the water changes and small waves occur. Because of this, artifacts such as glare, semi-glare, and refractive distortion of the image appear.

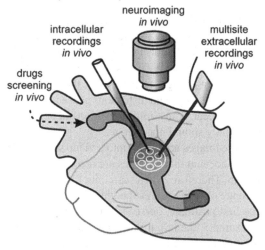

Fig. 2. Schematic of the experiment [3].

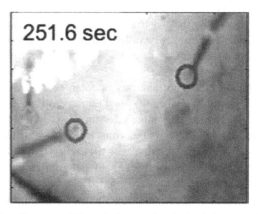

Fig. 3. Frame at 251 s. Orange and blue circles are the electrode bases, red circle is the pipette base. (Color figure online)

Glare is characterized by complete illumination of the image area and complete loss of information about it. A semi-glare is next to a glare, but unlike a glare, it does not completely destroy information. Refractive distortion is characterized by a change in the image picture because it acts like a lens.

Elimination of refractive distortions in the region where glare is absent is the goal of this study. Since it is easiest in this experiment to rely on objects that are clearly visible in the green spectrum, we will limit ourselves to the study of this spectrum only. Then we will have a video sequence, which is recorded in the format of 8 frames in the first third of a second.

In the present work, images obtained under green light will be processed.

2.2 Algorithm

Let us describe an algorithm that reduces refractive distortion. Postulate one: since one recording is performed over a stationary mouse and the camera is fixated, the captured images should not change practically during the experiment, except for relative brightness or contrast. This means that the positions and shapes of the vessels, electrodes, pipettes, and holder should not change. In the image, the position of glare, brightness and contrast of the image may change and distortions caused by changes in the curvature of the liquid surface may appear. Thus, initial positions of separate parts of images in the video sequence practically should not change.

Postulate two: since the images are linked into a video sequence, they are dependent on each other. Taking into account that 8 frames are recorded per second, the changes in the video are quite smooth. Therefore, when searching for the shift of an image element, it is sufficient to investigate only the nearest neighborhood to the previous position.

Then, based on the first postulate, one can conclude that for successful restoration some base image (for example, the initial image) is needed, with which one can check during image restoration. Such a frame will be called a source frame. To understand how the initial frame should be formed, one can refer to the first postulate. It does not follow from the postulate itself that one can determine the real size of objects in the image or the real position of objects relative to each other. In this case, it does not matter what frame will be taken as a basis for the construction of the original frame. But since a video sequence is a sequential set of images recorded in time, it makes sense to take the very first frame from the video sequence under consideration. This choice is preferable, first of all, for visual perception.

Also, from the image histogram analysis one can see that in the current video sequence, information is lost only when the pixel brightness value approaches the maximum (equal to 255). There is no darkening effect in this case. That is, the information is lost only when there is a full illumination. Thus, if it is possible to segment glare and semi-glare, one can try to fill these segments with the darkest pixels from the next frames in the video sequence, based on observations about glare movements in space. In doing so, the problem with this approach must be singled out. Dark pixels using which one tries to fill the loss of information in a pixel can themselves be shifted due to refraction effects, especially in view of the fact that earlier there was a glare in this place, which subsequently shifted. However, firstly, this paper does not aim to reconstruct the image under the glare. Such areas will be used only as additional, but not as reference information in the restoration. Secondly, even the distorted part of the image, restored in this way, will carry some information about the elements located under the water, unlike the glare, which completely destroys the information and represents dynamic objects of the video sequence.

In order to create the original image, which will be used to reconstruct other images in the video sequence, it is necessary to eliminate glare as much as possible. As mentioned above, this can be done by replacing the illuminated pixel with a pixel with a minimum intensity value throughout the video sequence. To determine the set of pixels to which one will need to apply this operation, the Sobel filter will be used. Then, using the information about the changes, applying a certain threshold value, one will get a mask that will single out the glare in the image. Next, passing through the images of the entire video sequence, the value of each pixel from the set singled out by the mask in the original image will be compared versus the value of the same pixel in another image from the video sequence. If it turns out that the brightness of the pixel is smaller, this value is taken as the value of the brightness of the pixel in the original image. In this way, the lost part of information in the original image is restored.

Next, let us proceed to the construction of the iterative tracking algorithm. **The window** will refer to the investigated sub-area of the image. The size of the window can be arbitrary within the boundaries of the image, but in the present paper, a size of 7 x 7 is chosen. The reason for this choice is the limitations of the metrics described below. The window is needed to keep track of a group of pixels. Let us select the center of such a square window 7×7. One will call the neighborhood the area denoted by the step by which it is necessary to shift to obtain a new window. That is, the minimum neighborhood is step 0. Then the center of the window will remain at the same point (x, y). Let us consider a neighborhood of size 1. That is, the coordinates of the window center can be already in the points $(x + dx, y + dy)$, where dx and dy take values $-1, 0$ or 1.

This algorithm will be largely based on the second postulate. Its idea is to take windows in $i + 1$ frame in the neighborhood of the window position in frame i. Let us compare each such window from the neighborhood with a window from the i-th frame and conclude whether it matches the neighborhood in the i-th frame. The check algorithm is as follows:

1. Make sure the glare (maximum pixel value is high) is reached, otherwise skip.
2. Find the neighborhood of the current window of frame i in frame $i + 1$.
3. Collect into an array many windows from the vicinity of frame $i + 1$.
4. In a loop, using the selected metric, compare windows from the array with the window from the i-th frame:
5. If the value of the metric is the best, that is, the windows are most similar to each other, then assign the window position value from the current instance.
6. Otherwise, do not change the position of the window.

This algorithm should be called every time it is required to loop from i frame to $i + 1$. Thus, one will loop through the images of the whole video sequence, but it will be done only for one particular window centered at (x, y). In order to have complete information about shifts of each pixel with a certain accuracy, it is necessary to work out this cycle for all points of the image, i.e. different centers of windows. Then by shifts of the window center in the video sequence it will be possible to trace how refractive distortions affect the image. Subsequently, the image returns to "its place". An example of window movement is shown in Fig. 4.

It is worth noting that the algorithm can work independently for each window, i.e. this process can be parallelized by performing calculations for each window separately.

After the calculations have been performed and the window offsets for each frame have been found, it is possible to "return" all windows to their places. In this process, one can both use pixel values of windows without overlap and combine matching pixels of different windows on each other, for example, by averaging their values (as in the present paper).

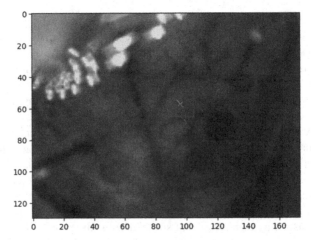

Fig. 4. Example of window trajectory.

2.3 Metrics for Assessing the Similarity of Contours and Images

In order to infer which window of the next frame is closer to the "reference" window, it is necessary to be able to effectively evaluate how similar two images are to each other. This evaluation can be done using existing metrics. Let us consider the metrics used in the present paper.

IoU Metric

Intersection over Union (IoU) or Jaccard index is a metric originally intended for calculating the similarity of any sets, proposed by Paul Jaccard. This metric is based on operations with sets. Note that images can also be represented as sets, namely sets of pixels. The values of the metric are represented between 0 and 1 and 0 refers to the absence of common elements and 1 refers to a complete match. The IoU formula is as follows:

$$\text{IoU} = \frac{\text{target} \cap \text{prediction}}{\text{target} \cup \text{prediction}} \tag{1}$$

Usually in the field of image processing, this metric is used in detection and segmentation tasks [15]. It is difficult to apply this metric directly to our images because the pixels in the image have quite a large range of values (from 0 to 255), and even the elements that are close in value will be perceived as different. To avoid this, one needs to ignore small variations that are caused by recording noise. Thus, it is necessary to reduce the number of classes of different elements (pixel brightness values). To do this, the values will be separated into groups, as is done when constructing histograms. Or one can binarize the image according to different methods, distributing the pixels of the image into two groups. This will allow selecting a set of pixels belonging to one or another structure. If the number of such structures is small, taking into account that the frames in the sequence do not differ much from each other, then with the help of Jaccard index it is possible to estimate their structural features. However, such a metric will not work correctly in case of sharp changes in brightness. Relative simplicity of calculation can also be attributed to the advantages of such a metric.

SSIM

SSIM (Structure similarity index metric) is a metric for evaluating the similarity of one image with respect to another image [16, 17]. This metric shows how similar two images are to each other. The values of the metric vary between 0 and 1, where 1 reflects the absolute identity of the images with respect to the metric and 0 reflects a complete mismatch. SSIM compares images based on several metrics: brightness, contrast, structure:

$$\text{SSIM}(X, Y) = \frac{(2 * \mu_X \mu_Y + C_1) * (2 * \sigma_{XY} + C_2)}{(\mu_X^2 + \mu_Y^2 + C_1) * (\sigma_X^2 + \sigma_Y^2 + C_2)}, \tag{2}$$

where X, Y are matrices (set of pixel brightness values of two windows) of equal size $N*N$; μ_X and μ_Y are average values of matrices X, Y, respectively. σ_X^2 and σ_Y^2 are the variance of the values of these matrices. σ_{XY} is the covariance of X and Y; C1, C2 are constants close to zero, helping to avoid division by zero.

To get a high value of the SSIM metric, the images must be similar in brightness, i.e. in the average of the pixel brightnesses. It is also important that the images should have a similar pattern (possibly with different brightness). In other words, the pattern that is present in the images should match. It is the combination of luminance, contrast, and an estimate of the structural component of the two images, which is achieved by calculating the covariance matrix, that makes this metric stand out among the others in the context of the current task. The metric allows the small shifts and changes in brightness that inevitably appear during the experiment to not be heavily penalized. The covariance matrix will allow assessing how related the pixels in the image are to each other. The latter means evaluation of the similarity of some pattern between two images. The disadvantage of this metric is that it is more difficult to calculate than the other metrics described above.

In our task, the SSIM metric will be used. This metric is well suited for evaluating successive images that are not very different.

3   Results

Let us consider two ways of applying the proposed algorithm to our image set. The first method is as follows. On each frame, the windows "nearest" to the initial windows are found according to the SSIM metric. The center pixel of the initial window is replaced with the center pixel of the found window, thus filling the entire frame except for a narrow strip along the border with a width of 3 pixels (dark green perimeter strip in Fig. 5a). Going through the whole frame, a new record is formed. The result of this method is shown in Fig. 6a.

In the second method, the closest windows are also found first, but when overlapping, not only the center pixels are considered, but also the pixels of the whole matrix. In case the pixels of separate windows are overlapped, the average value of all overlapped pixels is calculated. Obviously, for a step of one pixel frequent overlapping of windows occurs

(Fig. 5a). In this case, the whole middle part of the frame is yellow. As the window motion step increases, the number of overlapping window elements decreases. This can be noted in Figs. 5a–5d. Frames recovered at different window movement steps are shown in Figs. 6a–6d.

Our task is actually to leave the original image static in its structure, allowing only changes in color shades and brightness. In the experiment on mice, this will correspond to the processes of increasing and decreasing blood supply to separate parts of the brain.

Let us estimate how much the frame elements have shifted. To do this, let us take a random frame from the dataset. Let us choose a region on the frame, which undergoes changes under the action of refraction. Let us get three images of this region: initial, restored and unrestored. The binarization operation is applied to each of them using the cv2.adaptiveThreshold(frame, 255, cv2.ADAPTIVE_THRESH_MEAN_C, \ cv2.THRESH_BINARY, 11, 2) method.

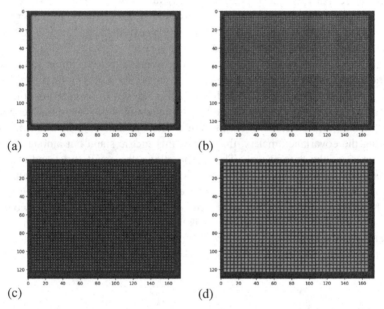

Fig. 5. Diagram showing overlapping windows with different steps: a) 1 pixel spacing between windows, b) 2 pixel spacing between windows, c) 3 pixel spacing between windows, d) 4 pixel spacing between windows. The closer the color is to yellow, the greater the number of overlaps; the closer the color to dark green, the fewer the number of overlaps. (Color figure online)

Black and white images are obtained that can be evaluated by the IoU metric. The comparison results are summarized in Table 1.

4   Discussion

The results presented in Table 1 show that without averaging the result is significantly worse than with averaging. In our experiment, we managed to improve image stabilization by almost 10%. Note that the result obtained by the IoU metric between the original (initial) and unrestored images is 0.7055.

Figure 7 shows the estimated region. Figure 8 shows the reconstructed and binarized regions.

Let us calculate the computational complexity of the algorithm. The experiment is conducted on an Intel Core i5 10300h processor, with 4 physical and 8 logical cores and 16 GB of RAM. All computations presented in Table 2 are performed in parallel in 8 threads. The Python 3 language library Joblib is used.

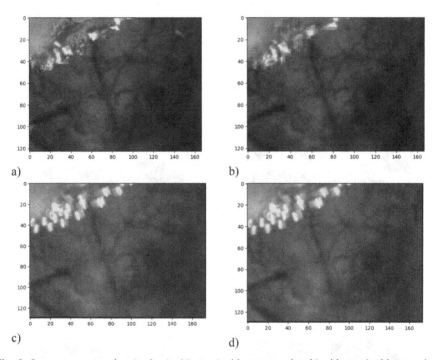

Fig. 6. Image reconstruction result: a) with step 1 without averaging, b) with step 1 with averaging, c) with step 2 with averaging, d) with step 3 with averaging.

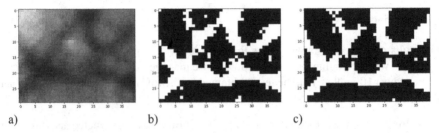

a)   b)   c)

Fig. 7. Estimated image sub-area. a) initial image, b) initial image binarized, c) same sub-area part, current image, binarized.

Table 1. Estimation of image differences at different window movement steps.

Step, px	1 px, only px	1 px	2 px	3 px	4 px	5 px	6 px	7 px
IoU	0.3613	0.7726	0.7718	0.7554	0.7636	0.7480	0.7256	0.7095

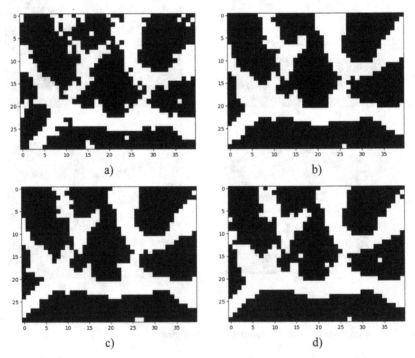

a)   b)

c)   d)

Fig. 8. Reconstructed binarized region: a) step 1 without averaging, b) step 1 with averaging, c) step 2 with averaging, d) step 3 with averaging.

Table 2. Calculation costs for different window movement steps.

Step, px	1 px, only px	1 px	2 px	3 px	4 px	5 px	6 px	7 px
time, hours	9	9	2.1	0.67	0.57	0.35	0.15	0.11
steps on x	123	123	62	41	31	25	21	18
steps on y	167	167	83	55	41	33	27	23
total steps	20541	20541	5146	2255	1271	825	567	414
time, hours	9	9	2.1	0.67	0.57	0.35	0.15	0.11

5 Conclusion

An algorithm for video sequence image restoration in the presence of refractive distortions is proposed. The algorithm is based on tracking of individual zones in the video sequence and subsequent calculation of the "correct" pixel position. SSIM is chosen as the metric evaluating the tracking.

Different values of window movement steps during tracking are considered. It is concluded that the best result is achieved at the minimum step equal to one pixel, taking into account overlapping of windows on each other. In this case, the improvement in the accuracy of restoring the initial frame from the current frame amounted to almost 10%.

Acknowledgment. This paper has been supported by the Kazan Federal University Strategic Academic Leadership Program.

References

1. Shumkova, V., Sitdikova, V., Rechapov, I., Leukhin, A., Minlebaev, M.: Effects of urethane and isoflurane on the sensory evoked response and local blood flow in the early postnatal rat somatosensory cortex. Sci. Rep. **11**, 9567 (2021)
2. Tuliabaeva, D., Tumakov, D, Elshin, L.: On the recognition of weakly blurred, highly contrasting objects by neural networks. In: Proceedings SPIE 13065, Third International Conference on Optics, Computer Applications, and Materials Science (CMSD-III 2023), p. 1306507 (2024)
3. Suchkov, D., Shumkova, V., Sitdikova, V., Minlebaev M.: Simple and efficient 3D-printed superfusion chamber for electrophysiological and neuroimaging recordings in vivo. eNeuro **9**(5) (2022)
4. Jung, Y.-H., Kim, G., Yoo, W.S.: Off-site distortion and color compensation of underwater archaeological images photographed in the very turbid yellow sea. J. Cons. Sci. **38**(1), 14–32 (2022)
5. Haitao, L., et al.: 3D point cloud capture method for underwater structures in turbid environment. Meas. Sci. Technol. **32**(2), 025106 (2021)
6. Thapa, S., Li, N., Ye, J.: Learning to remove refractive distortions from underwater images. In: Proceedings of the IEEE/CVF International Conference on Computer Vision (ICCV), pp. 5007–5016 (2021)

7. Li, T., Yang, Q., Rong, S., Chen, L., He, B.: Distorted underwater image reconstruction for an autonomous underwater vehicle based on a self-attention generative adversarial network. Appl. Opt. **59**(32), 10049–10060 (2020)

8. Li, N., Thapa, S., Whyte, C., Reed, A. W., Jayasuriya, S., Ye, J.: Unsupervised non-rigid image distortion removal via grid deformation. In: Proceedings of the IEEE/CVF International Conference on Computer Vision (ICCV), pp. 2522–2532 (2021)

9. Sun, H., Du, H., Li, M., Sun, H., Zhang, X.: Underwater image matching with efficient refractive-geometry estimation for measurement in glass-flume experiments. Measurement **152**, 107391 (2020)

10. Dutta, A., Mondal, A., Dey, N., et al.: Vision tracking: a survey of the state-of-the-art. SN Comput. Sci. **1**(1), 57 (2020)

11. Yedjour, H.: Optical flow based on Lucas-Kanade method for motion estimation. Artif. Intell. Renew. Towards Energy Transit. **4**, 937–945 (2020)

12. Zhong, L., Meng, L., Hou, W., Huang, L.: An improved visual odometer based on Lucas-Kanade optical flow and ORB feature. IEEE Access **11**, 47179–47186 (2023)

13. Du, K., Bobkov, A.: An overview of object detection and tracking algorithms. Eng. Proc. **33**(1), 22 (2023)

14. Luo, W., Xing, J., Milan, A., Zhang, X., Liu, W., Kim, T.-K.: Multiple object tracking: a literature review. Artif. Intell. **293**, 103448 (2021)

15. Eelbode, T., et al.: Optimization for medical image segmentation: theory and practice when evaluating with dice score or jaccard index. IEEE Trans. Med. Imaging **39**(11), 3679–3690 (2020)

16. Nilsson, J., Akenine-Möller, T.: Understanding SSIM. arXiv preprint arXiv 2006.13846 (2020)

17. Starovoytov, V., Eldarova, E., Iskakov, K.: Comparative analysis of the SSIM index and the pearson coefficient as a criterion for image similarity. Eurasian J. Math. Comput. Appl. **8**(1), 76–90 (2020)

Quantum Fourier Transform in Image Processing

D. T. Mukhamedieva[1]($\boxtimes$) (ID), R. A. Sobirov[1] (ID), N. M. Turgunova[1] (ID), and B. N. Samijonov[2] (ID)

[1] Tashkent Institute of Irrigation and Agricultural Mechanization Engineers National Research University, 39, Kari Niyaziy Street, Tashkent, Uzbekistan 100000
dilnoz134@rambler.ru

[2] Sejong University, 209, Neungdong-ro, Gwangjin-gu, Seoul, South Korea

Abstract. This paper presents an approach to apply quantum Fourier transform (QFT) to image processing using quantum computing. The use of quantum computing for image analysis and processing is becoming increasingly relevant in modern science and technology. A quantum QFT circuit is presented, implemented using the Qiskit framework, which is a tool for programming quantum computers. The paper presents the basic steps of QFT and their application to a state vector representing the pixel intensities of an image. The influence of quantum transformation on the image structure is studied and the results are presented in the form of graphs and visualizations. In addition, we have introduced QFT quantum circuit inference capabilities for a more visual representation of the algorithm. The results highlight the potential of quantum computing in the field of image processing and open new prospects for the use of quantum technologies in the field of computer vision.

Keywords: Quantum Computing · Image Processing · Qiskit · Qubits · Quantum Circuit Simulation · Image Conversion · Quantum Circuit · Visualization of Results · Fourier Transform

1 Introduction

With the development of quantum technologies, new opportunities appear for solving computational problems, including in the field of image processing. Traditional image processing methods often face limitations in speed and efficiency, especially when dealing with large volumes of data. In this context, the application of quantum computing for image processing represents a promising research direction. Quantum algorithms, such as the Quantum Fourier Transform (QFT), can provide more efficient data processing by using the principles of quantum mechanics. In this paper, we propose research on the application of QFT to images using quantum computing, which may lead to more efficient and faster image processing methods. This approach is relevant in light of the constant development of quantum technologies and their potential impact on the field of computer vision and image analysis [1].

A. Gibadullin (Ed.): ITIDMS 2023, CCIS 2112, pp. 143–151, 2024.
https://doi.org/10.1007/978-3-031-60318-1_12

With the development of quantum computing and the expansion of its scope, new opportunities in the field of data processing arise. One exciting area of research is the application of quantum methods to image processing. Traditional methods, although effective, often face limitations, especially when working with large amounts of information. Quantum computing represents a promising tool for creating new, more efficient methods of image processing. In particular, QFT has attracted the attention of researchers for its ability to efficiently process data in a quantum environment [2].

The purpose of this work is to review and analyze the application of QFT to images using quantum computing. We explore the key steps of quantum transformation in the context of image processing and consider the impact of this method on the structure of images. We also present a new aspect in the form of the output of QFT circuit for a clear demonstration of the algorithm [3].

This work aims to expand understanding of the capabilities of quantum computing in the field of image processing and contribute to the development of new data analysis methods using quantum technologies. The benefits of quantum computing, such as parallelism and superposition, promise to speed up the solution of certain problems, such as factoring large numbers or simulating complex molecular systems. This could have huge implications for fields ranging from cryptography to the development of new materials and drugs. However, for now, quantum computing is still in its infancy, and there are a number of technical and algorithmic hurdles that need to be overcome before it can become widely available. Despite this, the potential of quantum computing to revolutionize our ability to predict physical phenomena is exciting [4, 5].

2 Materials and Methods

The basic idea of quantum computing is to use quantum bits, or qubits, instead of classical bits. Unlike classical bits, which can be in either a 0 or 1 state, qubits can be in a superposition state, which means they can be both 0 and 1 at the same time. This property of superposition allows qubits to process information in parallel, which makes quantum calculations in some cases are much more efficient than classical ones. Additionally, qubits can be linked to each other in a phenomenon known as quantum entanglement, allowing them to jointly encode and process information. The use of qubits and their unique properties opens the door to the creation of new algorithms that can solve problems more efficiently than classical algorithms [6].

One of the main mysteries of quantum computing is its fragility and complexity. While quantum computers promise significant benefits in solving certain problems, they also face several technical and physical challenges. One such problem is decoherence, or the loss of quantum superposition due to environmental influences. This may occur due to unpredictable fluctuations in the surrounding electromagnetic field or thermal fluctuations. Controlling these effects is a complex task that requires the development of high-precision methods for isolating and stabilizing quantum systems. Another problem is errors in quantum computing due to non-ideal quantum elements and operations. For example, noise can occur in quantum gates, and interaction errors between qubits can occur in quantum circuits. Work is underway to improve error correction algorithms and develop more accurate quantum devices, but this still remains a challenge [7].

Thus, although quantum computing holds much promise, its successful implementation requires overcoming many technical and physical obstacles associated with its fragility and complexity. Converting quantum information into a format compatible with classical computers represents a significant obstacle to the practical use of quantum computing. This process, called dequantization, requires the development of specialized methods and algorithms to read and interpret the results of quantum calculations by classical devices. Despite the significant difficulties associated with dequantization, it is important to note that classical computers are also improving towards simulating quantum processes. New algorithmic strategies and optimizations allow classical computers to more efficiently simulate some aspects of quantum systems, which in certain cases can compete with the advantages provided by quantum computing [8].

This fact emphasizes the importance of further research and development of both quantum and classical computing methods. Both fields can complement each other, because some problems can be effectively solved using both quantum and classical approaches. Integrating classical and quantum methodologies represents a potentially powerful approach for improving computation and solving complex problems. This approach, known as hybrid computing, leverages the strengths of both classical and quantum computing to solve problems more efficiently than is possible with either method alone. For example, classical computers can be used to process and pre-train data, and then quantum computers can be used to perform complex quantum algorithms, analysis or optimization. The results can then be processed and interpreted using classical methods. This approach not only benefits from the benefits of both types of computation, but can also mitigate some of the limitations faced by both classical and quantum systems. As a result of integration, we can achieve higher efficiency and accuracy in solving complex problems, from cryptography to artificial intelligence optimization [9].

To conduct the study, a digital image of interest for analysis was selected. The image can be either monochrome or color to view the effect of quantum transformation on different types of data. The image is converted into a format suitable for processing, such as black and white. The image size can also be reduced to the nearest lesser power of two to facilitate the application of QFT [10, 11].

Each pixel in the image is converted to intensity and a state vector is generated. This vector is prepared for use in a quantum circuit. A quantum circuit is implemented to apply QFT to the image state vector. The Qiskit library for the Python programming language is used for this. Each element of the state vector represents the probability amplitude on the corresponding qubit [12].

The impact of QFT on image structure is studied. State vectors before and after transformation, as well as the resulting images, are analyzed. Visualization of results is used for a clearer understanding of the process. To visually represent the QFT algorithm in a quantum circuit, the Qiskit library is used. A quantum circuit is derived taking into account the application of QFT to the input data [13].

The experiment is carried out with various variants of images and QFT parameters to identify the features and influence of quantum transformation on the structure of the input data. To implement a quantum circuit, the program uses the Qiskit library, which provides the ability to work with quantum circuits in the Python programming language. The quantum circuit includes the following steps [14]:

Quantum bits are created that will be used to represent the input image state vector. The number of qubits is equal to the nearest lesser power of two to the image size (for example, if the image size is 64×64, then 6 qubits are used) [15, 16].

The quantum circuit describing the QFT is represented by the following mathematical formula [17]:

For n quantum bits (qubits), the state of the input vector $|x\rangle$ is given as [18].

$$|x\rangle = \frac{1}{\sqrt{2^n}} \sum_{k=0}^{2^n-1} e^{\frac{2\pi i \cdot kx}{2^n}} |k\rangle \tag{1}$$

where $|k\rangle$ is the binary representation of the number k.

The QFT is applied to this state and its transformation matrix QFT_n is defined as follows [19]:

$$QFT_n = \frac{1}{\sqrt{2^n}} \begin{bmatrix} 1 & 1 & 1 & \cdots & 1 \\ 1 & e^{\frac{2\pi i}{2^n}} & e^{\frac{2\pi i \cdot 2}{2^n}} & \cdots & e^{\frac{2\pi i \cdot (2^n-1)}{2^n}} \\ 1 & e^{\frac{2\pi i \cdot 2}{2^n}} & e^{\frac{2\pi i \cdot 4}{2^n}} & \cdots & e^{\frac{2\pi i \cdot 2(2^n-1)}{2^n}} \\ \vdots & \vdots & \vdots & \ddots & \vdots \\ 1 & e^{\frac{2\pi i \cdot (2^n-1)}{2^n}} & e^{\frac{2\pi i \cdot 2(2^n-1)}{2^n}} & \cdots & e^{\frac{2\pi i \cdot (2^n-1)^2}{2^n}} \end{bmatrix} \tag{2}$$

where each element of the matrix $QFT_n[j, k]$ is calculated by the formula:

$$QFT_n[j, k] = \frac{1}{\sqrt{2^n}} e^{\frac{2\pi i \cdot jk}{2^n}} \tag{3}$$

where j and k take values from 0 to $2^n - 1$.

3 Results

Fourier transform of images is widely used in digital image and video processing due to its efficiency and power in signal analysis and processing. The Fourier transform of an image transforms an image from the spatial domain to the frequency domain. This means that it converts the image from a pixel representation to a frequency representation. Specifically, the Fourier transform of an image allows the image to be decomposed into a set of sine (or cosine) functions of different frequencies. These frequencies represent different details and structures in an image.

After the Fourier transform is performed, the image is represented in a two-dimensional frequency space, with low frequencies at the center and high frequencies at the periphery. Thus, a frequency domain image allows you to analyze the frequency components it contains, which can be useful for tasks such as noise filtering, sharpening, edge detection, etc. Visualizing the Fourier transform of an image allows you to see the contribution of different frequencies to the image, which can help in understanding its structure and characteristics.

This code creates a quantum circuit that applies a quantum Fourier transform to an image. All the pixels in the image are represented as quantum bits and the Fourier transform is then applied.

The program begins by loading a grayscale image from a file. We use the OpenCV (cv2) library for this purpose.

The original image is plotted in the first plot using Matplotlib. This allows us to visualize what the image looks like before applying the Fourier transform.

Determining the number of bits that are needed to represent each pixel in an image in binary form. This is necessary to determine the size of the quantum circuit.

Creating a quantum circuit for Fourier transform using the Qiskit library. In this circuit, we apply QFT. To do this, control rotations (cr) and Hadamar rotations (H) are used.

Drawing a quantum circuit using the circuit_drawer function from the Qiskit library. We use the *output = 'mpl'* parameter to get color graphical output.

Simulation of a quantum circuit. We use the Qiskit simulator to execute the quantum circuit. In this case, we use the state vector simulator, which builds the exact state of the quantum system.

Visualization of the results: We obtain the simulation results in the form of the number of dimensions for each possible state of the quantum bits. We then use the plot histogram function from the Qiskit library to plot a histogram of these results.

Thus, the program loads an image, applies a quantum Fourier transform to it using a quantum circuit, simulates the results and visualizes both the circuit itself and the results, and also displays the image before and after the Fourier transform (Fig. 1 and 2).

The QFT program has been developed for an image represented as a vector of pixel intensities. The quantum circuit presented in this program performs the Fourier transform on quantum qubits. The Fourier transform is a mathematical transformation that has applications in various fields, including classical and quantum information science. A quantum circuit uses quantum bits, which are the quantum analogues of classical bits. Qubits can be in a linear combination of states $|0\rangle|0\rangle$ and $|1\rangle|1\rangle$ due to the phenomenon of quantum interference [19, 20].

The Fourier transform in this context is performed on quantum bits. This transform is the quantum analogue of the classical Fourier transform, which is applied to a sequence of values.

Fig. 1. Quantum Fourier transform circuit

The circuit uses quantum gates such as Hadamard gates (H), controlled phase gates R_ϕ, and controlled phase gates (C).

The initial state of the quantum system is initialized with an image, and then a quantum transformation is performed. The qubits are then measured to obtain classical information. The results of quantum transformation are visualized using graphs, allowing you to see how the state vector and image change after the transformation. Such a quantum circuit can be used to study quantum transformations in images and in the context of quantum data processing algorithms.

This program performs a quantum Fourier transform (QFT) on an image represented as a vector of pixel intensities. Let's look at the results of each stage of the program:

The original grayscale image is displayed.

The pre-QFT state vector shows the pixel intensity values represented as the state vector before the quantum transformation is applied.

State Vector after QFT Displays the state vector after applying the quantum transformation. This vector shows how the state amplitudes changed after applying QFT.

The transformed image after QFT is a rendering of the transformed image after quantum transformation. The image is formed based on the amplitudes of the states of the quantum bit.

Constructing an amplitude histogram for visual analysis of the distribution of amplitudes of states after quantum transformation.

It is important to note that the results of the program may depend on the choice of the number of quantum bits and the image itself. Also, the Fourier transform can highlight certain patterns in an image.

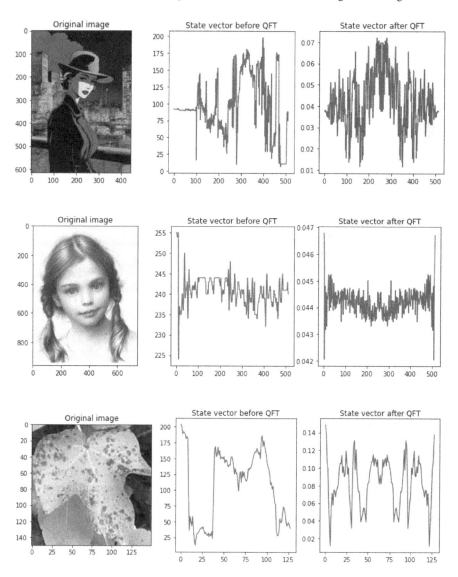

Fig. 2. Quantum Fourier transform.

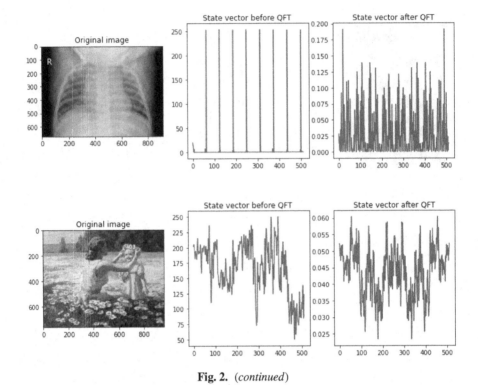

Fig. 2. (*continued*)

4 Conclusion

In this work, the application of QFT in the context of image processing was analyzed. Experimental results show that quantum transformation can affect the structure of images, leading to changes in pixel amplitudes. The efficiency of quantum conversion was assessed using images using different numbers of quantum bits. Increasing the number of bits resulted in higher transformation granularity, but required more computational resources. The amplitude histogram after QFT can serve as an indicator of important image characteristics. However, it must be taken into account that the results can greatly depend on the image itself and the parameters of the quantum circuit. It also highlighted areas of application where quantum image processing techniques could be most useful, such as highlighting singular points and patterns. However, it should be noted that quantum image processing methods have their limitations, and the performance of such approaches can be improved with further research and optimization.

These results highlight the promise of using quantum approaches in image processing, providing new opportunities for analyzing and modifying visual data. Further research in this area will help optimize the parameters of quantum circuits and expand the scope of their application in practical image processing problems.

References

1. Yao, X., et al.: Quantum image processing and its application to edge detection: theory and experiment. Phys. Rev. X **7**, 031041 (2017). https://doi.org/10.1103/physrevx.7.031041
2. Sysoev, S.: Introduction to Quantum Computing. In: Quantum Algorithms: Textbook. Allowance, St. Petersburg, pp. 140–144 (2019)
3. Park, J.E., Quanz, B., Wood, S., Higgins, H., Harishankar, R.: Practical application improvement to Quantum SVM: theory to practice. Cornell University (2020)
4. Rieffel, E., Polak, W.: Quantum computing: a gentle introduction. Choice Rev. Online **49**, 49–0911 (2011). https://doi.org/10.5860/choice.49-0911
5. Kopczyk, D.: Quantum machine learning for data scientists. Cornell University (2018)
6. Weber, J.R., et al.: Quantum computing with defects. Proc. Natl. Acad. Sci. U.S.A. **107**, 8513–8518 (2010). https://doi.org/10.1073/pnas.1003052107
7. Cong, I., Choi, S., Lukin, M.D.: Quantum convolutional neural networks. Nat. Phys. **15**, 1273–1278 (2019). https://doi.org/10.1038/s41567-019-0648-8
8. Kaye, P., Laflamme, R., Mosca, M.: An introduction to quantum computing (2006). https://doi.org/10.1093/oso/9780198570004.001.0001
9. Oh, S., Choi, J.W., Kim, J.: A tutorial on quantum convolutional neural networks (QCNN). In 2020 International Conference on Information and Communication Technology Convergence (ICTC), pp. 236–239 (2020). https://doi.org/10.1109/ictc49870.2020.9289439
10. Fitzsimons, J.F.: Private quantum computation: an introduction to blind quantum computing and related protocols. Npj Quant. Inf. **3**, 23 (2017). https://doi.org/10.1038/s41534-017-0025-3
11. Deng, L.: The MNIST database of handwritten digit images for machine learning research [best of the web]. IEEE Signal Process. Mag. **29**, 141–142 (2012). https://doi.org/10.1109/msp.2012.2211477
12. Harper, R., Flammia, S.T.: Fault-Tolerant logical gates in the IBM quantum experience. Phys. Rev. Lett. **122**, 080504 (2019). https://doi.org/10.1103/physrevlett.122.080504
13. Steffen, M., DiVincenzo, D.P., Chow, J.M., Theis, T., Ketchen, M.B.: Quantum computing: an IBM perspective. IBM J. Res. Dev. **55**, 13:1-13:11 (2011). https://doi.org/10.1147/jrd.2011.2165678
14. Han, X., Rasul, K., Vollgraf, R.: Fashion-MNIST: a novel image dataset for benchmarking machine learning algorithms. Cornell University (2017)
15. Muhamediyeva, D.: Fuzzy logical model for assessing soil salinity. IOP Conf. Ser. Earth Environ. Sci. **1206**, 012019 (2023). https://doi.org/10.1088/1755-1315/1206/1/012019
16. Recht, B., Roelofs, R., Schmidt, L., Shankar, V.: Do CIFAR-10 classifiers generalize to CIFAR-10? Cornell University (2018)
17. Muhamediyeva, D.: Application of artificial intelligence technologies to assess water salinity. IOP Conf. Ser. Earth Environ. Sci. **1206**, 012020 (2023). https://doi.org/10.1088/1755-1315/1206/1/012020
18. He, K., Zhang, X., Ren, S., Sun, J.: Deep residual learning for image recognition. 2016 IEEE Conference on Computer Vision and Pattern Recognition (CVPR), pp. 770–778 (2016). https://doi.org/10.1109/cvpr.2016.90
19. Muhamediyeva, D.T., Niyozmatova, N.A.: Monitoring of biodiversity of water communities. In: E3S Web of Conferences, vol. 411, p. 02042 (2023)
20. Howard, J., Gugger, S.: FastAi: a layered API for deep learning. Information **11**, 108 (2020). https://doi.org/10.3390/info11020108

Choosing an Information Protection Mechanism Based on the Discrete Programming Method

Alexandr Kanareykin(✉) 📷

Sergo Ordzhonikidze Russian State University for Geological Prospecting, Miklouho-Maclay
Street 23, 117997 Moscow, Russia
kanareykins@mail.ru

Abstract. The article formulates and solves the problem of choosing a set of
countermeasures to protect the software of a corporate information network. The
problem is formalized by analogy with the open model of the assignment problem
in the integer formulation. An example of a numerical implementation of the problem of choosing the optimal software protection mechanism based on the decay
vector method is considered. The implementation of the algorithm of the method
is written in the Java language. The resulting solution is a set of countermeasures
recommended to neutralize security threats to the software.

Keywords: Information · Hardware and Software · Decay Vector Method ·
Information Protection Mechanism · Integer Optimization · Java

1 Introduction

The use of programming systems in various industries in a competitive environment
becomes profitable for both the designer [1] and the customer. From an economic point
of view, the costs of purchasing or developing and maintaining the system are compen-
sated by the speed of project launch, a reduction in the number of employees involved,
an increase in quality (at least, errors caused by human factors are eliminated) and
compliance of documentation with current norms, rules and standards [2].

It should also be noted that modern systems, as a rule, meet the highest level of
complexity, since automation of a separate part of the design process does not lead to
significant improvement of the process as a whole, and sometimes even creates additional
difficulties, for example, related to the development of specific calculation programs [3].

Due to the constant increase in the global load on resources and the environment, as
well as the continuous development of the process of marketization of electric energy,
users place increasingly high demands on the quality of work and reliability [4–7].

Information security in the production process plays an important role in the organization. Improving the security quality of an information system can only be achieved
through a set of data protection measures. The result of the work of the information
system should be a clear understanding of production, which allows making managerial
decisions, as well as ensuring the security of the transmitted information [8–10].

© The Author(s), under exclusive license to Springer Nature Switzerland AG 2024
A. Gibadullin (Ed.): ITIDMS 2023, CCIS 2112, pp. 152–163, 2024.
https://doi.org/10.1007/978-3-031-60318-1_13

In the modern information society, where digital technologies penetrate into all spheres of human activity, the issues of human interaction with machines and computers are becoming more relevant and complex.

Since a priori there is no data on the probability of threats and damages from them (lack of statistical data), an assessment of these indicators by level values based on expert assessment should be carried out. Since expert assessments are qualitative and subjective in real situations, it becomes necessary to use the apparatus of odd sets to assess the damage from the implementation of a specific threat through existing constraints, and therefore the risk of information security.

It is known that in traditional applied mathematics, a set is understood as a set of elements having some common property. For any element, only two possibilities are considered: either this element belongs to this set, or it does not belong. Thus, the description of a set in the usual sense should contain a clear criterion that allows one to judge whether or not any element belongs to a given set.

However, when trying to mathematically describe complex systems operating in conditions of uncertainty, the language of ordinary sets turns out to be insufficiently flexible. The available information about the system can often be formulated only in the language of fuzzy concepts that cannot be mathematically formalized using ordinary sets.

The mechanism for obtaining risk assessments based on fuzzy logic makes it possible to replace approximate tabular methods of rough risk assessment with a modern mathematical method adequate to the problem under consideration. The knowledge base, when assessing risks based on fuzzy logic, consists of rules reflecting the logic of the relationship between input values and risk. In general, this is a logic reflecting real relationships that can be formalized using production rules.

The mechanism of fuzzy logic requires the formation of estimates of key parameters and their representation in the form of fuzzy variables. At the same time, it is necessary to take into account the variety of sources of information and the quality of the information itself. In general, this is a rather difficult task, but in each specific case, sufficiently convincing solutions can be found and formally justified.

The essence of any approach to risk management is to make adequate decisions on their processing and analysis of related factors. Risk factors are the seven main parameters that we use when evaluating: asset, damage, threat, vulnerability, control mechanism, average annual loss and return on investment.

Thus, based on the results of the assessment, it is possible to obtain a description of risks exceeding the acceptable level and a real idea of their magnitude. The latter is determined by the size of the average annual losses. Next, it is necessary to make a decision on risk management, i.e. to answer questions about the choice of risk management options, control mechanisms for minimizing them and the degree of effectiveness.

The increase in the number of attacks aimed at information flows leads to the fact that information used to ensure the operability of various phases of the life cycle of both enterprises and people's lives must be protected due to the presence of confidential information in it. The purpose of this work is to analyze and develop an approach to assessing the survivability of the system, which means the ability of the system to fulfill its functional purpose without deterioration of quality indicators in the conditions of an attack on the system, as well as recommendations for ensuring survivability.

2 Materials and Methods

The purpose of this article is to describe an approach to choosing a mechanism for protecting information systems software based on solving a discrete programming problem. The procedure for searching for a plan to neutralize the identified vulnerabilities of information system software based on the selection and application of information security mechanisms available to the information security administrator is presented as a combinatorial integer optimization problem in a binary formulation.

3 Results

3.1 Setting the Task

The modern concept of integrated information protection is based on the following basic principles: consistency; complexity; continuity of protection; reasonable sufficiency; flexibility of management and application; openness of algorithms and protection mechanisms; ease of use of protective measures and tools.

Situational information security risk management, as is known, is a purposeful process of developing and implementing control actions corresponding to the state of the object and the surrounding environment and aimed at bringing the information protection mechanism to an optimal state.

A detailed analysis of open publications covering various aspects of the problem of protecting information systems software and the experience of detecting and eliminating the consequences of network attacks has shown that the cost of protection mechanisms offered by developers is often commensurate with the cost of protected software products. On the other hand, a decrease in the level of software security due to insufficient financing of the policy of upgrading the means of protecting this critical resource can lead to the successful implementation of threats to information security and to a violation of the functionality of the entire information system. At the same time, the damage caused by cyber-attacks through software vulnerabilities can greatly exceed the cost of purchasing (developing or updating) security tools. This circumstance underlines the importance of a systematic approach to the problem of analyzing the security of software and to the issues of predictive assessment of information security risks.

The existing software protection mechanisms can be divided into two groups: universal and specialized.

These and some other universal software protection mechanisms based on the experience of ensuring information security requirements are reflected in the corporate security policy. All efforts to ensure the internal security of information systems are focused on creating reliable and convenient mechanisms for regulating the activities of all its legitimate users and service personnel in order to force them to unconditionally comply with the discipline of access to network resources of information systems established in the organization.

The use of specialized protection mechanisms is local in nature, since they are focused on reflecting specific threats to information security, taking into account possible defects (vulnerabilities and errors) of the application software. We will highlight several protection mechanisms that have been proven in practice and have the potential for further development and adaptation, taking into account the specifics of use.

One method of the mechanism for monitoring the integrity of executable programs is based on the analysis of their activity using the implementation of an auxiliary hybrid network. The analysis of the program behavior is based on the idea of profile identification, taking into account the statistics of program accesses to the operating system core based on the methods of the theory of fuzzy neural (hybrid) networks.

Another way to audit the security of computer programs is based on dynamic binary code analysis. Dynamic analysis consists in monitoring the program's actions when performing various security-related functions: installation, changing permissions, forwarding passwords, clearing memory, etc. The implementation of these protection mechanisms is aimed at identifying vulnerabilities in the binary code of the program and refers to preventive information security measures.

In order to weaken the effect of targeted network attacks on information and software, the author proposed a mechanism for dynamic redistribution of local databases between network nodes. However, for the practical implementation of this protection mechanism, it is necessary to justify the procedure for identifying the vector of a network attack and procedures for finding an optimal solution in real time.

In practice, situations of active interaction between means of attack and defense often develop according to a game scenario. In this regard, there are certain prospects for protection mechanisms that use obfuscation (obfuscation) methods to protect software. The beneficial effect of using such protection mechanisms is manifested, for example, in the fact that the program functions during code generation are randomly arranged in the created object file or random memory gaps are inserted between the local variables of the function on the stack (padding). In the program assembled in this way, it is difficult to exploit vulnerabilities related to incorrect memory operation. Each binary copy of the distributed program acquires the property of uniqueness, which prevents an attacker from creating a universal robot cracker of all copies of the program.

3.2 Description of the Algorithm

The problem of Boolean programming is generally considered an NP-complete problem, given that checking the admissibility of any solution requires simulation experiments, which may have a high numerical complexity, the use of accurate methods is practically impossible due to the high computational complexity of the problem.

Approximate methods can be used to solve such problems, for example, the decay vector method based on the motorization of a discrete space and the introduction of the concept of a neighborhood of a point in a discrete space. The method provides obtaining a local optimum in polynomial time. However, it is not always convenient to use this method directly for tasks with implicit constraints, taking into account the possible high computational complexity of implementing a simulation model.

The problem of Boolean programming is generally considered an NP-complete problem, given that checking the admissibility of any solution requires simulation experiments, which may have a high numerical complexity, the use of accurate methods is practically impossible due to the high computational complexity of the problem.

Approximate methods can be used to solve such problems, for example, the decay vector method based on the metrization of a discrete space and the introduction of the concept of a neighborhood of a point in a discrete space. The method provides obtaining a local optimum in polynomial time. However, it is not always convenient to use this method directly for tasks with implicit constraints, taking into account the possible high computational complexity of implementing a simulation model.

Let's first consider the classical model of the assignment problem.

The classic assignment task is a distributive task in which each job requires one and only one resource, and each resource can be used on one and only one job. In other words, in the classical version, it is assumed that resources are indivisible between jobs, and work is indivisible between resources. Let the following be given: m - the number of available resources; n - the number of works; A_i, $i = 1, 2,..., m$ - a single amount of resource; B_j, $j = 1, 2,..., m$ - a single amount of work; r_{ij} - quality characteristics (positive effect) due to the performance of work with the help B_j of a resource A_i.

The desired parameter x_{ij} - the indicator for assigning a resource to work A_i is equal to B_j:

$$x_{i,j} = \begin{cases} 0, & \text{if } i \text{ not assigned } j, \\ 1, & \text{if } i \text{ assigned } j. \end{cases} \tag{1}$$

The mathematical model of the assignment problem has the form:

$$f(X) = \sum_{i=1}^{m}\sum_{j=1}^{n}(r_{i,j}\cdot x_{i,j}) \rightarrow \max, \tag{2}$$

$$\begin{cases} \sum_{i=1}^{m} x_{i,j} = 1, \; j = 1, ..., n, \\ \sum_{j=1}^{n} x_{i,j} = 1, \; i = 1, ..., m, \end{cases} \tag{3}$$

$$x_{i,j} = \{0, 1\}; i = 1, ..., m; j = 1, ..., n.$$

In our case, the assignment task model will have the following features:

1. As a result of solving the problem, it is required to propose such a software protection plan that will allow to "close" previously identified vulnerabilities and achieve minimal average damage when carrying out malicious attacks with the least expenditure of computing resources.

Separate information protection mechanisms can be used for integrated resource protection, which is manifested in the possibility of simultaneous neutralization of several correlated vulnerabilities in software. Let's assume the additional condition that m ≤ N and it is permissible to neutralize two different vulnerabilities simultaneously using the same protection mechanism. Formally, taking into account this circumstance requires loosening the restrictions, in particular, instead of the second ratio in expression (2), it is proposed to write the inequality:

$$1 \le \sum_{j=1}^{n} x_{i,j} \le 2, \quad i = 1, ..., m.$$ (4)

2. The implementation of the resource protection plan consists in activating the m (m ≤ N) available protection mechanisms.

3. The assessment of the implemented information protection mechanism is characterized by the cost of computing resources, expressed in monetary terms, and the average prevented damage caused by the successful neutralization of a possible malicious attack on the software components of information systems.

Taking into account these comments, we define a generalized indicator of the optimal set of protection measures as follows:

$$F(X) = \frac{F_1(X)}{F_2(X)}$$ (5)

where $F_1(X)$ is the value of the total prevented damage in value terms; $F_2(X)$ is the value of the total cost of implementing the activated protection mechanism in value terms. Expression (5) is an indicator formed in accordance with the generalized criterion "efficiency/cost".

Let's consider an example of choosing a plan to neutralize security threats focused on exploiting software vulnerabilities. Let's assume that according to the results of the first stage of the internal audit of information security software for information system nodes, n vulnerabilities have been identified. Suppose that the security administrator has at his disposal several ways A_i, i = 1, 2,..., m to neutralize vulnerabilities B_j, j = 1, 2,...,. Each of the methods gives a certain final effect in the specific conditions of the implementation of existing threats and the rules of operation of the software. To assess the effectiveness of a set of protection measures, a matrix of private indicators is introduced

$$R = \{r_{i,j}\}, \quad i = 1, ..., m, \quad j = 1, ..., n \; ; \; 0 \le r_{i,j} \le 1$$ (6)

in which the rij element characterizes the relative effectiveness of protecting software components while neutralizing the vulnerability of Bj based on the Ai protection mechanism

In order to simplify the numerical solution of the optimization problem, we will carry out according to the criterion of maximum prevented damage, determined by the functional

$$F_1(X) = \sum_{i=1}^{m} \sum_{j=1}^{n} (r_{i,j} \cdot x_{i,j}) + \sum_{i=1}^{n} \sum_{\substack{j,k=1 \\ j \ne k}}^{n} (d_{j,k} \cdot v_{j,k} \cdot x_{i,j} \cdot x_{i,k}) \; \rightarrow \; \max,$$ (7)

where

$$d_{j,k} = \begin{cases} 0, & if \; B_j \; and \; B_k \; - \; independent \; ; \\ 1, & if \; B_j \; and \; B_k \; - \; addicted. \end{cases}$$ (8)

Here $v_{j,k}$ is an element reflecting a particular positive effect, which is associated with the simultaneous neutralization of vulnerabilities B_j and B_k.

For the finiteness of the resources involved in software protection, the system of constraints (2) of the task is supplemented by an inequality that takes into account the limitation on the allowed total costs C in the implementation of protection mechanisms:

$$F_2(X) = \sum_{i=1}^{m} [\sum_{j=1}^{n} (c_{i,j} \cdot x_{i,j}) - \sum_{\substack{j,k=1 \\ j \neq k}}^{n} (d_{j,k} \cdot c_{i,j} \cdot x_{i,j} \cdot x_{i,k})] \leq C. \tag{9}$$

A numerical solution to the problem of optimizing the software protection plan in Boolean variables is obtained on the basis of an author's application implementing the well-known decay vector method.

3.3 Description of the Algorithm

To solve the assignment problem, we will use the well-known method of the decline vector.

The idea of the decay vector method is that at each step the neighborhood of some point corresponding to an acceptable solution of the problem is considered and the transition is carried out by calculating the components of the decay vector to the point of the neighborhood that has the largest (smallest) value of the objective function. The process continues until the local maximum (minimum) of the task is obtained.

We present an algorithm of one of the modifications of the decay vector method to solve the problem of optimal choice of options for protection against security threats.

Step 0 (preliminary). We select the initial acceptable approximation. For example, we will use all acceptable means of protection, in this case $xj = 1$, $\forall j \in M$ (this solution will always be acceptable if the problem is posed correctly, i.e. if the constraints allow us to specify at least one acceptable solution). We set the value of the radius $r = 1$.

Step k (k $\geq$ 1)

1. We define for each point, which is permissible according to the above constraints, the neighborhood of the component of the decay vector σ.
2. We determine the point of the neighborhood for which the component of the decay vector is negative and is minimal (since the minimization problem is solved) among all points of the neighborhood, then we take this point as the next approximation _X(k) and proceed to step $k + 1$.
3. If there is no such point, then the algorithm is completed, and a local minimum point is obtained at step $k - 1$.

3.4 The Text of the Program in Java

The implementation of the algorithm for choosing an information protection mechanism based on the method of the decline vector is performed in Java, Java has a lot of advantages, due to which many developers choose it.

Simplicity is the first technical advantage of Java. It has clear syntactic rules and clear semantics. Rationality and brevity are very useful for processing code by machines with limited resources. A special Java Micro Edition platform has been created for embedded devices.

An Object-Oriented Approach. For 3 decades, it has proven its effectiveness. The bottom line is that the focus is on data (objects), interfaces and algorithms are secondary. In other words, we depend on the result when choosing tools and how to use them.

Safety. The most important criterion, considering the use of the language in network/distributed environments. The developers have done a lot of work to protect the Java platform. And it continues. It is extremely difficult to circumvent or crack the protection mechanisms. Example: Using digitally signed classes. Full rights are granted only with full confidence in the author of the class.

For example, symmetric encryption can be implemented in java. Symmetric cryptosystems (symmetric encryption) is a method of encryption in which the same cryptographic key is used for encryption and decryption. In asymmetric encryption, the cryptographic encryption and decryption keys are different; encryption is performed using a public key, and decryption using a private key.

Efficiency. Initially, it raised questions. New versions of Java dynamic compilers are not inferior to traditional ones from other platforms. A powerful increase in processing speed is provided by optimizing those code fragments that are executed more often. If necessary, certain optimization techniques are enabled or canceled by the JIT compiler.

Reliability is One of the Most Important Advantages. Java programs work stably in any environment. The compiler is able to detect errors even before code execution, that is, at early stages. Execution control allows you to prevent memory failures (for example, due to an inaccurate pointer). The pointers themselves can be used not everywhere, but only where necessary (for example, when working with linked lists).

Independence from Hardware and OS. It is only important to have an execution environment and a JVM. And computer architecture as a whole does not matter. The bytecode is easily interpreted on any machine. The approach has proven its worth largely due to dynamic compilation. The interface implemented in the system libraries also differs in cross-platform form.

Dynamism and Adaptability. This feature allows Java not to be used in an ever-changing environment. If necessary, you can add new objects and methods to the libraries. At the same time, you do not need to touch applications that use library data. It is very easy to track information about the structure of objects, their behavior, and the progress of the program.

Convenient and Efficient Network Capabilities. Applications are able to find the necessary objects on the network and open access to them. Moreover, it is as easy as if we are dealing with a local file system. There is a wide software library for data transmission over the most widespread protocols: FTP, HTTP, TCP/IP. The mechanism for calling remote methods is working.

Below is a Java program that implements the algorithm of the decline vector method in relation to solving the problem of choosing options for protection against security threats.

3.5   The Text of the Program in Java

```java
import java.util.Arrays;
public class GradientSearch {
private double[] threatProb;
private double[] threatDamage;
private double[] toolPrice;
private double[][] preventionProb;
private double minDamage;
private int stepCount;
private int[] optChoice;
private long time;
public void init(double[] threatProb,
double[] threatDamage,
double[] toolPrice,
double[][] preventionProb,
double minDamage) {
this.threatProb = threatProb;
this.threatDamage = threatDamage;
this.toolPrice = toolPrice;
this.preventionProb = preventionProb;
this.minDamage = minDamage;
}
public void run() {
long start = System.currentTimeMillis();
int[] optChoice = new int[toolPrice.length];
Arrays.fill(optChoice, 1);
step(optChoice, objectiveFunc(optChoice));
time = System.currentTimeMillis() - start;
}
private void step(int[] optChoice, double value) {
stepCount++;
int index = -1;
double minValue = value;
for (int i = 0; i < toolPrice.length; i++) {
if (optChoice[i] == 1) {
optChoice[i] = 0;
if (constraintFunc(optChoice) >= minDamage) {
double newMinValue = value - toolPrice[i];
if (newMinValue < minValue) {
minValue = newMinValue;
index = i;
}
```

```
        }
      optChoice[i] = 1;
      }
    }
    if (index != -1) {
      optChoice[index] = 0;
      step(optChoice, minValue);
    }
  }
  public int[] getOptChoice() {
    return optChoice;
  }
  public long getTime() {
    return time;
  }
  public int getStepCount() {
    return stepCount;
  }
  public double objectiveFunc(int[] choice) {
    double result = 0;
    for (int i = 0; i < toolPrice.length; i++) {
      result += toolPrice[i] choice[i];
    }
    return result;
  }
  public double constraintFunc(int[] choice) {
    double result = 0;
    for (int threat = 0; threat < threatProb.length; threat++) {
      double maxPreventionProb = 0;
      for (int tool = 0; tool < toolPrice.length; tool++) {
        double tmp = preventionProb[threat][tool]
        choice[tool];
        if (tmp > maxPreventionProb) {
          maxPreventionProb = tmp;
        }
      }
      result += threatDamage[threat]
      threatProb[threat]
      maxPreventionProb;
    }
    return result;
  }
}
```

4 Discussion

Taking into account the specifics of the implementation of the situational information security risk management strategy, the choice of the optimal set of countermeasures for protecting hardware and software information security is proposed, characterized in that the selection problem is presented as a combinatorial assignment problem of an open type, and the well-known decay vector method is used to determine its numerical solution.

The proposed approach to choosing the optimal set of countermeasures to neutralize threats to information systems software reduces the requirements for accuracy and completeness of the presentation of initial data and thereby increases the stability of the protection mechanism in real conditions.

The method of the decline vector is considered. This method belongs to the group of gradient methods and is designed to solve discrete optimization problems, it provides a local solution.

A general description of the method is given, and a Java program has been prepared that implements the algorithm of the decline vector method in relation to solving the problem of choosing protection options against threats to the security of an enterprise computer network.

The use of an accurate algorithm is unacceptable when solving a problem with a large number of considered protection options.

The price for high speed is the low accuracy of the solutions found by the algorithm of the decay vector, which can serve as an obstacle to its use.

5 Conclusion

The article considers a method for solving the problem of choosing information security tools, which can be applied within the framework of an optimization-simulation approach. In this approach, the problem of choosing security tools is formulated as a discrete programming problem with a linear quality indicator that determines the cost of the selected tools, and implicit limitations, the essence of which is to verify the admissibility of a possible solution using experiments on the implementation of an information security system simulation model.

The article proposes and tests a modification of the decay vector method, which requires m + 1 steps, where m is the number of unknown variables of the Boolean vector.

The modification is applicable to the tasks of choosing information security tools within the framework of an optimization-simulation approach, when at each step, simulation modeling is required to verify the feasibility of a possible solution.

References

1. Kanareykin, A.: Computer-aided design of heat supply systems for individual construction. In: E3S Web of Conferences, vol. 389, p. 06011 (2023)
2. Fugarov, D.D.: Methods for Revealing Hidden Failures of Automation System for Technological Processes in Oil and Gas Sector. J. Phys. Conf. Ser. **1118**, 012055 (2018)
3. Solomentsev, K.: Interference elimination in digital controllers of automation systems of oil and gas complex. J. Phys. Conf. Ser. **1015**, 032179 (2018)
4. Sukhinov, A.I.: Accounting method of filling cells for the solution of hydrodynamics problems with a complex geometry of the computational domain. Math. Models Comput. Simul. **12**(2), 232–245 (2020)
5. Chernyshev, Y.O.: Swarm-intelligence-based algorithm of connections permutation between pins. J. Theor. Appl. Inf. Tech. **80**(1), 466–473 (2015)
6. Fugarov, D.: Technological control of the granulometric composition of active materials of chemical current sources. Lect. Notes Netw. Syst. **510**, 1417–1423 (2023)
7. Purchina, O.: Securing an information system via the SSL protocol. Int. J. Saf. Secur. Eng. **12**(5), 563–568 (2022)
8. Agibalov, O.: On the issue of using intuitionistic fuzzy sets for describing the expediency of solving optimization problems by genetic algorithms with given parameters. In: E3S Web of Conferences, vol. 224, p. 01008 (2020)
9. Liu, S., Song, H.: Research on computer network security technology in the data age. Wirel. Internet Technol. **16**(21), 126–127 (2019)
10. Zhang, C.: Opportunities and challenges facing accounting theory in the era of "Internet +" big data. Account. Study **18**, 114–115 (2020)

Application of Machine Learning Methods for Annotating Boundaries of Meshes of Perineuronal Nets

Anton Egorchev[1]([✉]), Aidar Kashipov[1], Nikita Lipachev[1], Dmitry Derzhavin[1], Dmitry Chickrin[1], Albert Aganov[1], and Mikhail Paveliev[2]

[1] Kazan (Volga Region) Federal University, 18, Kremlin Street, Kazan 420008, Russia
anton@egorchev.ru
[2] University of Helsinki, 8, Haartmaninkatu, 00290 Helsinki, Finland

Abstract. The article explores the use of neural networks to solve the problem of determining boundaries of meshes of perineuronal nets. The confocal stacks' image layers of rat brains are used as initial data. This article presents a comparison of two alternative methods to solving the problem. The first method is based on the generation of boundaries through the use of a neural network based on the DCGAN architecture. The second method is based on solving the problem of semantic segmentation using a neural network based on the U-Net architecture, that is widely used in biomedicine. For both neural networks, architectural changes are presented to achieve greater generalizability of the models. Some learning strategies are considered to solve the problem of overfitting that is typical for small samples. Both solutions showed results comparable in quality to the semi-automatic algorithm. A solution based on the U-Net architecture provides good tools for further solving the problem of boundary ambiguity and allows customizing the algorithm for various criteria for boundaries of the perineuronal nets.

Keywords: Generative Adversarial Networks · U-Net · Medical Image Analysis · Confocal Stacks · Microscopic Images · Perineuronal Nets

1 Introduction

One of the most important areas of modern molecular neuroscience is the study of the role of the extracellular matrix in the function of the brain and spinal cord in normal state as well as in pathology. A special place in this topic is occupied by the study of the structure and function of perineuronal nets, a highly structured type of extracellular matrix covering large subpopulations of neurons of the central nervous system and surrounding synapses on the bodies of neurons and proximal segments of dendrites. To date, the most important role of perineuronal nets in the mechanisms of neuronal plasticity of the central nervous system in ontogenesis as well as their participation in synaptic plasticity and the pathophysiology of a number of diseases, such as schizophrenia, epilepsy, stroke, Alzheimer's disease, deficiency of post-traumatic regeneration of the spinal cord, i.e. pathologies carrying huge social burden on society, have been shown.

© The Author(s), under exclusive license to Springer Nature Switzerland AG 2024
A. Gibadullin (Ed.): ITIDMS 2023, CCIS 2112, pp. 164–177, 2024.
https://doi.org/10.1007/978-3-031-60318-1_14

In a number of structural studies, it has been shown that a mesh of the perineuronal net creates a spatial shell of a synapse on the surface of the plasma membrane of a neuron. The combination of microscopy, molecular biology, and electrophysiology data allows concluding that the meshes of the perineuronal net have important effects on synaptic transmission and synaptic plasticity in the brain. At the same time, the spatial structure of the meshes of the perineuronal net surrounding synapses remained poorly studied until recently.

We and others published previously some quantitative studies of the microstructure of the perineuronal net meshes [1–3]. Furthermore, a set of quantitative methods for semi-automatic analysis of the microstructure of the meshes of the perineuronal net [4] as well as the complex of the presynaptic terminal with the surrounding perineuronal net [5] were developed. At the same time, a change in the microstructure of meshes was shown in the experimental models of schizophrenia [4] and neonatal sensory deprivation [5]. The parameters of the two-dimensional geometry of perineuronal nets in the confocal plane such as the area and shape of the meshes, the distribution of intensity of the fluorescent signal of specific markers of chondroitin sulfates were investigated. The parameters of three-dimensional geometry including the thickness of the meshes and the distribution of local maxima of the color brightness of chondroitin sulfates in the three-dimensional space of confocal stacks were also studied. In addition, a comparative analysis of two mesh tracing methods was reported [4, 5].

To date, we have moved on to the next stage of analyzing the microstructure of perineuronal nets, that is development of an automatic method for the mesh contour detection using machine learning methods. This method has a potential to speed up significantly the analysis of the microstructure of perineuronal nets, and may be also innovative for solving such problems using artificial intelligence. Therefore our report suggests a new approach to the structural studies of the extracellular matrix surrounding synaptic contacts in normal state as well as in pathology. In the present work, we compare two methods for analyzing the contours of perineuronal nets based on machine learning algorithms. This will allow us to move on to studying the structure of perineuronal nets in the ketamine model of schizophrenia.

Since perineuronal nets are considered as a new biomarker and a pharmacological target, understanding its structural and functional aspects is important for the development of methods for the diagnosis and therapy of diseases associated with its impaired functioning.

Within the framework of this work, the application of neural networks, namely neural networks with DCGAN and U-Net architectures, is investigated to solve the problem of determining mesh boundaries of perineuronal nets. At the end of the article, the results of comparing the two approaches are described.

2 Material and Methods

2.1 Materials

In this section, we describe the datasets used (examples are shown in Fig. 1), as well as the methods that led to the result.

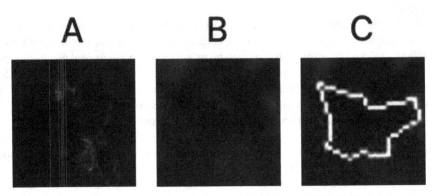

Fig. 1. Datasets used. a) Stack image layer. b) Mesh image. c) Identified mesh image.

Here we use two sets of data. The first one is completely composed of confocal stacks of perineuronal nets in parvalbumin-positive neurons of the IV and V layers of the cerebral cortex of adult rats and was previously described in [4]. The size of the confocal images is 100×100 microns (1024×1024 pixels). Voxel size is $99 \times 99 \times 170$ nm. Here we use the dataset of 28 confocal stacks (560 confocal images in total).

The second one consists of two subsets including a small subset containing 569 images of the boundaries of individual meshes annotated by neuroscientists, and a large subset containing 7127 images of the boundaries of individual meshes, which are the result of the work of a semi-automatic algorithm [4], that passed the stage of manual selection by a specialist. It is especially important that the perineuronal net meshes by it selves are not easy to find. The problem is similar to some extent to the detection of whole cell perineuronal nets in low resolution fluorescent microscopy images. Ciampi co-authors, for example, in [6] highlighted the problem of errors in the annotation, namely the ambiguity of the presence of the perineuronal net in the image. The assessment depends on the opinion of an expert in the field, and the main feature of both large and small subsets is that the annotation of the internal structure of the perineuronal net depends even more on the expert and sometimes does not undoubtedly represent the structure visible on the image texture. The difficulty of obtaining an error-free visual assessment is aggravated by the small size and the uneven distribution of the chondroitin sulfate staining signal along the contour of a mesh of the perineuronal net. As a result, one specialist can annotate the boundaries of the mesh in the area of the image layer where the other will not see the structure.

In addition to all of the above, the texture of the obtained layer images is subject to nonlinear noise, which does not allow experts to come to an agreement on its actual boundary in an unambiguously determined mesh.

2.2 Preprocessing

The images are filtered, after which the matrix of input pixels I turns into in Eqs. (1) and (2).

$$I'(x) = \frac{1}{W} \sum_{x_i \in \Omega}^{I} (x_i) f_r(\|I(x_i) - I(x)\|) g_s(\|x_i - x\|), \tag{1}$$

$$W = \sum_{x_i \in \Omega}^{I} (x_i) f_r(\|I(x_i) - I(x)\|) g_s(\|x_i - x\|), \tag{2}$$

where I' is the filtered image; I is the input image; x is the coordinate of the filtered pixel; Ω is a filter window with pixels x_i in it; f_r is a kernel to smooth out differences in intensity; g_s is a kernel to smooth the differences in coordinates; W is a normalizing coefficient.

Filtering does not allow getting rid of the features of the perineuronal net structure, such as ambiguity of borders, but it smooths the texture with a dense gradient inside the mesh, leaving the mesh shell unbiased in the pixel-by-pixel sense.

2.3 Architecture of Models

The first of the selected objects of research related to solving the problem of contour selection represents one of the most significant architectural variations of the U-Net precision neural network. Since its release in 2015, U-Net has found wide application in biomedical image segmentation tasks [7]. The architecture of the neural network consists of two parts including an encoder that accepts the input image, and a decoder that returns an annotated map of the same size as the input image from a high-dimensional vector. The decoder and encoder layers are additionally combined by skip connections from the output of each encoder block to the input of each decoder block. Skip connection is the transfer for subsequent concatenation of the tensor of features from the early layers of the model to the later ones, skipping the intermediate layers.

The encoder, by convolving the input tensor with 3×3 filter kernels and further reducing the feature map due to maxpulling layer in Eq. (3), encodes the image into an embedding vector with its key features. The decoder with using similar convolution layers and upsampling layers in Eq. (4), i.e. deconvolution layers [8], extracts the segmented image map pixel by pixel:

$$\begin{aligned} out(N_i, C_j, h, w) &= \max pool2d\left(input(N_i, C_j, h + m, w + n)\right) \\ &= \max_{m=0,\ldots,kH-1} \max_{n=0,\ldots,kW-1} input(N_i, C_j, h + m, w + n) \end{aligned}, \tag{3}$$

where output feature map is a tensor of dimension (N, C, H, W).

$$C1(y_i) = \frac{\lambda}{2} \sum_{c=1}^{K_0} \left\| \sum_{k=1}^{K_1} z_k^i \oplus f_{k,c} - y_c^i \right\|_2^2 + \sum_{k=1}^{K_1} \left| z_k^i \right|^p, \tag{4}$$

where z_k^i is a feature map and f is filter kernels with optimized weights.

Another approach under study in this paper is the generative–adversarial GAN network. It consists of two different models, a generator and a discriminator. The task of the generator is to create "fake" images that look like training images. The task of the discriminator is to look at the image and deduce from the generator whether it is a real training image or a fake one. During training, the generator constantly tries to outsmart the discriminator by generating all the best fakes, while the discriminator works to become the best detective and correctly classify real and fake images.

The generator is made up of the same encoder and decoder that are described in U-Net; however, in this case, the main feature of the generative model is the discriminator. Neural network training is based on binary cross-entropy as the fundamental component of the error function; as a result, the discriminator takes on great importance in the learning process [9]. The discriminator, in turn, is a primitive binary classifier.

2.4 Optimized Architectures

As a result of experiments, we have verified that the data sets obtained, due to the weak reliability in the annotation, are not sufficient to obtain a stable solution from scratch. The encoder block in two solutions has been completely replaced by the first five blocks of the vgg16 classifier, which is typical for image processing [10]. Each block consists of a cascade of 2 or 3 convolutional layers. During the analysis, images from the dataset were convolved with filter kernels of the first layer of classifier. The analysis showed that vgg16 copes well with the selection of simple shapes in the image. However, the construction of a linear regression model on these kernel weights did not show convincing generalizability, so it was decided to build a non-linear model around them.

2.5 Encoder in U-Net and DSGAN Architectures

Schematically, the encoder is shown in Fig. 2. Each sequence inside the encoder consists of a convolutional layer, a normalization layer with zero mean and one standard deviation, and a nonlinear layer with ReLU as activation function [11] (see Fig. 2(a)). Each block in Fig. 2(b) consists of three sequences and an output maxpull layer of size 2×2. The well-known "bottle neck" problem, namely the 1024×1 vector of features, was solved by transferring a $2 \times 2 \times 512$ tensor to the decoder. Moreover, it was decided to add a trainable drop-out layer [12], which helped to get rid of the instability of the model training. The presence of skip connection from the first block in the course of the study showed a tendency to retraining, and the connection was subsequently deleted. The decoder scheme is shown in Fig. 2(c) and is common to both U-Net and DCGAN.

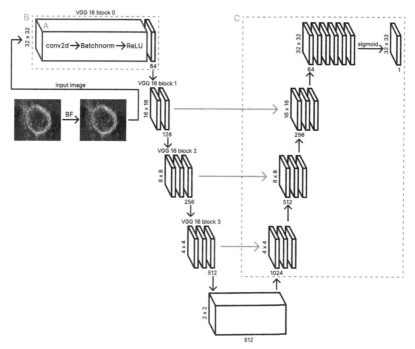

Fig. 2. Scheme of U-Net architecture. a) The layer of vgg16, which consists of 3×3 convolutional layer, batch normalization and non-linear ReLU activation function. b) vgg16 block, which consists of 2 or 3 vgg16 layers. c) U-Net decoder architecture, which analyses output feature tensor from encoder.

2.6 Hyperparameters

The loss function vector of the model is shown in Eq. (5).

$$\ell(x, y) = L = [1 \ldots, l_N]^T, \tag{5}$$

where l_N is the loss function value on a single image.

U-Net encoder-decoder loss function is shown in Eq. (6).

$$l_n = -w_n\big[y_n \cdot \log x_n + (1 - y_n) \cdot \log(1 - x_n)\big] + 1 - \frac{2 \cdot y_n \cdot x_n + 1}{y_n + x_n + 1} + \lambda \cdot |x_n - y_n|, \tag{6}$$

DCGAN encoder-decoder loss function is shown in Eq. (7).

$$l_n = -w_n\big[D(y_n) \cdot \log D(G(x_n)) + (1 - D(y_n)) \cdot \log(1 - D(G(x_n)))\big] \\ + \lambda \cdot |G(x_n) - y_n|, \tag{7}$$

where D is the function of discriminator; G is the function of generator; λ is the weight of L1 loss presented in Table 1.

DCGAN discriminator loss function is shown in Eq. (8).

$$l_n = \frac{1}{2}(BCE(D(G(x_n)),\ 1) + BCE(D(x_n)),\ 0), \tag{8}$$

where BCE is binary cross entropy.

All other hyperparameters in **Error! Not a valid bookmark self-reference.**.

Table 1. Other hyperparameters.

	U-Net	DCGAN
Optimizer	Adam	Adam
Adam's β	$\beta_1 = 0.05\ \beta_2 = 0.99$	$\beta_1 = 0.05\ \beta_2 = 0.99$
Learning rate	0.0002	0.0001
L1 λ	30	100
Batch size	64	64

2.7 Learning Process

The learning process of a neural network based on the U-Net architecture consists of 2 alternating stages:

- The first stage involves fixing the encoder weights in a constant position, and optimizing strictly the decoder weights. The duration of this stage is about 20 epochs.
- The second stage involves fixing the decoder weights in a constant position and a short-term optimization of the encoder weights. Under conditions of a small sample size, retraining at this stage may occur as early as 5–6 epochs, causing an irreparable collapse in model training. The duration of this stage varies from 1 to 5 epochs and depends on the values of errors in training and validation.

The change of the error function value in training and validation is shown in Fig. 3.

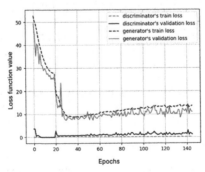

Fig. 3. Graph of loss function value of DCGAN model.

The learning process of a neural network based on the DCGAN architecture has a similar character, and can also be divided into two alternating stages with only one addition:

– The first stage involves fixing the discriminator weights and duplicates the U-Net learning process. The feature separator block on the discriminator in this configuration is also replaced by the vg 16 weights, as shown in Fig. 4.
– The second stage involves fixing the generator weights and optimizing the discriminator weights, also repeating the process described in U-Net training.

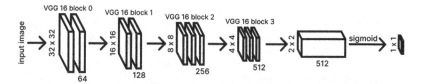

Fig. 4. Scheme of discriminator, where the first 4 sequencies are vgg16 blocks.

The change of the error function value in training and validation is shown in Fig. 5.

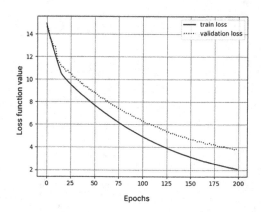

Fig. 5. Graph of loss value of U-Net model.

3   Results

3.1 Outputs of Models

The results of the neural networks of the two architectures discussed in this part are shown in Fig. 6. The images supplied to the model and the images representing the annotated layers are also demonstrated.

The first model based on the DCGAN architecture was used to solve the problem of generating boundaries of meshes of a perineuronal net. The output of the neural network is a generated image containing the borders annotated by the model. In Fig. 6, the result of solving the task is shown in the corresponding column.

The second model based on the U-Net architecture was used to solve the problem of semantic segmentation of mesh boundaries of the perineuronal net. The output of the model is an image size matrix, each value in which indicates the confidence of the model in belonging to the pixel boundary at the corresponding position. In the corresponding column of Fig. 6, the result of solving the problem is shows.

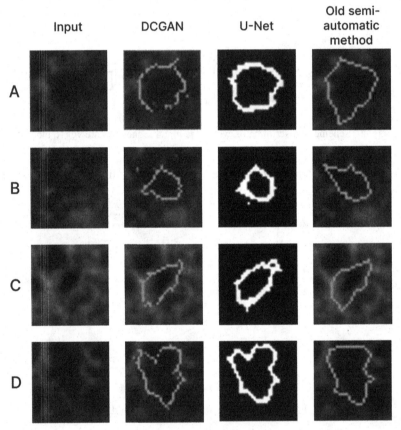

Fig. 6. A figure caption is the result of the DCGAN models (corresponding DCGAN column): the output tensor is a reconstructed image with a generated single-pixel boundary (marked in blue), and U-Net (corresponding U-Net column): the output matrix is interpreted as the values of the probability of each pixel belonging to the mesh boundary. Pixels with a probability exceeding the threshold of 0.6 are marked in white. (Color figure online)

3.2 Metrics Calculation

In a previous article, our group published the results of a semi-automatic algorithm for annotating mesh boundaries of a perineuronal net [10]. This section presents a comparison of the operation of two automated algorithms with a semi-automatic algorithm. The following metrics were used for comparison:

- Mesh area
- Mesh perimeter
- Roundedness of the mesh
- Axial ratio

Figure 7 and Fig. 8 present the results of a comparison of automated boundary annotation algorithms based on the neural network architectures U-Net and DCGAN with a semi-automatic algorithm. For calculating a correlation between results of previous semi-automatic and presented models, Pearson's correlation coefficient R (see Fig. 7(c-f)) and Spearman's correlation coefficient Sp (see Fig. 7(c-f)) were used.

In Fig. 9, the result of a Roundedness comparison of automated boundary annotation algorithms based on the neural network architectures U-Net and DCGAN is presented. In plots A and D (see Fig. 9), two extreme cases of images with a complex structure, in which either DCGAN or U-Net makes a non-correlated error in the annotation, is shown. In plots B and C, round and non-round mesh boundaries are represented, respectively.

In Table 2, the calculation of the recall metric for both models, which shows a similar result of the accuracy of border selection, is represented.

Table 2. Recall value

	U-Net	DCGAN
Recall value	0.7537	0.7698

4 Discussion

The use of neural networks to annotate mesh boundaries of perineuronal nets is a new approach in this field. The existing algorithm was implemented on the basis of directional gradients and tended to annotate more rounded borders in cases where the mesh had a smooth shape. In the algorithms discussed in this article, this problem has been solved, as can be seen when comparing the results of calculating the roundness metric. Both solutions showed results commensurate in quality with semi-automatic algorithms. The solution based on the U-Net architecture provides a good toolkit for further solving the problem of boundary ambiguity and makes it possible to adjust the algorithm to various criteria of the perineuronal net boundaries. Moreover, the presented algorithms show similar results and are not correlated with errors in extreme cases. In the future, it is planned to continue research on the complexity of the architecture and the search for a single optimal method for allocating the boundaries of the perineuronal net meshes.

Based on the above results, the use of neural networks in the field of microscopic image analysis is promising.

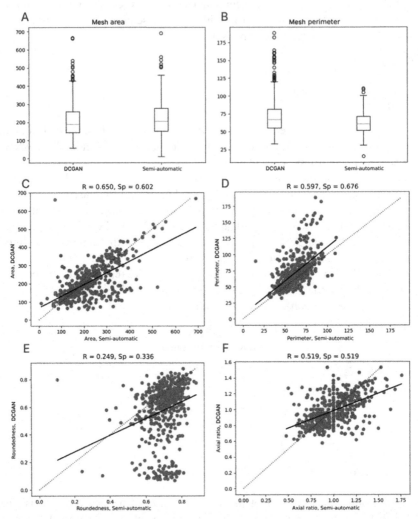

Fig. 7. Set of graphs of metrics calculation result by the DCGAN model. a) Mesh area metric. b) Mesh perimeter metric. c) Correlations of mesh areas. d) Correlations of mesh perimeters. e) Roundedness correlations. f) Correlations of axials ratios.

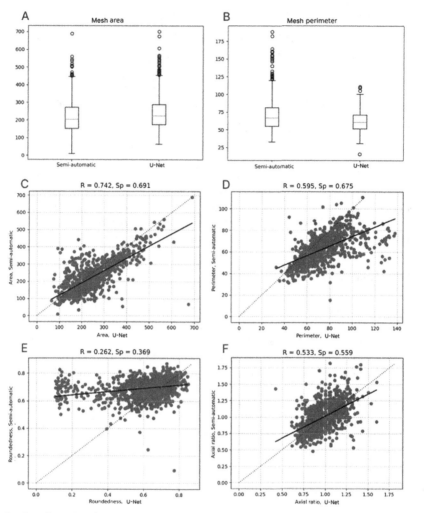

Fig. 8. Set of graphs of metrics calculation result by the U-Net model. a) Mesh area metric. b) Mesh perimeter metric. c) Correlations of mesh areas. d) Correlations of mesh perimeters. e) Roundedness correlations. f) Correlations of axial ratios.

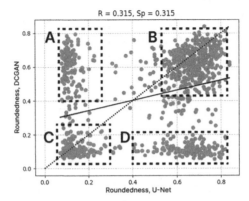

Fig. 9. Graph of Roundedness metric calculation result by the U-Net model and DCGAN model. a) Domain of error for U-Net model. b) Domain of meshes with rounded border. c) Domain of meshes with non-rounded border. d) Domain of error for DCGAN model.

5 Conclusion

The article describes a comparison of two alternative methods to the allocation of mesh boundaries of the perineuronal net and presents the main results of the study. The introduction of automatic algorithms is a priority task, because their application will significantly accelerate the analysis of the microstructure of perineuronal nets, and will also become the world's first method for solving such problems using artificial intelligence.

Acknowledgments. This paper has been supported by the Kazan Federal University Strategic Academic Leadership Program ("PRIORITY-2030"), Strategic Project #4.

We are thankful to Alexander Dityatev for providing the confocal dataset.

References

1. Arnst, N., et al.: Spatial patterns and cell surface clusters in perineuronal nets. Brain Res. **1648**(Pt A), 214–223 (2016)
2. Dzyubenko, E., Manrique-Castano, D., Kleinschnitz, C., Faissner, A., Hermann, D.: Topological remodeling of cortical perineuronal nets in focal cerebral ischemia and mild hypoperfusion. Matrix Biol. **74**, 121–132 (2018)
3. Sigal, Y., Bae, H., Bogart, L., Hensch, T., Zhuang, X.: Structural maturation of cortical perineuronal nets and their perforating synapses revealed by superresolution imaging. Proc. Natl. Acad. Sci. **116**(14), 7071–7076 (2019)
4. Kaushik, R., et al.: Fine structure analysis of perineuronal nets in the ketamine model of schizophrenia. Eur. J. Neurosci. **53**(3), 3988–4004 (2020)
5. Lipachev, N., et al.: Postnatal development of the microstructure of cortical GABAergic synapses and perineuronal nets requires sensory input. Neurosci. Res. **182**(8), 32–40 (2022)
6. Ciampi, L., et al.: Learning to count biological structures with raters' uncertainty. Med. Image Anal. **80**, 102500 (2022)
7. Weng, W., Zhu, X.: INet: convolutional networks for biomedical image segmentation. IEEE Access **9**, 16591–16603 (2021)

8. Zeiler, M., Krishnan, D., Taylor, G., Fergus, R.: Deconvolutional networks. In: 2010 IEEE Computer Society Conference on Computer Vision and Pattern Recognition, pp. 2528–2535. IEEE (2010)

9. Goodfellow, I., et al.: Generative adversarial nets. In: Advances in Neural Information Processing Systems, vol. 27, pp. 139–144 (2014)

10. Simonyan, K., Zisserman, A.: Very deep convolutional networks for large-scale image recognition. https://arxiv.org/abs/1409.1556 (2014)

11. Shi, W., et al.: Real-time single image and video super-resolution using an efficient sub-pixel convolutional neural network. In: 2016 Proceedings of the IEEE Conference on Computer Vision and Pattern Recognition (CVPR), pp. 1874–1883. IEEE (2016)

12. Isola, P., Zhu, J.Y., Zhou, T., Efros, A.: Image-to-image translation with conditional adversarial networks. In: 2017 IEEE Conference on Computer Vision and Pattern Recognition (CVPR), pp. 1125–1134. IEEE (2017)

Diagnostics of Animals Diseases Based on the Principles of Neutrosophic Sets and Sugeno Fuzzy Inference

D. T. Mukhamedieva[1] 🆔 and L. U. Safarova[2(✉)] 🆔

[1] Tashkent Institute of Irrigation and Agricultural Mechanization Engineers National Research University, Tashkent, Uzbekistan
[2] Samarkand State University of Veterinary Medicine, Livestock and Biotechnologies, Samarkand, Uzbekistan
lola.safarova.81@inbox.ru

Abstract. This study is devoted to the development of improved methods for diagnosing cattle diseases based on the principles of neutrosophic sets and Sugeno fuzzy inference. The study proposed new algorithms and models that can effectively process fuzzy and uncertain information characteristic of veterinary diagnostics. The goal of the work is to create a diagnostic system that will have high accuracy and the ability to adapt to various conditions and characteristics of specific disease cases. The expected result of the study is aimed at developing an effective tool for the early detection of diseases in cattle, which will significantly improve the efficiency of veterinary practice and animal welfare.

Keywords: Diagnostic System · Fuzzy Logic · Fuzzy Sugeno Model

1 Introduction

Currently, animals in many countries are susceptible to various diseases. Improvement and implementation of systems based on modern information technologies for the development of methods for early diagnosis of diseases in animals is one of the key tasks. This is important not only to ensure the health and welfare of animals, but also to prevent the spread of diseases that can have serious consequences for livestock production, human health and the economy as a whole. The use of modern information technologies, such as machine learning, data analytics, sensors and telemedicine, can significantly improve diagnostic capabilities, enabling rapid detection and response to diseases, which contributes to effective control and control [1, 2].

Research based on mathematical modeling using fuzzy logic and neutrosophical fuzzy sets is actively being conducted in the world scientific community. These works are aimed at improving and developing computer diagnostic systems designed to identify various types of diseases and their causes in the early stages, as well as to improve treatment methods in veterinary medicine. In this regard, the creation of models for diagnosing animal diseases based on fuzzy logic and neutrosophical fuzzy sets, the

A. Gibadullin (Ed.): ITIDMS 2023, CCIS 2112, pp. 178–185, 2024.
https://doi.org/10.1007/978-3-031-60318-1_15

development of appropriate algorithms and programs for predicting and identifying diseases of cattle is one of the priority tasks. These efforts are aimed at improving the quality of life of animals, effectively managing their health, and promoting agricultural development and food security [3, 4].

The purpose of this work is to develop models and algorithms for identifying diseases of cattle using the Sugeno fuzzy inference method and the concept of neutrosophical fuzzy sets. This will make it possible to create a diagnostic system capable of efficiently processing fuzzy and uncertain information about the health status of animals. Using fuzzy logic and neutrosophical fuzzy sets will allow us to take into account various aspects of uncertainty and fuzziness inherent in veterinary diagnostics, which will make the system more flexible and adaptive to a variety of conditions and situations. The expected result of the study will be the creation of an effective tool for the early identification of diseases in cattle, which contributes to their more successful treatment and prevention of the development of complications [5–7].

The purpose of this research is to develop improved algorithms and models for disease identification in cattle using neutrosophic sets and Sugeno fuzzy inference. This includes the creation of effective methods for processing the fuzzy and uncertain information characteristic of veterinary diagnostics, as well as the development of algorithms that can adapt to a variety of conditions and characteristics of specific disease cases. The main goal is to ensure accurate and rapid identification of diseases in cattle with a minimum number of false positive and false negative results. Successful completion of this task will significantly increase the efficiency of veterinary practice and improve animal health [8, 9].

The use of neutrosophic fuzzy sets and decision-making methods represents a promising approach to solve the problem of diagnosing osteodystrophy, secondary osteodystrophy, hypomicroelementosis and ketosis in cattle. Given that the symptoms of these diseases are interrelated and may overlap, and given the possibility that one disease can cause another, accurately identifying the type of disease can be difficult for veterinarians.

Issues related to the methodology for solving the problem of identifying diseases for studying the structure of classes of cattle, and identifying diseases based on neutrosophic fuzzy sets and decision-making methods, are relevant and promising in modern veterinary science and practice [10].

Studying the class structure of cattle using fuzzy set technologies allows us to take into account various factors, such as genetic, morphological and behavioral characteristics, which may influence their classification. This can be useful for more accurately determining breed quality, meat quality, milk quality or other characteristics, as well as for improving breeding programs and breeding methods. Defining diseases using neutrosophical fuzzy sets and decision-making methods makes it possible to take into account various symptoms and signs of diseases, as well as their interrelationship and influence on each other. This can be useful for more accurately diagnosing diseases, determining their severity and choosing optimal treatment and prevention strategies. Such approaches offer new prospects for improving the diagnosis, treatment and health management of cattle, which can lead to increased productivity and quality of livestock products, as well as improved animal welfare and reduced losses in livestock production.

Single-valued neutrosophical fuzzy sets and interval neutrosophical fuzzy sets are subclasses of neutrosophical fuzzy sets and a generalization of intuitive fuzzy sets and interval intuitive fuzzy sets. The properties of single-valued neutrosophical fuzzy sets and interval neutrosophical fuzzy sets are independently described by degrees of truth, uncertainty and falsity. The main advantage of neutrosophical fuzzy sets is that they provide a powerful formalism for handling information that may be incomplete, uncertain, and contradictory. Unlike conventional fuzzy sets, neutrosophical sets are able to effectively take into account this uncertainty and inconsistency, which makes them more flexible and universal in solving real problems [11].

Recently, various algorithms and methods have been proposed in various studies to deal with single-valued neutrosophical fuzzy sets and interval neutrosophic fuzzy sets [12, 13]. These works introduced basic operations on single-valued and interval neutrosophical fuzzy sets, such as addition and multiplication, as well as corresponding aggregation operators. The basic operational laws for elementary neutrosophical fuzzy sets, including single-valued and interval neutrosophical fuzzy sets, are determined. Weighted mixing aggregation operators were also proposed to combine elementary neutrosophical fuzzy information, which were then applied to the feature decision set [14, 15]. These developments promote more efficient and flexible use of neutrosophical fuzzy sets and their application in various fields, including veterinary medicine, for decision making based on fuzzy and uncertain information.

In work [16], shortcomings of some laws of functioning of unambiguous neutrosophical fuzzy sets were identified. As part of the study, certain principles of the functioning of interval neutrosophical fuzzy sets used for some aggregation operators were also improved. These improved principles were then explored through their application to the decision set based on interval neutrosophical fuzzy information.

In [17–21], a new operator was proposed, which is called the elementary weighted average interval neutrosophical fuzzy advantage operator. This operator was designed for use in a variety of feature-based decision making. The peculiarity of this operator is that, unlike previous works, where the main component was the clear values (weights) of single-valued or interval neutrosophical fuzzy sets, a new approach is introduced here. This approach allows us to take into account a wider range of uncertainty and inconsistencies in the data, which makes it more flexible and adaptive for solving decision-making problems in a fuzzy environment.

Problems with the protein and sugar -protein ratio in the diet of cows, especially if it falls below 0.7–0.79, can lead to the development of dystrophic changes in the liver of animals. This is especially true in case of deficiency of microelements such as copper, cobalt, zinc, manganese, and certain minerals, which can cause metabolic disorders. Micronutrient deficiency can lead to decreased development of microflora in the rumen, increased acidity and ammonia levels in the blood, which in turn causes acidosis and chronic intoxication.

Secondary osteodystrophy, osteodystrophy, microelementosis and ketosis in cattle can be caused by various factors, including diets deficient in calcium, phosphorus and other nutrients, and low sugar to protein ratios in the diet. Symptoms of deficiency of iodine, cobalt, vitamins A and D in cows kept in radioactively contaminated areas include various manifestations, such as dryness and parakeratosis of the skin, enophthalmos, bradycardia and others. This highlights the need for careful control and balancing of livestock nutrition, as well as regular monitoring of micronutrient and vitamin levels in animals to maintain their health and productivity.

Symptoms of deficiency of iodine, cobalt, and vitamins A and D in cows living in areas exposed to radioactive contamination can be varied and include the following: 86.7% of animals have dryness and parakeratosis of the skin, 26.7% have enophthalmos, in 90% - whitening of the conjunctiva, as well as bradycardia in 57.8% of cows. An enlarged thyroid gland and signs of mexidema were found in 3.35% of animals. In addition, anemia occurs in 92.6% of dairy cows, hypocalcemia in 93.8–100% of animals, and hypophosphatemia in 50–92.6%. There is also a decrease in the content of copper, cobalt and zinc in the blood serum in 90% of animals. These data highlight the serious consequences of deficiencies of important microelements and vitamins in animal diets, especially in conditions of radioactive environmental contamination. Providing cows with adequate nutrition and monitoring their nutrient levels play an important role in maintaining their health and productivity.

2 Methods and Models

This paper presents a new interval neutrosophic logic, which expands previous models, such as interval fuzzy logic- a logical method that uses ranges of values to describe the degree of uncertainty or fuzziness, intuitionistic fuzzy logic- a logical method that uses ranges of values to describe the degree of uncertainty or fuzziness and paraconsistent logic-logical approach in which states are possible that do not contradict themselves, taking into account not only the degree of truth or falsity of the statement, but also the degree of uncertainty. This allows additional information to be taken into account more reliably under conditions of uncertainty. The paper introduces mathematical definitions of interval neurosophical propositional calculus and interval neutrosophic predicative calculus. A general method for developing an interval neutrosophic logic system is also proposed, incorporating neutrosophics, neutrosophic inference.

The resulting intersection of two interval neutrosophic sets A and B, denoted C, is an interval neutrosophic set that includes elements present in both set A and B, which includes elements present in both set A and B. and in set B. Thus, the elements in set C are evaluated taking into account the fuzziness and uncertainty in both set A and set B.

Mathematically this can be represented as:

$C = A \cap B$

$\inf T_C(x) = \min(\inf T_A(x), \inf T_B(x))$, $\sup T_C(x) = \min(\sup T_A(x), sup T_B(x))$,

$\inf I_C(x) = \max(\inf I_A(x), \inf I_B(x))$, $\sup I_C(x) = \max(\sup I_A(x), \sup I_B(x))$,

$\inf F_C(x) = \max(\inf F_A(x), \inf F_B(x))$, $\sup F_C(x) = \max(\sup F_A(x), \sup F_B(x))$,

where C is an interval neutrosophic set representing the intersection of sets A and B.

This paper presents a new intervallic neutrosophical logic that extends previous models such as interval fuzzy logic, intuitionistic fuzzy logic and paraconsistent logic by taking into account not only the degree of truth or falsity of a statement, but also the degree of uncertainty. This allows additional information to be taken into account more reliably under conditions of uncertainty. The paper introduces mathematical definitions of interval neurosophical propositional calculus and interval neutrosophic predicative calculus. A general method for developing an interval neutrosophic logical system is also proposed, including neutrosophics, neutrosophic inference, neutrosophic rule base, neutrosophic type reduction, and deneutrosophics.

R^k: IF $x_1 = \; < T_{A_1^k}(x_1), I_{A_1^k}(x_1), F_{A_1^k}(x_1) >$ and $x_2 = \; < T_{A_2^k}(x_2), I_{A_2^k}(x_2), F_{A_2^k}(x_2) >$ and $, ...,x_n = \; < T_{A_n^k}(x_n), I_{A_n^k}(x_n), F_{A_n^k}(x_n) >$, Then $y_j = b_{j,0} + b_{j,1}x_1 + \ldots + b_{j,n}x_n$.

Here A_i^k is an interval neurosophical set defined in space X_i with a truth membership function, $T_{A_i^k}(x_i)$, an uncertainty membership function $I_{A_i^k}(x_i)$ and a falsity membership function $F_{A_i^k}(x_i)$, where $T_{A_i^k}(x_i), I_{A_i^k}(x_i), F_{A_i^k}(x_i) \subseteq [0, 1], 1 \leq i \leq n$. B^k is an interval neutrosophic set defined by a space Y with a truth membership function $T_{B^k}(y)$, an uncertainty membership function $I_{B^k}(y)$ and a falsity membership function $F_{B^k}(y)$, where $T_{B^k}(y), I_{B^k}(y), F_{B^k}(y) \subseteq [0, 1]$.

If $x_1 = \langle [0.05, 0.2], [0.1, 0.15], [0.65, 0.8] \rangle \wedge x_2 = \langle [0.75, 0.95], [0.1, 0.15], [0.1, 0.2] \rangle \wedge$
$x_3 = \langle [0.6, 0.75], [0.1, 0.2], [0.2, 0.25] \rangle \wedge x_4 = \langle [0.5, 0.6], [0.2, 0.25], [0.25, 0.35] \rangle \wedge$
$x_5 = \langle [0.05, 0.2], [0.1, 0.15], [0.65, 0.8] \rangle \wedge x_6 = \langle [0.4, 0.5], [0.2, 0.3], [0.35, 0.45] \rangle \wedge$
$x_7 = \langle [0.05, 0.2], [0.1, 0.15], [0.65, 0.8] \rangle$

Then $y_1 = 4, 9 + 7, 8x_1 - 6, 9x_2 - 1, 5x_3 - 0, 3x_4 + 0, 37x_5 + 0, 06x_6 - 0, 003x_7 y_1 = 4, 9 + 7, 8x_1 - 6, 9x_2 - 1, 5x_3 - 0, 3x_4 + 0, 37x_5 + 0, 06x_6 - 0, 003x_7$

If $x_1 = x_1 = \langle [0.05, 0.2], [0.1, 0.15], [0.65, 0.8] \rangle \wedge x_2 = x_2 = \langle [0.05, 0.2], [0.1, 0.15], [0.65, 0.8] \rangle \wedge$
$x_3 = x_3 = \langle [0.3, 0.4], [0.15, 0.25], [0.45, 0.5] \rangle \wedge x_4 = x_4 = \langle [0.4, 0.5], [0.2, 0.3], [0.35, 0.45] \rangle \wedge$
$x_5 = x_5 = \langle [0, 0.05], [0.05, 0.01], [0.8, 0.95] \rangle \wedge x_6 = x_6 = \langle [0.05, 0.2], [0.1, 0.15], [0.65, 0.8] \rangle \wedge$
$x_7 = \langle [0.3, 0.4], [0.15, 0.25], [0.45, 0.5] \rangle$

Then $y_2 = -0, 6 - 1, 45x_1 + 1, 7x_2 + 0, 34x_3 - 0, 1x_4 - 0, 2x_5 - 0, 07x_6 - 0, 03x_7 y_2 = -0, 6 - 1, 45x_1 + 1, 7x_2 + 0, 34x_3 - 0, 1x_4 - 0, 2x_5 - 0, 07x_6 - 0, 03x_7$

If $x_1 = x_1 = \langle [0.6, 0.75], [0.1, 0.2], [0.2, 0.25] \rangle \wedge x_2 = x_2 = \langle [0.6, 0.75], [0.1, 0.2], [0.2, 0.25] \rangle \wedge$
$x_3 = x_3 = \langle [0.75, 0.95], [0.1, 0.15], [0.1, 0.2] \rangle \wedge x_4 = x_4 = \langle [0.5, 0.6], [0.2, 0.25], [0.25, 0.35] \rangle \wedge$
$x_5 = x_5 = \langle [0.75, 0.95], [0.1, 0.15], [0.1, 0.2] \rangle \wedge x_6 = x_6 = \langle 0.3, 0.4], [0.15, 0.25], [0.45, 0.5] \rangle \wedge$
$x_7 = \langle [0.75, 0.95], [0.1, 0.15], [0.1, 0.2] \rangle$

Then $y_3 = -3, 42 - 0, 6x_1 + 7, 8x_2 + 1, 7x_3 - 0, 2x_4 - 0, 04x_5 - 0, 19x_6 - 0, 9x_7 y_3 = -3, 42 - 0, 6x_1 + 7, 8x_2 + 1, 7x_3 - 0, 2x_4 - 0, 04x_5 - 0, 19x_6 - 0, 9x_7$

3   Results

The program was developed and the results were collected. The report includes precision, recall, F1 measure, and support information for each class, as well as overall precision, macro-average precision, weighted precision, and overall support. The confusion matrix shows the number of correctly and incorrectly classified examples for each class (Fig. 1).

Classification Accuracy: 0.8888888888888888
Classification report:
precision recall f1-score support

ketoz 1.00 0.86 0.93 22
mastitis 0.77 1.00 0.87 23
pneumonia 1.00 0.78 0.88 18

accuracy 0.89 63
macro avg 0.92 0.88 0.89 63
weighted avg 0.91 0.89 0.89 63

Confusion Matrix:

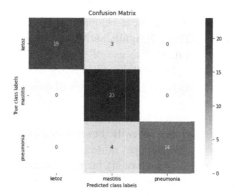

Fig. 1. Confusion Matrix.

Classification Accuracy This is the percentage of correctly classified samples from the entire data set. In this case, the classification accuracy is 88.89%, which means that the model correctly classified 88.89% of the samples.

Classification report: Classification report:

– Precision: This is the proportion of correctly classified positive samples among all positive samples predicted by the model. For example, for the class "ketoz" the accuracy is 100%, which means that all samples predicted as "ketoz" are actually "ketoz".

– Recall (recall): This is the proportion of correctly classified positive samples among all real positive samples in the data set. For example, for the class "mastitis" the recall is also 100%, which means that the model has detected all real examples of the class "mastitis".

– If 1-score: This is the harmonic average of precision and recall. It shows the balance between accuracy and completeness of classification. The F1-measure is close to 1 if both precision and recall are high.

– Support: This is the number of samples in each class.

Confusion Matrix (Confusion Matrix):

It is a square matrix where the rows represent the actual classes and the columns represent the predicted classes by the model. Each element of the matrix shows the number of samples that were classified correctly (diagonal elements) or incorrectly (off-diagonal elements).

4 Conclusion

This study develops improved methods for diagnosing diseases in cattle based on the principles of neutrosophic sets and Sugeno fuzzy inference. The proposed algorithms and models are able to effectively process fuzzy and uncertain information that is typical for veterinary diagnostics. The goal of the study is to create a diagnostic system that is highly accurate and capable of adapting to various conditions and characteristics of specific disease cases.

The expected result of the work is the development of an effective tool for the early detection of diseases in cattle. This will significantly improve the efficiency of veterinary practice and ensure animal welfare. The use of modern information technologies in combination with mathematical modeling based on fuzzy logic and neutrosophical sets makes it possible to create a diagnostic system capable of quickly responding to diseases and preventing their spread.

The model demonstrated good classification accuracy, amounting to 88.89%. This means that most of the samples were classified correctly. Analysis of the classification report allows us to see that the model copes quite successfully with the classification of all three classes (ketosis, mastitis, pneumonia), having high accuracy, completeness and F1-measure. This confirms the good performance of the model. The confusion matrix allows you to visually evaluate which classes were correctly or incorrectly classified. From the matrix, it can be seen that most of the samples were classified correctly, but there are a small number of errors in the classification of some samples. Based on this information, we can conclude that the model copes well with the classification task, but may require some improvement to improve accuracy and reduce the number of errors.

These results have important implications not only for animal health and welfare, but also for the economy and society as a whole. An effective diagnostic system will help improve control of animal diseases, reduce the risk of spreading infections and ensure sustainable development of agriculture.

References

1. Borisevich, V.B., Borisevich, Y.: Enzootic osteodystrophy of cattle in Poselye. J. Vet. Med. **5**, 41–43 (2005)
2. Samokhin, V.T., Ermoleva, T.G.: Correction of energy metabolism in dairy cows. J. Vet. Med. **9**, 44–45 (2004)
3. Firk, R., Stamer, E., Junge, W., Krieter, J.: Improving oestrus detection by combination of activity measurements with information about previous oestrus cases. Livest. Prod. Sci. **82**, 97–103 (2003)
4. Freddy, F.: Fuzzy classification of phantom parent groups in an animal model. Genet. Sel. Evol. **1297**, 41–42 (2009)

5. Orazbayev, B., Ospanov, E., Kissikova, N., Mukataev, N., Orazbayeva, K.: Decision-making in the fuzzy environment on the basis of various compromise schemes. Procedia Comput. Sci. **120**, 945–952 (2017)
6. Marzhan, Y., Talshyn, K., Kairat, K., Belginova, S., Karlygash, A., Yerbol, O.: Smart technologies of the risk-management and decision-making systems in a fuzzy data environment. Indonesian J. Electric. Eng. Comput. Sci. **28**(3), 1463–1474 (2022)
7. Mukhamedieva, D.T., Safarova, L.U.: Main problems and tasks of intellectualisation of information processing system. Int. J. Innov. Technol. Explo. Eng. **8**(9.3), 158–165 (2019)
8. Guo, Y., Sengur, A., Ye, J.: A novel image thresholding algorithm based on neutrosophic similarity score. Measurement **58**, 175–186 (2014)
9. Ye, J.: Single valued neutrosophic minimum spanning tree and its clustering method. J. Intell. Syst. **23**(3), 311–324 (2014)
10. Wang, H., Smarandache, F., Zhang, Y.Q., Sunderraman, R.: Single valued neutrosophic sets. Multispace Multistructure **4**, 410–413 (2010)
11. Zhang, H.Y., Wang, J.Q., Chen, X.H.: Interval neutrosophic sets and their application in multicriteria decision making problems. Sci. World J. **15**, 1–16 (2014)
12. Suyunov, A.S., Mirzayev, A.A., Urakov, O.A., Suyunov, S.: Field studies of electronic total stations in a special reference satellite geodetic basis. Proc. SPIE Int. Soc. Opt. Eng.E Int. Soc. Opt. Eng. **12564**, 125640Y (2023)
13. Liu, P.D., Wang, Y.M.: Interval neutrosophic prioritized OWA operator and its application to multiple attribute decision making. J. Syst. Sci. Complex. **29**(3), 681–697 (2016)

The Technique of Processing Non-Gaussian Data Based on Artificial Intelligence

Viktor Gnatuk[1], Oleg Kivchun[1(✉)], and Sofia Mozhaeva[2]

[1] Immanuel Kant Baltic Federal University, Kaliningrad, Russia
`oleg_kivchun@mail.ru`
[2] Technion – Israel Institute of Technology, Haifa, Israel

Abstract. The article discusses the technique of parametric adaptation of big data. The basis of this technique is vector rank analysis, developed within the framework of the technocenological theory of Professor B.I. Kudrin. The novelty of the technique lies in the fact that for the first time, together with technocenological methods, the possibility of using elements of artificial intelligence has been realized. The main stages of the methodology are: loading "raw" data, forming matrices of verified and approximated data, as well as checking their adequacy based on vector rank analysis methods. These steps are performed in parallel using ChatGPT based on the proposed artificial intelligence methods.

Keywords: Data Processing · Non-Gaussian Data · Artificial Intelligence · Parametric Adaptation · Big Data · Criterion of Predictive Capabilities · Vector Rank Analysis

1 Introduction

In the modern world, there is an increase in the use of new digital technologies. Their field of application covers the entire spectrum of human activity. Digital technologies are of great importance in the industry and economy.

The introduction of digital devices in workshops, structural divisions and infrastructure facilities made it possible to collect large amounts of data on resources, financial resources, nomenclature of technical products, logistics, etc. with the necessary accuracy over the required time interval. One of the advantages of the introduction of digital metering devices is the ability to simultaneously capture data from all objects, including those located in remote territories. This allows decision makers at facilities to obtain complete information about the facilities, thereby substantiating and making the most effective decisions. Automated control systems (ACS), which include elements of artificial intelligence, can also be used as a LPR. In addition, the ability to receive huge amounts of data and transfer them to removable media allows you to create scientifically sound procedures for their collection, organization, visualization and modeling.

In this regard, a number of problems arise, which consist in the need for high-quality data processing in order to preserve their completeness, value, reliability and

A. Gibadullin (Ed.): ITIDMS 2023, CCIS 2112, pp. 186–195, 2024.
https://doi.org/10.1007/978-3-031-60318-1_16

variability. To this end, research in the field of big data "Big Date" is being implemented all over the world. The works of foreign scientists: R. Kitchin and G. McArdle [1, 2] describe the fundamental foundations of the definition of big data. Scientists D. Boyd and K. Crawford [3, 4] work in the field of big data aggregation and the formation of links to them. At the same time as O'Malley and J. Michael conducts scientific research in the field of survey and correlation of various data in order to form search and query systems [5]. Methods for ensuring the reliability of big data are described in the works of L. Floridi, Ph. Illari, S. Zhu, S. Leonelli , A. Loettgers, J. Bogen [7–10]. The works of M. Bowker, W. Edwards, and S. Lagoze are devoted to studies of data variability [10–12]. The evidence of the value of the data is reflected in the works of S. Leonelli, N. Tempini [14].

The research of Russian scientists in the field of completeness, value, reliability and variability of data is reflected in the works of Yu. Konstantinova, I. Barilo, A. Baryshev, T. Ivanova, V. Kryukov, Yu. Lagutin, Yu. Mezentsev, B. Makoklyuev and others [15, 16].

Recently, research in the field of non-Gaussian data by scientists of the scientific school of Professor B.I. Kudrin has been of particular interest. The main research area in this scientific school is the technocenological theory, with the help of which scientifically based models and techniques have been developed that allow cleaning, formatting, verification, adaptation of measurement results, and data cubing. The leading scientists in this field are B.I. Kudrina [9, 10], V.I. Gnatyuk, D.V. Lutsenko, A.A. Sheinin, P.Y. Dundik, A.A. Merkulova and others [16–21]. Their research is based on the assertion that big data is a fractal-like, discounting medium with non-Gaussian properties.

2 The Technique of Parametric Adaptation of Big Data

It is advisable to study such environments based on the methods of rank analysis, the main sections of which are functional, combinatorial and vector rank analysis. Based on the provisions of vector rank analysis, a technique for parametric adaptation of big data has been developed (Fig. 1).

For a more understandable description of the stages of the methodology, the concept of parametric adaptation of big data should be introduced. It is a continuous verification of the values obtained as a result of importing from metering devices according to the criterion of maximum predictive capabilities in order to select the best layer of big data for further implementation of calculation methods [1, 11].

The main purpose of the big data parametric adaptation technique is to study vector rank distributions using four algorithms: processing and formatting "raw" data, generating verified big data, approximating big data by various methods and checking the adequacy of "raw", verified and approximated big data [21].

The algorithms are implemented in strict sequence. The first algorithm – processing and formatting of "raw" big data – is designed for the primary processing of measurement results obtained from metering devices via various communication channels, as well as manually collected. The processing and formatting of measurement results are operations to eliminate syntactic errors, bring them to a single digital format and process metainformation. After the algorithm is completed, the final matrix of "raw" big data is formed. "Raw" data should be understood as the simplest data format containing raw values, which avoids information loss and does not have a clear specification [21].

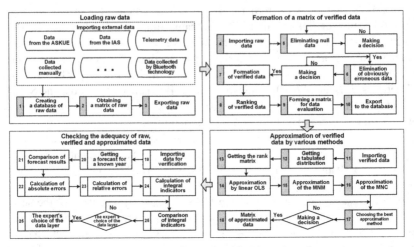

Fig. 1. The structure of the methodology for parametric adaptation of power consumption data: OLS is the method of least squares; MNM is the method of least modules.

The second algorithm allows you to create a matrix of verified data. To do this, the "raw" data is checked for the presence of zero values, equal (atypical) and obviously erroneous values. The recovery of null data is carried out using spline interpolation and the method of numerical extrapolation [16, 21].

Further, obviously erroneous data (outliers) are eliminated, resulting from gross measurement errors that deviate significantly from the distribution center. Their elimination is carried out by replacing them with spline interpolation or extrapolation, and at the output a matrix of verified values is formed, which is exported back to the database. The next stage of the technique allows you to approximate the verified data. To do this, a tabulated rank distribution of verified data and a rank vector are generated. The approximation is implemented by three methods: the linear least squares method, the least modulus method and the classical least squares method [16, 17, 21].

Based on the results of the correlation analysis of the obtained approximation values, the decision maker (LPR) chooses the best method for approximating the verified data. The results of the first three stages of the methodology, the system describing the operations of verification, ranking and approximation of the initial data on the power consumption of the REC, can be presented as follows:

$$
\begin{cases}
\{W_k^{RAW}\}_{k=1}^n \xrightarrow[\text{Verific}]{} \{W_k^{VER}\}_{k=1}^n; \\
\{W_k^{VER}\}_{k=1}^n \xrightarrow[\text{Rangin}]{} \{W_k^{RAN}\}_{k=1}^n; \\
\{W_k^{RAN}\}_{k=1}^n \xrightarrow[\text{Approx}]{} \{W_k^{APP}\}_{k=1}^n,
\end{cases}
\tag{1}
$$

$$\{W_k^{RAW}\}_{k=1}^n \quad - \quad \text{a lot of raw values of power consumption;}$$

$$\{W_k^{VER}\}_{k=1}^n \quad - \quad \text{multiple verified values;}$$

$$\{W_k^{RAN}\}_{k=1}^n \quad - \quad \text{multiple ranked values;}$$

$$\{W_k^{APP}\}_{k=1}^n \quad - \quad \text{the set of approximated values.}$$

The presented system (1.1) includes sets that form vectors of "raw", verified and approximated data, forming four primary layers of data on REC power consumption.

A distinctive feature of this technique is the possibility of implementing elements of artificial intelligence. Figure 2 shows a parallel algorithm for implementing big data verification procedures using ChatGPT. As can be seen from the figure, the user simultaneously requests the same operations from ChatGPT while implementing the main software package developed in the Mathcad 15 environment.

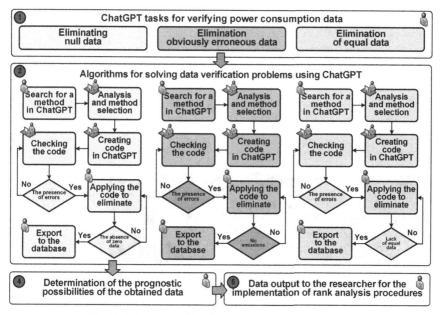

Fig. 2. Big Data verification algorithm using Chat GPT.

Within the framework of requests to ChatGPT, the best codes for the implementation of calculation programs are generated to eliminate zero, obviously erroneous and equal big data. Figure 2 shows the operations performed by the user using the "little man" figure, and the "little man with a computer" icon shows the operations performed using Chat GPT. Figure 3 shows a fragment of the work of the user and Chat GPT to eliminate null data.

Next, the user forms a question about creating an algorithm for eliminating null data, proposed by ChatGPT (Fig. 4).

At the final stage of the methodology, an algorithm is used to verify the adequacy of "raw", verified and approximated data. The purpose of implementing this algorithm is to obtain a reference data layer with the best predictive capabilities. This will allow us to obtain the most accurate results in the future when implementing other control procedures.

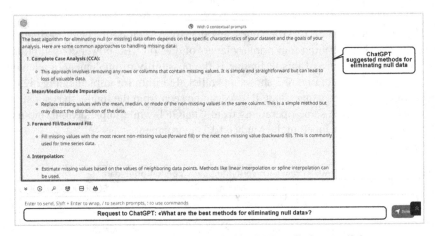

Fig. 3. A fragment of working with ChatGPT to eliminate null data.

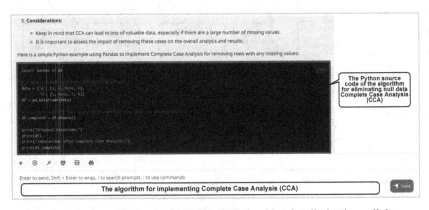

Fig. 4. A fragment of the proposed ChatGPT algorithm for eliminating null data.

3   The Results of Testing the Methodology of Parametric Adaptation of Big Data

To verify the adequacy of big data, matrices obtained from the sets of the system (1) and a vector of known values are imported, which is selected as a verification one. Usually, the verification vector represents data on power consumption for the last known year or month (Fig. 5). The matrices of "raw", verified and approximated data have a certain size, which allows to fully implement the procedure for predicting power consumption. For example, for annual data, the working matrix should include power consumption values for five to seven years. Next, forecasting is performed using several methods for a known year based on the data of each matrix. Forecasting is carried out by several methods. In this case, the user used forecasting methods: SSA-R, a technocenological forecasting method with a fixed first point (SPT) and based on rank phase angles (RFU). As an example, monthly data from 2017 to 2022 were processed for the implementation of the parametric adaptation of big data. The last one, 2022, was chosen as a test year. And the matrices of raw, verified and approximated data were the values from 2017 to 2021. Figure 5 shows a fragment of the prediction results and a verification vector.

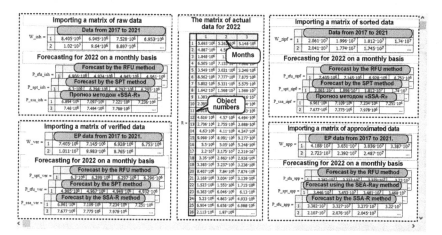

Fig. 5. Formation of the initial data for verification.

Using ChatGPT, the user selected the following forecasting methods: ARIMA, Gradient Boosting Machines (GBM), Recurrent Neural Networks (RNNs). Figures 6 and 7 show a request to ChatGPT and an algorithm for implementing the ARIMA method.

After receiving the forecast values, their accuracy was checked based on the calculation of the total relative forecast error, relative forecast error, total absolute error, average relative error, maximum relative error:

$$
\begin{cases}
sa = \sum_{i=1}^{n} |w_i - y_i|; \quad so_i = 100 \frac{|w_i - y_i|}{w_i}; \\
ss = \frac{\left| \sum_{i=1}^{n} w_i - \sum_{i=1}^{n} y_i \right|}{\sum_{i=1}^{n} w_i}; \quad \overline{so} = \frac{1}{n} \sum_{i=1}^{n} so_i; \quad mo = \max_{1 \le i \le n}(so_i),
\end{cases}
\tag{2}
$$

$i = 1, \ldots, n$ –   formal index; n – number of objects;

y_i –   projected power consumption of the i-th object;

w_i –   the actual power consumption of the i-th object;

ss   –   the total relative error of the forecast for the entire system, %;

so_i –   relative forecast error for the i-th object;

sa   –   total absolute error, kWh;

$\overline{so}$ –   average relative error, %;

mo   –   maximum relative error, %.

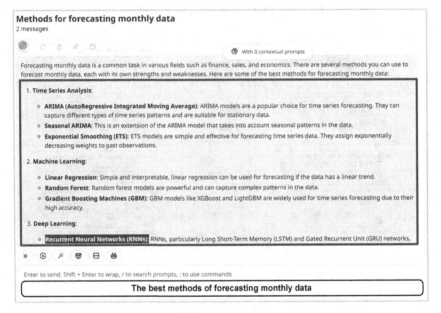

Fig. 6. A fragment of a ChatGPT query about the best forecasting methods.

After evaluating the accuracy of forecasting, the following results were obtained (Tables 1, 2 and 3).

As a result of the analysis of Tables 1, 2 and 3, integral indicators of predictive capabilities were formed by the method of additive convolution (Table 4).

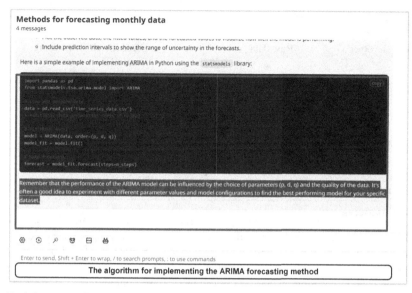

Methods for forecasting monthly data
4 messages

○ Include prediction intervals to show the range of uncertainty in the forecasts.

Here is a simple example of implementing ARIMA in Python using the statsmodels library:

```
import pandas as pd
from statsmodels.tsa.arima.model import ARIMA

data = pd.read_csv('time_series_data.csv')

model = ARIMA(data, order=(p, d, q))
model_fit = model.fit()

forecast = model_fit.forecast(steps=n_steps)
```

Remember that the performance of the ARIMA model can be influenced by the choice of parameters (p, d, q) and the quality of the data. It's often a good idea to experiment with different parameter values and model configurations to find the best performing model for your specific dataset.

Enter to send, Shift + Enter to wrap, / to search prompts, : to use commands

The algorithm for implementing the ARIMA forecasting method

Fig. 7. A fragment of the proposed ChatGPT source code for implementing the ARIMA method.

Table 1. Results of estimation of forecasting accuracy based on "raw" data.

Name of the error	Raw data			Forecasts obtained using ChatGPT		
	SPT	RFU	SSA-R	ARIMA	GBM	RNNs
Total absolute error, 10^7	4.6	8.8	8.9	4.3	6.1	6.5
Average relative error, %	10	15	18	8	7	8
Total relative error, %	3	8	6	9	5	6

Table 2. The results of the assessment of the accuracy of forecasting based on verified data.

Name of the error	Verified data			Forecasts obtained using ChatGPT		
	SPT	RFU	SSA-R	ARIMA	GBM	RNNs
Total absolute error, 10^7	4.1	7.8	7.9	3.3	2.1	4.5
Average relative error, %	9	11	13	8	3.1	6
Total relative error, %	4	6	5	4	3	5

Table 3. The results of the assessment of the accuracy of forecasting based on approximated data.

Name of the error	Raw data			Forecasts obtained using ChatGPT		
	SPT	RFU	SSA-R	ARIMA	GBM	RNNs
Total absolute error, 10^7	4.8	9.8	10.9	5.3	7.1	7.5
Average relative error, %	15	14	19	9	9	10
Total relative error, %	7	9	9	12	8	9

4 Conclusion

Thus, one of the modern methods of big data processing is the technique of parametric adaptation of big data. The basis of this technique is vector rank analysis, developed within the framework of the technocenological theory of Professor B.I. Kudrin.

The novelty of the technique lies in the fact that for the first time, together with technocenological methods, it became possible to apply elements of artificial intelligence. The main stages of the methodology are: loading "raw" data, forming matrices of verified and approximated data, as well as checking their adequacy based on vector rank analysis methods. These steps are performed in parallel using ChatGPT based on the proposed artificial intelligence methods.

At the final stage, the best data layer is selected based on integral indicators of predictive capabilities. As a result of the implementation of the proposed methodology on the monthly data of a large enterprise from 2017 to 2022, two results were obtained. The first result is that the best data layer is selected – verified data obtained at the second stage of the methodology. The second result is that for this type of data, the most powerful forecasting method has been defined – the Gradient Boosting Machines (GBM) method, since it has the lowest integral indicator of predictive capabilities equal to 2.7.

References

1. Kitchin, R., Thousand, O.: The data revolution: big data, open data, data infrastructures and their consequences. J. Regional Sci. **56**(4), 722–723 (2016)
2. McArdle, G., Kitchin, R.: What makes big data, big data? https://www.researchgate.net/publication/295253316 last accessed 2023/10/26
3. Boyd, D., Crawford, K.: Six provocations for big data. A decade in internet time: symposium on the dynamics of the internet and society https://ssrn.com/abstract=1926431, https://doi.org/10.2139/ssrn.1926431. Accessed 21 Nov 2023
4. Boyd, D., Marwick, A.E.: Social Privacy in networked publics: teens' attitudes, practices, and strategies. a decade in internet time: symposium on the dynamics of the internet and society, September 2011
5. O'Malley, M.J.: Learning strategies in second language acquisition. Conference. Oxford, England. Publication. Cambridge University Press Collection in library; print disabled; internet archive books. Cambridge, New York, 260 p. (1990)
6. Floridi, L., Illari, Ph.: The Philosophy of Information Quality. Springer International, 15–22 (2014)

7. Zhu, C.: Earning surprise and implied volatility: could new information increase uncertainty? SSRN: https://ssrn.com/abstract=2591742 or https://doi.org/10.2139/ssrn.2591742. Accessed 08 Oct 2023
8. Leonelli, S.: Documenting the emergence of bio-ontologies: or, why researching bioinformatics requires HPSSB. Hist Philos Life Sci **32**(1), 105–126 (2019)
9. Bogen, J.: Noise in the world. Philos. Sci. **77**(5), 778–791 (2016)
10. Bowker, M.: Shifting Perspective on Indexicals. Pragmatics **32**(4), 518–536 (2022)
11. Edwards, P.N.: A Vast Machine: Computer Models, Climate Data, and the Politics of Global Warming. The MIT Press, Cambridge (2010)
12. Edwards, Paul N., M.S. Mayernik, A.L. Batcheller: Science friction. Data, Metadata, and Collaboration. Social Studies of Science 41(5), 667–690 (2011)
13. Lagoze, C.: Big data, data integrity, and the fracturing of the control zone. Big Data Soc. **1**(2), 45–56 (2014)
14. Tempini, N.: Till data do us part: understanding data-based value creation in dataintensive infrastructures. Inf. Organ. **27**, 191–210 (2017)
15. Sarkisova, A.Y.: Big data and problems of society: collection of articles based on the results of the International Scientific Conference (Kirov, May 19–20, 2022) (2022)
16. Gnatyuk, V.: The law of optimal construction of Technocenoses: monograph. http://gnatukvi.ru/ind.html. Accessed 23 Oct 2023
17. Haitun, S.D.: Problems of quantitative analysis of science, 280 p. (1989)
18. Gnatyuk, V.I., Kivchun, O.R., Dorofeev, S.A., Bovtrikova, E.V.: Mathematical model of parametric virtualization of technocenosis data. In: CEUR Workshop Proceeding, pp. 90–99 (2021)
19. Mukhamedieva, D.T., Safarova, L.U. Main problems and tasks of intellectualisation of information processing system. Int. J. Innov. Technol. Explor. Eng. **8**(9.3), 158–165 (2019)
20. Gnatyuk, V.I., Kivchun, O.R., Lutsenko, D.V.: Digital platform for management of the regional power grid consumption. In: IOP Conference Series: Earth and Environmental Science, vol. 689, no. 1, p. 012022 (2021)
21. Orazbayev, B., Ospanov, E., Kissikova, N., Mukataev, N., Orazbayeva, K.: Decision-making in the fuzzy environment on the basis of various compromise schemes. Procedia Comput. Sci. **120**, 945–952 (2017)
22. Marzhan, Y., Talshyn, K., Kairat, K., Belginova, S., Karlygash, A., Yerbol, O.: Smart technologies of the risk-management and decision-making systems in a fuzzy data environment. Indonesian J. Electr. Eng. Comput. Sci. **28**(3), 1463–1474 (2022)
23. Gnatyuk, V.I., Kivchun, O.R., Ilyshin, P.S.: Parametric adaptation of data on electrical appliances of objects of the regional energy system based on color analysis. Industrial Energy **10**, 48–56 (2020)
24. Kivchun, O.R.: Vector rank analysis: a treatise. http://gnatukvi.ru/vran.pdf. Accessed 10 Sep 2023
25. Suyunov, A.S., Mirzayev, A.A., Urakov, O.A., Suyunov, S.A.: Field studies of electronic total stations in a special reference satellite geodetic basis. In: Proceedings of SPIE - The International Society for Optical Engineering, vol. 12564, 125640Y (2023)

Development of Automation and Control System of Waste Gas Production Process Based on Information Technology

Bobir Toshmamatov$^{(\boxtimes)}$ (iD)

Karshi Engineering Economics Institute, Karshi, Uzbekistan
boburissiqlik@gmail.com

Abstract. Achieving energy and resource efficiency through the application of modern information technologies, calculation algorithms, automatic management and control systems to the process of waste gas production from solid household waste is an urgent issue today. In the article, the author analyzed the system of automatic management and control of the process of heliothermic processing of solid household waste based on information technology. The thermal scheme of the automatic and control system of the exhaust gas production process from municipal solid waste is proposed. ATmega8 microcontroller, which allows automatic management and control of all technological and thermochemical processes of waste gas production, was used in the heliothermic waste gas processing unit. At the same time, all technological processes of waste gas production, collection and use are automated, anaerobic fermentation (50 ÷ 55 °C) in the device, automatic control of heat distribution processes between layers in the waste reactor, waste protection, technological process parameters, order charging and energy saving is ensured. Automation and control of the solid waste heliothermic processing plant is carried out by the application of information technologies, the information resource of the system, working pressure, temperature, temperature range, humidity, consumption of raw materials, the level of the mixture in the waste reactor, the pH indicator, as well as the control of the operation of the valves.

Keywords: Municipal Solid Waste · Waste Reactor · Waste Gas · Automation And Control · Energy And Resource Saving · Microcontroller · Anaerobic Fermentation

1 Introduction

The rational use of natural fuel and energy resources is one of the global problems of the countries of the world, and its successful solution will be crucial not only for the further development of the world community, but also for maintaining environmental stability. One of the promising ways to solve this problem is the use of new energy-saving technologies using renewable energy sources [1–3].

The depletion of traditional fossil fuels (coal, oil, and gas) and the environmental consequences of burning them has led to a significant increase in interest in energy

© The Author(s), under exclusive license to Springer Nature Switzerland AG 2024
A. Gibadullin (Ed.): ITIDMS 2023, CCIS 2112, pp. 196–205, 2024.
https://doi.org/10.1007/978-3-031-60318-1_17

devices and technologies based on renewable energy sources in almost all developed countries of the world in recent years [3–6].

Energy devices based on renewable and alternative energy sources are energy-saving and environmentally friendly "GREEN" technologies that provide savings on traditional energy sources: natural gas, liquid, solid organic fuels, and electricity [7, 8].

Therefore, the issue of reconstruction of the energy base and finding ways to use environmentally friendly renewable energy sources is urgent.

Today, the problem of waste is becoming one of the most urgent environmental, social and energy issues on a global scale. Analyzes show that household and industrial emissions have been increasing year by year in recent years. Especially in the 21st century, the increase in the volume of household waste began to have a very negative impact on environmental stability.

Consistent efforts are being made in our country to protect the environment, ensure public health, rational use of natural resources, and improvement of sanitary and ecological conditions.

This problem is especially relevant for Uzbekistan, because the annual accumulation of all types of waste is very large, and the rate of their reuse does not exceed 30%. The southern regions of our republic, especially the Kashkadarya region, are distinguished by the high potential of renewable energy resources (solar energy, biomass energy). In particular, the well-developed agricultural and horticultural sectors of the Kashkadarya region means that it has a high concentration of cheap raw materials (solid household, organic and agro-industrial waste) for the production of waste gas. In such areas, there is a possibility of a continuous and stable supply of agro-industrial complexes, social sector objects with completely cheap, ecologically clean energy resources, alternative fuel (biogas, exhaust gas), and energy units equivalent to heat and electricity.

The purpose of this work is to automate a solar device for the processing of small-scale municipal solid waste, which allows to improve the production of waste gas and high-quality biohumus as a result of heliothermal processing of municipal solid waste, increases its quality and reduces human participation in labor-intensive processes [9].

For energy-efficient and continuous operation of the heliothermic solid waste treatment plant, all parameters of the technological process (solid household waste amount, loading and unloading of solid household waste, temperature regime, exhaust gas pressure, working pressure, humidity regime, management and control of valves and valves) it is necessary to develop an automation unit that monitors and controls [10–18].

1.1 Statement of the Problem

Automation means the introduction of technical tools that manage technological processes without human intervention. Automation is a new stage of the industry in which no man is involved in the production process, in which the function of controlling the technological and production processes is performed by automatic devices. The introduction of automation leads to the improvement of the main technical and economic indicators of production, i.e. the increase in the quantity and quality of the produced products and the decrease in their cost. That is why it is important to automate the operation process of the heliothermic processing unit of solid household waste, increase the continuity of the process and quality indicators by reducing the human factor.

The purpose of automation is to automate, optimize, and manage plans to increase the efficiency and productivity of solid waste processing and the quality of production, freeing people from working in harmful conditions. It is the result of the general development of science and technology. The development of automation of technological processes began mainly in the 50-60s. The degree of automation in various areas of chemical production has increased due to the goal-oriented technical policy. The integrity of the technological equipment and the implementation of the management of the technological processes mastered it in the technological process constitute the management of the technological object. A human-machine system that provides automated collection and processing of information and is necessary for optimal management in various areas of human activity is called an automated management system [16–20].

In this work, the solar device designed for the processing of solid household waste and the automatic management and control of the processes taking place in it are carried out in three stages.

Firstly, automatic control provides the necessary conditions for the automatic reception and processing of fast data in the processing of solid household waste.

Secondly, automatic adjustment - in the processing of solid household waste, thermal-technical parameters of waste, and thermal-physical parameters of the substrate loaded into the waste reactor are maintained at the required level using automatic adjustment devices, and a stable temperature regime is provided. In this case, the person controls only the correct operation of the automatic adjustment system.

Thirdly, automatic management is the development of a certain consistency of the effects on the object of management in the sequence of automatic execution of the specified processes in the processing of solid household waste.

It helps to significantly increase productivity with minimal human resources, which is implemented with the help of programmable microprocessors and relevant information sensors [7].

2   Materials and Methods

Components of the technological process of waste gas production. The number of countries that are developing renewable and alternative energy sources and increasing their share in the energy balance is increasing in the conditions of the constant increase in the prices of traditional energy resources, their limited reserves, as well as the depletion of the Earth's hydrocarbon resources. it is aimed to increase its share to 15%. One of the alternative energy sources is biomass energy, bioenergy, and biogas, waste gas. A heliothermic solid waste processing unit is a technological complex consisting of the following working parts [8, 12, 20]:

- Collection of solid household waste and separation of household organic waste;
- Loading and unloading of household organic waste;
- Providing heat energy;
- Waste gas and biohumus production;
- Purification and storage of waste gas;
- Electricity and thermal energy production;

– An automated control system for a solar device designed for the processing of solid household waste.

Heliothermic solid waste treatment plant and raw material preparation system (separation of organic household waste from solid waste) and mixing of primary organic household waste with water to ensure the required raw material moisture content (85%) controlled by a humidity sensor, as well as the mixture used to feed the waste reactor. The mixture (organic household waste + water) is loaded into the waste reactor of the considered solid household waste heliothermic processing unit using a screw conveyor.

The waste reactor of the heliothermic solid waste treatment plant is hermetically sealed, the activity of waste gas-producing bacteria is observed in an airless environment, and the generated waste gas accumulates in the upper part of the waste reactor, creates pressure, and passes to the filter.

The temperature of the mixture loaded into the waste reactor must be maintained at an optimal level (50 ÷ 55 °C), which ensures the normal functioning of the relevant anaerobic bacteria and increases the level of gas release. The reaction in the waste reactor itself is exothermic, but if the ambient temperature is lower than the required temperature, it is necessary to ensure the temperature regime in the waste reactor. The difficulty is that the raw materials loaded into the waste reactor must be kept at the same temperature and the temperature must be kept within the specified limits. Determination of the optimal temperature regime for methanogenesis depends on the morphological composition of the processed waste. The devices, reflectors, and solar air heating collectors installed in the heliothermic processing unit of solid household waste must ensure the temperature regime of the unit, pressure, and control of the technological process.

It is necessary to organize periodic mixing of raw materials, which ensures efficient and stable operation of the heliothermic processing unit of solid household waste. The raw material loaded into the waste reactor tends to separate into fractions during the reaction. It is recommended to mix the raw materials slowly every 5–6 h.

Mixing also ensures uniform heating of raw materials between layers. The heliothermic solid waste processing unit is equipped with a pneumatic mixer, and optimal mixing of raw materials increases the efficiency of waste gas output up to 50 ÷ 60%. The produced waste gas can be cleaned in a filter and sent to a storage tank, and then used in mini-thermal power plants or cogeneration devices to generate heat and electricity. A part of the received heat energy is used to cover the private needs of the device (45–55% of the rest is provided by solar energy).

The operation of the automation unit is based on the data collected by several sensors, namely the temperature of the raw material in the waste reactor, the amount of raw material in the reactor, the operating pressure and humidity in the waste reactor. Based on this information, as well as on the basis of timer signals, the automation unit turns on and off the heating system, the mixing system, and also gives a signal about the beginning and end of loading, filling and discharge of raw materials.

Devices that ensure the progress and control of the technological process. Devices that control the technological process in a waste reactor include:

– A screw conveyor that loads the sorted household organic waste from the initial tank to the waste reactor. The operation of the screw transmission is automatically controlled;

- A screw mixer that allows mixing of raw materials loaded into the waste reactor;
- The heating system necessary to provide the raw materials in the waste reactor with a stable temperature regime (50 ÷ 55 °C). The side and bottom of the waste reactor consist of an air duct, and the bottom of the air duct is connected to a solar air heating collector with a flat reflector with a heat accumulator with the help of an electric heater and a valve.
- Automatic valves (L1–L8). Ensures normal operation of automated valves and valves;
- The timer transmits signals to the microcontroller at 10-min intervals, which turns on and off the raw material heating and mixing system, and also informs about the need to remove and fill the raw material from the waste reactor;
- pH sensor, which records and displays the acidity value of the raw material in the waste reactor;
- A micromanometer sensor, which records and displays the value of the working pressure in the waste reactor.

Heliothermic Solid Waste Processing Unit Consists of the Following Systems

1. The waste reactor for the anaerobic processing of solid household waste by helio-thermic method is designed in the form of a parallelepiped in two layers with the dimensions of 1200 × 1000 mm, a pneumatic mixer is installed, and it is provided with a filter and a gas holder.
2. The side and bottom of the waste reactor consist of an air channel, and the bottom of the air channel is connected to a solar air heating collector with a heat accumulator flat reflector with a useful surface of 1.8 m^2 using an electric heater and a valve. The energy of the solar air heating collector to increase its efficiency, parallel flat reflectors with a useful surface of 1.8 m^2 are installed. As a heat accumulator, water and transformer oil are used. As a result, a solar air heating collector with a flat reflector with a heat accumulator serves as an active solar heating system for processing solid household waste in the waste reactor at a temperature range of 50 ÷ 55 °C.
3. A transparent cover (glass, polycarbonate glass, and 1, 2, 3 layers of polyethylene film) is installed on the upper part of the waste reactor in a triangular shape, which serves as a passive solar heating system for the waste reactor. To increase the energy efficiency of the device, flat reflectors of size 1200 × 1000 mm are installed parallel to it from the back and upper part of the waste reactor, which transmits the incoming solar radiation to the passive solar heating system.

To run a heliothermal solid waste treatment plant, a low-power power source such as solar panels, a diesel unit, or batteries is required, as well as a source of water and waste.

Figure 1 shows a heliothermal waste treatment plant and its automatic control system, which uses various sensors and automation system blocks.

Here, 1-waste reactor, 2-loading tank, 3-screw pump, 4-raw material loading valve, 5-passive solar heating system, 6-hinged reflector, 7-air channel, 8-solar air heating collector with flat reflector with heat accumulator. 9- electric heater, 10- screw mixer, 11- filter, 12- gas holder, 13- micromanometer, 14- temperature sensor, 15- pH sensor, 16- level sensor, 17- raw material release valve, 18- hot air air valve that transfers to channels, 19-valves for transferring hot air from cogeneration device to air ducts, 20-gas transfer valves, 21-cogeneration devices, 22-gas analyzers, 23-valves for loading local organic compound, 24-hot water generator tank, 25-humidity sensors, 26-1BLOCK, 27-2 BLOCK, 28-DD1-microcontroller, 29-timer, 30-bunker, 31-hot water valve, 32-steam gas mixture valve.

Heliothermic solid waste treatment plant and control system works in the following order.

The waste reactor 1 is designed in the form of a parallelepiped in two layers with dimensions of 1200 ×1000 mm, with 100 mm air ducts on the sides and bottom, and 100 mm thermal insulation on the sides and bottom of the waste reactor to prevent heat loss. An electric heater 9 is installed in the lower part of the air channel. A temperature sensor 14 is installed in the waste reactor to maintain the required temperature level. When the temperature drops below the required value (the pressure in the reactor is within normal limits), the temperature sensor sends a signal to the input of the DD1 microcontroller, which turns on the electric heater 9. When the temperature in the reactor rises, the microcontroller DD1 turns off the electric heater 9. Organic waste with different morphological compositions from valve 23, which loads the local organic compound into loading tank 2, hot water flow from the hot water generator tank through the hot water valve 31 is controlled by BLOCK 2. The temperature and humidity of the mixture are controlled by the DD1 microcontroller 28 and the timer 29 through the temperature sensor 14 and humidity sensor 25 installed in loading tank 2.

The loading of raw materials into the waste reactor 1 through the loading valve 4 of the mixture (waste + water (substrate)) formed in the loading tank 2 by means of a screw pump is controlled by BLOCK 2. Based on the amount indicated by the level sensor 16 installed on the side walls of the waste reactor 1, the substrate loading is stopped according to the signal from the microcontroller DD1. A transparent cover (glass, polycarbonate glass, and 1, 2, 3 layers of polyethylene film) is installed from the top of the waste reactor in a triangular shape, which serves as a passive solar heating

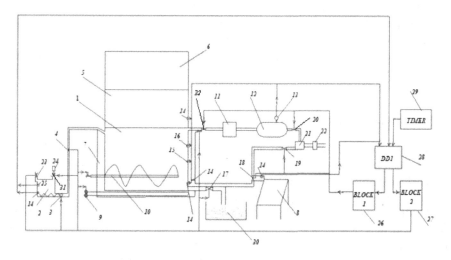

Fig. 1. Heliothermal solid waste treatment plant and control system.

system for the waste reactor. To increase the energy efficiency of the device, flat reflectors of 1200 × 1000 mm size are installed parallel to it from the back and upper part of the waste reactor, which transmits the incoming solar radiation to the passive solar heating system. is used to heat the substrate loaded into the reactor to the required temperature regime. A solar air heating collector 8 with a flat reflector with a heat accumulator to the air channel of the waste reactor transfers hot air to the air channels using valve 18 and heats the substrate based on heat conduction from the side and bottom walls of the waste reactor.

Temperature sensors 14 record the substrate and the air temperature in the air channel. If the temperature of the mixture in the waste reactor exceeds the set temperature regime of $50 \div 55$ °C, the microcontroller adjusts the consumption of hot air from valve 8, which transfers hot air to the air ducts, according to the signal from DD1.

According to timer 29 and the signal from BLOCK 2, the substrate loaded in the screw mixer waste reactor 1 is mixed.

During the maintenance of the waste reactor with a stable temperature regime, an anaerobic fermentation process, an exothermic reaction takes place, as a result of which water vapor, methane, and other compounds are released and make up the total waste gas (containing $55 \div 65\%$ methane). The generated gas is released on the free surface of the substrate, due to the relatively high temperature, the amount of water vapor in the exhaust gas decreases. Under the influence of the generated pressure, the waste gas passes through the filter 11 to the gas holder 12 after being cleaned of water vapor, carbonic anhydride, and hydrogen sulfide. The pressure in the gas holder is recorded by micromanometer 13. To increase the energy efficiency of the device, to provide additional heat and electricity on cloudy days and at night, a cogeneration device 21 is installed, and exhaust gas is supplied from the gas holder 12 using the gas transfer valve 20. The composition of waste gas is determined by gas analyzer 22.

The timer 32 and the pressure sensor 13 give a signal to the input of the microcontroller DD1, the output signal of which is given to BLOCK 1 (26). In this case, the timer provides the opening and closing of valves (20,32) at 10-min intervals.

The timer 32 and the pH sensor 15, the level sensor give a signal to the input of the microcontroller DD1, whose output signal is given to BLOCK 2 (27). In this case, the timer ensures the opening and closing of the valves (17) at 10-min intervals, and part of the substrate in the waste reactor is removed to the hopper 30. And so the process continues.

3   Results and Discussion

Figure 2 shows the block diagram developed for the automation and control of the heliothermal waste treatment plant with a DD1 (ATmega8) microcontroller.

Heliothermic solid waste processing device and control system (Fig. 1) based on the appropriate technological process, a block diagram of the device was developed, which allows to automation of the entire technological process of waste gas production, from the loading of raw materials into the waste reactor and its removal from the reactor includes processes that are.

Based on the block diagram in Fig. 2, a schematic diagram of the heliothermic treatment of solid household waste was developed (Fig. 3). The scheme is based on

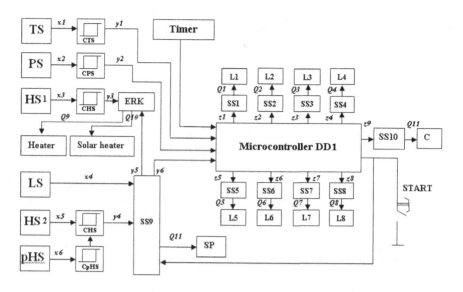

Fig. 2. Block diagram of a heliothermal waste treatment device with a DD1 (ATmega8) microcontroller (PS - pressure sensor; HS - temperature sensor; SS - level sensor; HS1, HS2 - humidity sensors; CTS, CPS, CHS, CpHS – comparators; ERK - electric relay switch; SS1-SS10 – semiconductor switches; L1–L8 - gas valves; C - compressor; SP - screw pump electric motor, DD1 – microcontroller).

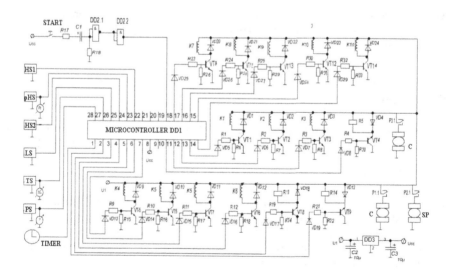

Fig. 3. Schematic diagram of a heliothermal waste treatment device.

the use of transistor electric relay switches, which ensures the absence of fluctuations when starting the system and powering the compressor, electric heater, solar air heating collector with a flat reflector with a heat accumulator, screw pump, and a stabilized voltage of 5 V.

4 Conclusions

It is possible to make block diagrams of the inputs and outputs of the ATmega8 microcontroller according to the elements of the heliothermic waste treatment device (Fig. 1).

Using modern information technologies, calculation algorithms, automatic management and control systems to the process of exhaust gas production from solid household waste, the heat- block schemes were developed and microcontrollers DD1 (ATmega8) were used in it.

The automated thermal scheme of the heliothermal processing unit of solid household waste, the block diagram of the heliothermal processing unit of solid household waste with microcontroller DD1 (ATmega8) was developed. The waste gas automation and control system proposed by the author is the heliothermic treatment of waste, providing the waste reactor with a stable temperature regime (50 ÷ 55 °C) and fully automating the process of continuous production of waste gas (containing 50 ÷ 65% methane) allows. The presented development makes it possible to use it for various modifications of thermal or heliothermic waste processing devices, as well as to make corrections to the technological process of the system.

Acknowledgements. I express my gratitude to Sh.Ergashev, docent of the Department of "Heat Power Engineering" and A.R. Toshboev and B.R. Arziev assistants of the Department "Alternative Energy Sources" at the Karshi Engineering Economics Institute.

References

1. Toshmamatov, B.: Determination of the energy efficiency of a flat reflector solar air heating collector with a heat accumulator. In: E3S Web of Conferences, vol. 402, p. 05010 (2023)
2. Rakhimov, O.D., Manzarov, Y.K., Azizov, S.L., Turdiev, S.S., Chorshanbiyev, Z.: Small universal unit for preparing, transporting and distributing liquid feed in small pig farms. BIO Web Conf. **71**, 01056 (2023)
3. Toshmamatov, B.: Improving the energy efficiency of a solar air heater with heat accumulator using flat reflectors. In: IE3S Web of Conferences, vol. 411, p. 01026 (2023)
4. Khuzhakulov, S.M., Faiziev, T.A., Sherkulov, B.G., Murodov, I., Samatova, S.Y.: Analysis of scientific research conducted to improve the efficiency of solar concentrator systems. BIO Web Conf. **71**, 02033 (2023)
5. Uzakov, G., Mamatkulova, S., Ergashev, S.: Thermal mode of the condenser of a pyrolysis bioenergy plant with recuperation of secondary thermal energy. In: E3S Web of Conferences, vol. 411, p. 01021 (2023)
6. Roman, M.: Renewable energy resources in students' opinions. Studia Ecologiae et Bioethicae **13**(3), 49–63 (2015)

7. Toshmamatov, B., Shomuratova, S., Safarova, S. Improving the energy efficiency of a solar air heater with heat accumulator using flat reflectors. In: E3S Web of Conferences, vol. 411, p. 01026 (2023)

8. Evgeniy, V., Tshovrebov, E., Niyazgulov, U.: Organizational, technical and economic fundamentals of waste management and monitoring. In: E3S Web of Conferences, vol. 164, p. 08031 (2020)

9. Sadia, I.: Bio-reclamation of strategic and energy critical metals from secondary resources. Metals 7(60), 207 (2017)

10. Khuzhakulov, S.M., Uzakov, G.N., Vardiyashvili, A.B.: Effectiveness of solar heating systems for the regeneration of adsorbents in recessed fruit and vegetable storages. Appl. Solar Energy (English Transl. Geliotekhnika) 49(4), 257–260 (2013)

11. Sattorov, B.: Increasing energy efficiency combined device solar dryer-water heater with heat accumulator. In: BIO Web of Conferences, vol. 71, p. 02024 (2023)

12. Vardiyashvili, A.B.: Utilization of conventional source waste heat in solar greenhouses. Appl. Solar Energy (English Transl. Geliotekhnika) 5(1), 20–23 (1999)

13. Mamatkulova, S.G.: Modeling and calculation of the thermal balance of a pyrolysis plant for the production of alternative fuels from biomass. In: IOP Conference Series: Earth and Environmental Science, vol. 1070, no. 1, p. 012040 (2022)

14. Uzakov, G.N.: Experimental study of the temperature regime of the solar pond in the climatic conditions of the south of Uzbekistan. In: IOP Conference Series: Earth and Environmental Science, vol. 1070, no. 1, p. 012026 (2022)

15. Arakelyan, M.K., Shepelin, A.V.: Methods for constructing automatic control systems for electric drives of pumps operating on long pipelines. Electr. Eng. 2, 35–40 (2001)

16. Orazbayev, B., Ospanov, E., Kissikova, N., Mukataev, N., Orazbayeva, K.: Decision-making in the fuzzy environment on the basis of various compromise schemes. Procedia Comput. Sci. 120, 945–952 (2017)

17. Kuznetsova, S.N., Kuznetsov, V.P., Kozlova, E.P., Potashnik, Y.S., Tsymbalov, S.D.: Transformational period of Russian development in the digital economy. In: Popkova, E., Sergi, B. (eds.) The 21st Century from the Positions of Modern Science: Intellectual, Digital and Innovative Aspects, ISC 2019, LNNS, vol. 91, pp 663–669. Springer, Cham (2020). https://doi.org/10.1007/978-3-030-32015-7_74

18. Filipov, A.I.: Automation of the control system in the foundry. Probl. Prospects Dev. Russia Youth View Future 3, 159–161 (2019)

19. Mukhamedieva, D.T., Safarova, L.U. Main problems and tasks of intellectualisation of information processing system. Int. J. Innov. Technol. Explor. Eng. 8(9.3), 158–165 (2019)

20. Marzhan, Y., Talshyn, K., Kairat, K., Belginova, S., Karlygash, A., Yerbol, O.: Smart technologies of the risk-management and decision-making systems in a fuzzy data environment. Indonesian J. Electr. Eng. Comput. Sci. 28(3), 1463–1474 (2022)

Machine Learning and Data Mining

Dmitry A. Kurasov[1]([✉]), Anton S. Kutuzov[2], Dmitry S. Zvonarev[1],
and Anton P. Devyatkov[1]

[1] University of Tyumen, 6, Street Volodarskogo, Tyumen 625003, Russia
`naukka@mail.ru`
[2] Chelyabinsk State University, 129, Street Kashirin Brothers, Chelyabinsk 454001, Russia

Abstract. The article discusses the main tasks of machine learning. The functional structure of a computer algorithm for solving machine learning problems and a data mining model are considered. The solution of the simplest machine learning problem using the classification method of linear regression is proposed. The analysis of existing learning algorithms based on a decision tree is carried out. Based on the analysis performed, a decision tree was selected for implementation using the so-called C4.5 algorithm. The article builds a decision tree using specific training data. The application of a simple and understandable algorithm for building trees is to create all possible trees, calculate the number of erroneously classified data for each of them and select a tree with a minimum number of errors. As a result, an optimal learning algorithm is formed for the decision tree in terms of data errors in the learning process. The top-down algorithm implemented in the article for building a decision tree selects the attribute with the largest increase in information at each step. Entropy is used as a metric of the amount of information in the training data set D. In the process of implementation, this algorithm is analyzed to identify opportunities for its application to a more complex task.

Keywords: Machine Learning · Decision Tree Learning · Entropy · Information Gain · Data Analysis

1 Introduction

Artificial intelligence serves to make computers able to perform various functional actions and tasks that humans are currently better at performing.

Humans by nature have more advanced educational abilities and skills to acquire new knowledge in comparison with computers. Because of this, it follows that the study of the mechanics of learning implementation and the modification of machine learning methods and algorithms at a qualitative level is one of the priorities of artificial intelligence.

A high level of demand for the practical use of machine learning capabilities is observed in the field of development and design of various software products. For example, the behavioral features of autonomous robots can be programmed on such principles. Depending on the purpose of use, the structural features of intellectual behavior may have a complicated description scheme. In some cases, the complexity becomes so high

A. Gibadullin (Ed.): ITIDMS 2023, CCIS 2112, pp. 206–216, 2024.
https://doi.org/10.1007/978-3-031-60318-1_18

that the behavior is difficult to program optimally. This applies not as it were to low-level, but indeed cutting edge high-level programming languages, such as PROLOG and Python. Machine learning calculations are presently finding commonsense utilize within the case of programming robots in a way that coincides with the existing way of human learning. In many cases, this is often a crossover combination of programmed and learned behavior.

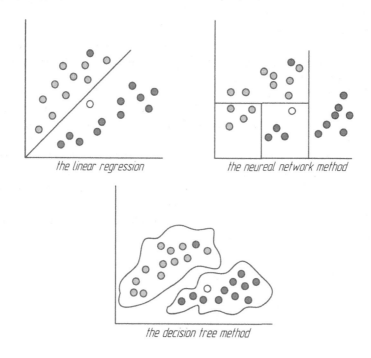

the linear regression

the neureal network method

the decision tree method

Fig. 1. Solving classification problems by various methods.

There are numerous viable errands within the humanities and connected scientific sciences to utilize machine learning. This incorporates, for illustration, considering the vocabulary and language structure of a outside dialect, memorizing specialized terms, and memorizing verse. For individuals, such errands are troublesome due to need of free time. The computing capabilities of computers make it conceivable to unravel these problems very effectively, since they vary as it were somewhat from the method of sparing content data to a record framework. In this way, the issue of memorization is of small esteem to artificial insights. The procurement of numerical abilities, on the other hand, essentially does not include the memorization handle. Within the case of addition of characteristic numbers, this does not apply at all, since each whole of $x + y$ corresponds to an interminable number of values. For each combination of two values x and y, it is vital to keep in mind the three $(x, y, x + y)$, which is essentially impossible. Within the case of decimal numbers, this possibility does not exist at all.

Right now, science instruction is based on the guideline of generalization. The educator tells the theoretical justification of a prepare, and the students work it out within the process of fathoming issues until, at a certain emphasis, they halt making botches in unused cases. For example, after 50 or 100 practical examples, the student understands how to apply a particular mathematical operation, which means he will be able to solve an infinite number of new examples seen for the first time. The use of machine learning [1–3] in this case can significantly reduce the complexity of such a process and allow the construction of generalized models that reduce the time of mastering mathematical knowledge.

The use of machine learning in applied tasks is reduced to the ordering and visual display of information characterized by a variety of features of a particular subject area.

In Fig. 1 conditionally shows the solution of the classification problem in several ways, followed by an assessment of the accuracy of the classification.

The problem of classification based on linear regression is solved using a perceptron (linear classifier). When considering features, the task is to find an (n – 1)-dimensional hyperplane in the n-dimensional feature space that best separates classes. Effective separation implies that the percentage of erroneously ordered objects is minimal. The classification problem can also be solved using the neural network method.

The classifier uses a feature description of an object to determine its class, usually from a limited number of alternatives. The desired display will also be the target function. If this objective function is not displayed in a limited range of values, then this is not a classification task, but an approximation task.

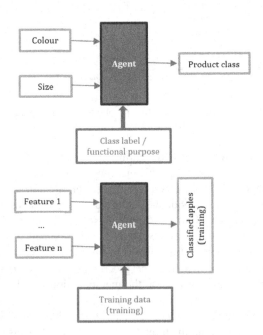

Fig. 2. Functional structure of the trained agent for apple sorting and general.

Formally, a prepared specialist could be a work that, employing a include portrayal, dis-plays a discrete esteem of a lesson or a genuine number in common. This work isn't programmatically characterized in development, instep it shows up and changes at the learning organize beneath the impact of preparing information (Fig. 2). At the same time, machine learning investigates computer calculations that move forward naturally based on its claim involvement.

One of the tasks of machine learning is data mining, which consists in the process of obtaining knowledge based on data, their correct presentation and application. Building a data mining model is part of a larger process, which can be represented as certain steps following each other (Fig. 3.).

Since the tasks of data classification and data mining are largely the same from a formal point of view, the main methods used are also similar. Therefore, there will not be much difference in the learning algorithms between the two directions.

The use of perceptron-based learning methods has a number of disadvantages. In this case, the knowledge available from the training programs is extracted concisely, which leads to loss of data and information, which ultimately leads to classification errors by certain characteristics or classes.

The use of methods using a decision tree makes it possible to correctly implement arbitrarily complex dividing lines with the necessary control of a possible error. The study and improvement of such methods and algorithms for their implementation is an urgent scientific area of research in machine learning problems.

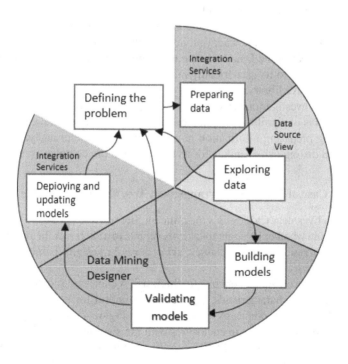

Fig. 3. Data Mining Model.

2 Materials and Methods

2.1 Solution Tree Training

Choice tree learning [4] is an amazingly vital calculation for counterfeit intelligence (AI) [5] since of its effortlessness and adequacy in extricating information from information. Compared to the closest neighbor learning calculation, this calculation has one exceptionally imperative advantage – the extricated information isn't fair accessible as a dark box, but can be effectively controlled by individuals within the shape of a lucid choice tree. This too makes this strategy an imperative apparatus for information mining.

When understanding real-world learning issues based on a choice tree, the so-called C4.5 calculation is utilized. The calculation itself showed up in 1993. It was introduced by Australian designer Ross Quinlan and was an progressed adaptation of his forerunner calculation ID3 [6]. The calculation is non-commercial and unreservedly accessible [7]. A afterward adaptation of the calculation, characterized by more noteworthy workflow productivity, can take into consideration the fetched of the arrangement includes a adjustment of the C5.0 [8].

The CART (Classification and Relapse Trees) calculation, proposed by Leo Breiman in 1984, works agreeing to standards comparable to C4.5 [9]. It has an intuitive graphical interface, but its utilize is exorbitant.

In 1964, J. Sonqvist and J. Morgan appeared the CHAID (Chi-square Programmed interaction finders) calculation, the capabilities of which permit programmed generation of choice trees. It has one eminent include:

CHAID stops the development of the tree some time recently it gets to be as well expansive. Be that as it may, nowadays it now not things much.

The KNIME (Konstanz Data Miner) data mining apparatus is additionally of considerable interest due to its user-friendly interface and the capacity to construct choice trees utilizing the Java library.

Based on the investigation performed, a strategy based on a choice tree utilizing the C4.5 calculation is of significant inquire about interest.5. In this article, the choice tree is built utilizing preparing information in arrange to at that point analyze the suitable calculation and distinguish openings for its utilize in a more complex assignment.

2.2 A Basic Case of Building a Arrangement Tree Utilizing Training Data

The skier, who lives near California's magnificent Sierra Crests, points to utilize a decision tree to decide whether he ought to take his vehicle to a ski resort. In this case, there's a issue of classification into two classes: ski or not (ski yes/no), based on the factors displayed in Table 1.

Figure 4 outlines a arrangement tree for this issue. A choice tree could be a tree whose inside hubs speak to characteristics. Each edge is mindful for the esteem of the trait. Each sheet metal hub encompasses a course esteem. Figure 4 on the proper side of the hubs appears the line numbers in enclosures with the significant train-ing information. Note that in a limited hub labeled SUN = YES, as it were two of the three ex-amples are classified accurately.

Table 1. Variables for ski classification task.

Variable	Meaning	Description
Ski (skiing) – target variable	Yes, no	Should I go to the nearest ski resort with enough snow?
Sun – sign	Yes, no	Is it sunny today?
Snow_Dist (snow_distance) – sign	≤100, >100	Distance to the nearest ski resort with good snow conditions (more/less than 100 km)
Weekend (weekends) – sign	Yes, no	Is it sunny today?

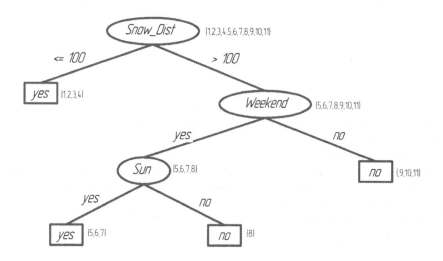

Fig. 4. Tree of solutions for the ski classification problem.

The data set used to build the tree is presented in Table 2. Each row cell in the table contains one day of information and is therefore sample data. There is a contradiction between the data in lines 6 and 7. It follows from this that none of the algorithms for ordering deterministic processes will be able to accurately classify all data, leading to one or more errors in the classification. Thus, it can be concluded that the tree in Fig. 4 provides optimal classification of data.

To create an information tree at the introductory arrange, you'll restrain yourself to discrete attributes with a limited number of values. Based on the restricted number of attributes accessible, each of which can be utilized as it were once, there's as it were a limited set of unique decision trees. The application of a basic and justifiable tree construction calculation is to make all conceivable trees, calculate the number of erroneously classified information for each of them, and select a tree with a least number of errors. As a result, an ideal learning calculation is shaped for the choice tree in terms of information mistakes within the learning handle.

Table 2. Data set for ski classification task.

Day	Snow_Dist	Weekend	Sun	Skiing
1	≤100	yes	yes	yes
2	≤100	yes	yes	yes
3	≤100	yes	no	yes
4	≤100	no	yes	yes
5	>100	yes	yes	yes
6	>100	yes	yes	yes
7	>100	yes	yes	no
8	>100	yes	no	no
9	>100	no	yes	no
10	>100	no	yes	no
11	>100	no	no	no

An obvious impediment of this calculation is that the execution time of its operations increments uniquely with the number of properties. But presently ready to utilize a heuristic calculation that will construct a choice tree beginning from the root hub and utilizing recursive methods. First, one hub with the biggest data pick up (Snow _ Dist) is chosen from the complete set of qualities as the root hub. For each attribute value (s 100, >100), there's a department within the tree. Presently, for each department, this handle is rehashed recursively. When creating a hub, the quality containing the foremost data among the unused data will continuously be chosen, ac-cording to the covetous methodology.

2.3 Entropy as an Pointer of the Sum of Data

The portrayed top-down calculation for building a choice tree chooses the attribute with the biggest increment in data at each step. Entropy can be utilized as a metric of the amount of data within the preparing information set D. When considering the twofold sort variable skiing within the over case, the dataset B can be depicted as: $D = ($yes, yes, yes, yes, yes, no, no, no, no, no$)$ with accepted probabilities:

$$p_1 = P(\text{yes}) = \frac{6}{11} \text{ and } p_2 = P(\text{no}) = \frac{5}{11} \tag{1}$$

Here the value of the probability distribution is: $p = (6/11, 5/11)$. In general, for n classes, the probability will then be $\sum_{i=1}^{n} p_i = 1$ where $p = (p_1, ..., p_n)$.

To find the amount of distribution information, it is necessary to consider two extreme cases. In the first case:

$$p = (1, 0, 0, \ldots, 0) \tag{2}$$

That's, the primary ordinal occasion of n occasions will unquestionably happen, and all the others will not be able to happen. As a result, instability approximately the result of the occasion is of negligible significance. On the opposite, for a uniform conveyance, vulnerability has the greatest esteem, since each occasion is similarly likely:

$$p = \left(\frac{1}{n}, \frac{1}{n}, \ldots, \frac{1}{n}\right) \tag{3}$$

It is vital to decide how numerous bits are needed to encode such an occasion. Within the particular case of Eq. (2), bits are needed, since we know that there's continuously one case. Within the case of a uniform conveyance agreeing to formula (3), there are n break even with openings. In this case, $\log_2 n$ bits are required to en-code the parallel sort. In this case, each person likelihood is numerically equal to $p = 1/n$, which compares to the encoding of $p_i = 1/n$, $\log_2(1/p_i)$ bits..

Within the generalized adaptation, $p = (p_1, \ldots, p_N)$, in case the likelihood of the most occasions contrasts from the uniform conveyance, the anticipated esteem of H for the number of bits is found. To do this, it is fundamental to grant a weight esteem to all values of $\log_2(1/p_i) = -\log_2 p_i$ relative to their probabilistic indicators:

$$H = \sum_{i=1}^{n} p_i(-\log_2 p_i) = -\sum_{i=1}^{n} p_i \log_2 p_i \tag{4}$$

A large number of bits for encoding the event leads to an increase in the uncertainty of the calculation result. Based on this, the entropy of H [10] as a metric for the uncertainty of the probability distribution can be found by the formula:

$$H(p) = H(p_1, \ldots, p_n) = -\sum_{i=1}^{n} p_i \log_2 p_i \tag{5}$$

Figure 5 shows the maximum value of the function at the point $P = 1/2$ and the symmetrical arrangement of the function relative to the transition process from P to $1 - P$.

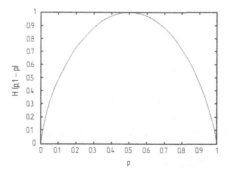

Fig. 5. The entropy function for the case of two classes.

3 Results and Discussion

Utilizing the concept and equation of entropy within the case of a skier leads to the taking after result:

$$H\left(\frac{6}{11}, \frac{5}{11}\right) = 0.994$$

Within the prepare of building a choice tree, the information set to boot isolated by each modern quality. The more a quality increments the sum of dissemination data conveyed by part information, the way better this trait is.

The increment in data G (D, A) utilizing trait A is defined as the difference between the normal esteem of the sum of data within the dataset $D = D_1 \cup D_2 \cup \ldots \cup D_n$ separated by the n-value of property A and the sum of information I(D) of the unified dataset:

$$G\,(D,A) = \sum_{i=1}^{n} \frac{|D_i|}{|D|} I(D_i) - I(D) \tag{6}$$

Using the ratio, you can get:

$$G\,(D,A) = \sum_{i=1}^{n} \frac{|D_i|}{|D|} I(D_i) - I(D) = \sum_{i=1}^{n} \frac{|D_i|}{|D|}(1 - H(D_i)) - (1 - H(D))$$

$$= H(D) - \sum_{i=1}^{n} \frac{|D_i|}{|D|} H(D_i)$$

If we use this formula for our Snow_Dust attribute, then we have:

$$G(D, \text{Snow\_Dist}) = H(D) - \frac{4}{11}H(D_{\leq 100}) + \frac{7}{11}H(D_{>100})$$

$$= 0.994 - \left(\frac{4}{11} \cdot 0 + \frac{7}{11} \cdot 0.863\right) = 0.445$$

Similarly, you can get:

$$G\,(D, \text{Weekend}) = 0.150$$

$$G\,(D, \text{Sun}) = 0.049$$

The Snow_Dust attribute now becomes the root node of the decision tree. The choice of this attribute is explained once again in Fig. 6. The graphical image allows you to determine which attribute provides the best distribution of data by class. The more distributions generated by an attribute deviate from a uniform distribution, the higher the information gain.

Two attribute values ≤ 100 and > 100 create two tree branches corresponding to subsets $D_{\leq 100}$ and $D_{>100}$. Obviously, the classification of a subset $D_{\leq 100}$ is yes. This means that the growth of the tree stops here. There is no clear result in the other branch $D_{>100}$.

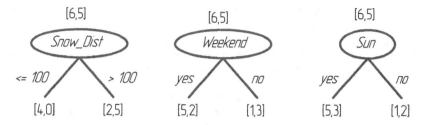

Fig. 6. The growth rate of various attributes.

Therefore, the algorithm is repeated recursively here. Of the two available attributes, Sun and Weekend, you need to choose the best one. To do this, we perform the calculation:

$$G(D_{>100}, \text{Weekend}) = 0.292$$

$$G(D_{>100}, \text{Sun}) = 0.170$$

Thus, the Weekend attribute is set for the root node. For the Weekend = no branch, the tree ends with the Sky = no solution. The increment of information here has a value of 0. For the Weekend = yes branch, the attribute has an increment of 0.171. Since further attributes are not available, the construction of the tree ends here, despite the fact that the example was classified incorrectly. We get the decision tree already familiar from Fig. 4.

4   Conclusions

Learning decision trees is the most popular method of classifying data. The reasons for this are its ease of use and high learning speed. Having training data in the set, the C4.5 algorithm spends a fraction of a second on training. This is a very good speed compared to other machine learning algorithms as a component of Industry 4.0 [11].

It is additionally critical for the client that the choice tree as a trainable demonstrates can be reasonable and potentially changeable. It is additionally simple to naturally change over a tree into an arrangement of "if-then-else" articulations and successfully implant it into an existing program.

In common, trees are conditionally ideal since they utilize a eager calculation when making and pruning trees. This created choice tree moreover encompasses a relative-ly moo mistake rate. Inclining toward the C4.5 eager look heuristic to small trees and traits with tall data substance at the best of the tree implies that there's continuously a more beneficial tree. For qualities with numerous values, the data pick up equation appears impediments, so there are elective arrangements.

References

1. Demin, A.V., Ponomaryov, D.K.: Machine learning with probabilistic law discovery: a concise introduction. Bull. Irkutsk State Univ. Ser. Math. **43**, 91–109 (2023)

2. Fedutinov, K.A.: Machine learning in decision support tasks in nature conservation management. Eng. Bull. Don **9**(81), 100–113 (2021)

3. Pandey, A.: Machine Learning. Int. J. Res. Appl. Sci. Eng. Technol. **11**(8), 864–869 (2023)

4. Kuzmin, O.V., Golikov, V.A.: Application of the "decision tree" method in the diagnosis of a malfunction of an internal combustion engine of a car. Mod. Technol. Syst. Anal. Model. **2**(70), 113–120 (2021)

5. Rich, E.: Artificial Intelligence. McGraw-Hill, New York (1983)

6. Simonov, D.A., Zernov, M.I.: Application of the ID3 algorithm for robot training. Energetika, informatics, innovations-2016, pp. 343–346. Universum, Smolensk (2016)

7. Nursikuwagus, A.: Implementation ID3 algorithm to predict. J. Eng. Appl. Sci. **12**(2), 204–207 (2017)

8. Quinlan, J.R.: C4.5: Programs for Machine Learning. Morgan Kaufmann Publishers, San Francisco (1993)

9. Kustiyahningsih, Y., Khotimah B.K., Anamisa D.R., Yusuf, M., Rahayu, T., Purnama, J.: Decision Tree C 4.5 algorithm for classification of poor family scholarship recipients. In: IOP Conference Series: Materials Science and Engineering, vol. 1125, no. 1, p. 012048 (2021)

10. Tuyakbasarova, N.A.: Entropy of the system and information. In: Modern Science: Issues of Theory and Practice: a Collection of Materials of the III Correspondence International Scientific and Practical Conference, pp. 168–176 (2018)

11. Kurasov, D. A: Digital technologies Industry 4.0. In: CEUR Workshop Proceedings, vol. 2843 (2021)

Author Index

A. Gibadullin (Ed.): ITIDMS 2023, CCIS 2112, pp. 217–218, 2024.
https://doi.org/10.1007/978-3-031-60318-1

Printed in the United States
by Baker & Taylor Publisher Services